Fro

Power, Conflict, and Democracy:

American Politics Into the Twenty-First Century

ROBERT Y. SHAPIRO, EDITOR

POWER, CONFLICT, AND DEMOCRACY:
AMERICAN POLITICS INTO THE TWENTY-FIRST CENTURY

Robert Y. Shapiro, Editor

AS IT EXAMINES THE POLITICAL
processes and major trends in politics that will affect the workings of
democracy and policymaking in the United States as it moves into the
twenty-first century, this series focuses on how the will of the people and
the public interest are promoted, encouraged, or thwarted. It aims to question not only the direction American politics will take as it enters the next
century, but also the direction American politics has already taken.

The series treats such diverse topics as the role of interest groups and
social and political movements; openness in American politics; important
developments in institutions such as the executive, legislative, and judicial
branches at all levels of government as well as the bureaucracies thus created; the changing behavior of politicians and political parties; the role of
public opinion; and the functioning of mass media. Because the characteristics of pressing problems drives politics, the series also examines
important policy issues in both domestic and foreign affairs.

Presented are all theoretical perspectives and the uses of different
methodologies and types of evidence that answer important questions
about trends in American politics.

From Tea Leaves to Opinion Polls

A Theory of

Democratic

Leadership

JOHN G. GEER

COLUMBIA UNIVERSITY PRESS   NEW YORK

Columbia University Press
New York   Chichester, West Sussex
Copyright © 1996 Columbia University Press

Library of Congress Cataloging-in-
Publication Data
Geer, John Gray.
    From tea leaves to opinion polls : a theory
of democratic leadership / John G. Geer.
        p.   cm. — (Power, conflict, and
democracy)
    Includes bibliographical references and
index
    ISBN 0-231-10280-1 (cloth : acid-free
paper).
    ISBN 0-231-10279-8 (pbk. : acid-free
paper)
    1. Political leadership. 2. Public opinion
polls. 3. Political leadership—United
States. 4. Public opinion—United States.
I. Title. II. Series.
JC330.3.G44   1996
303.3'4'0973—dc20   95-53114
                                CIP

Parts of this book have appeared in an
earlier form in "Critical Realignments and
the Public Opinion Poll" by John G. Geer
in *Journal of Politics* 53(2): 434–453 (by
permission of the author and Texas
University Press).

c 10 9 8 7 6 5 4 3 2 1
p 10 9 8 7 6 5 4 3 2 1

To

My parents, James H. and Jean A. Geer

and

My children, Megan R. and James D. Geer

Nothing is more dangerous than to live in the temperamental atmosphere of a Gallup poll, always taking one's pulse and taking one's temperature. . . . There is only one duty, only one safe course, and that is to try to be right and not to fear to do or say what you believe to be right.——*Winston Churchill*

I wonder how far Moses would have gone if he'd taken a poll in Egypt? What would Jesus Christ have preached if he'd taken a poll in Israel? . .. It isn't polls or public opinion of the moment that counts. It is right and wrong leadership ... that makes epochs in the history of the world.——*Harry S. Truman*

We elected a leader and we got a barometer.

——*A gay rights activist after Clinton announced his compromise on homosexuals in the military*

CONTENTS

LIST OF TABLES AND FIGURES

Tables

Figures

THIS BOOK IS ABOUT THE RELATION-
ship between politicians and public opinion. The starting point is simple
and obvious: the advent of polls has greatly increased the quality of information politicians have about public opinion. Less obvious, however, are
the implications that flow from this observation. Using a rational actor
framework, I develop a theory about how politicians behave in office that
provides a springboard for new ways to think about leadership, political
change, and democratic politics. The result is an argument that contends
polls have altered in systematic and important ways the behavior of
elected politicians.

My hope is that others will refine, extend, and test these arguments.
That process will, alas, refute some of my contentions. But that is part of
the scientific enterprise. Fortunately, it is not crucial that I be "right" about
all of the various ideas I tease out of my theory. I would, of course, like to
be right about a few things, but the more important matter is that others
begin to examine the relationship between politicians and information.
Social science needs to be prodded on this front. The changes over the last
fifty years in the availability of high-quality information are staggering,
and yet we have at best a limited grasp of the political and social impact of
these shifts. And as further advances in gathering information develop, it
will become even more important that we forge a better understanding of
these dramatic changes.

This book seeks to be part of that effort by building a simple theory
and then deriving implications from it. By focusing single-mindedly on

information and politicians, I have been able to explore this relationship in a number of interesting ways. My goal has been to draw not only a map to shed light on this general problem but also to provide a compass to other voyagers.

The downside, of course, is that important pieces of the political puzzle are missing from my story. Perhaps of most note is the absence of the news media, which so often—especially in the case of television—can be found at the center of most accounts of political change in the modern era. Consider Thomas Patterson's recent book *Out of Order*. He focuses almost exclusively on the changes the press has wrought on our electoral system. The arguments are interesting and worthy of serious consideration. Yet other changes have occurred during this period that deserve attention too. For example, Patterson talks about how the press tends to treat elections as games and not as serious discussions about policy. Why has this been the case? My theory offers a hypothesis not considered in standard treatments of the question; namely, that support-seeking politicians, armed with polls, are better able to identify the tough campaign issues that are best addressed in vague form, which has resulted in lessening many of the differences between competing candidates. With fewer sharp policy disputes at the center of today's campaigns, journalists have turned to the game as the "hook" for their stories. I do not want to argue that this hypothesis is "correct" (or even grant that Patterson is right about the changes in how members of the news media cover campaigns). My point is much more limited: other explanations for political change exist besides technological advances in our mediums of communication.

This strategy also has the advantage of allowing me to develop a general theory of politicians. The rise of television has not affected politics the same way in all countries. For instance, the controversy surrounding "sound bite" is *not* an inevitable outgrowth of television, as many observers of American politics often assume. First, one could argue that sound bites have always been part of politics—just consider what we remember of FDR's first inaugural address or Abraham Lincoln's famed debates with Stephen Douglas. In each case, we extracted a small nugget out of a much longer presentation. Perhaps it is inevitable that political observers boil down complicated arguments and ideas into a few simple themes. Hence, the sound bite may be an enduring part of politics that owes its origins to some force other than television.

Second, countries such as Sweden require candidates to debate each other in often long and serious exchanges that make it harder for glib statements to carry the day. In such nations, television is being used more effectively as a vehicle to exchange ideas. In sum, the news media are not just an independent variable in our political equations. They are also an dependent variable that is an outgrowth of the institutions and traditions that surround them.

In the end, my hope is that these pages will lead people to think more carefully about the import of information for how politicians behave. I do not expect people to agree with all I have written here. I have had more than a few doubts along the way myself, as I have wrestled with many of these arguments. Hence I will be shocked if anyone but my loyal Dachshund, Gretchen, buys into all my claims. And even with Gretchen I will never be sure, since a wagging tail hardly constitutes an unqualified endorsement.

ACKNOWLEDGMENTS

I HAVE BENEFITED TREMENDOUSLY from the advice and comments of Rich Dagger, Peter Esaiasson, Steve Finkel, Rick Herrera, Peter McDonough, Walt Stone, and Gunnar Vogt. Each of these people read the manuscript with great care, and pointed out numerous problems that demanded my attention. Dagger, Esaiasson, and Herrera pulled extra duty, since I forced them to spend many hours chatting about the ideas presented here. I greatly appreciate their generosity and friendship.

In addition, John Zaller, Jack Crittenden, and Steve Walker criticized parts of the manuscript, providing useful suggestions. My father, who is a psychologist at LSU, read the introduction, and gave me feedback on how the ideas might play to scholars in fields other than political science. In addition, I had assistance from a number of trusty graduate students: Gerald Duff, Toni McClory, Mike Morrell, and Cooper Drury. Gerald Duff, in particular, spent one semester pulling together a very disorganized bibliography. He was tireless in pursuit of the incomplete citation. During my time at Arizona State University, I also participated in a program called the "Junior Fellows." This program, started by Jack Crittenden, allowed me to tap the skills of a number of talented undergraduates who assisted with some of the library research. I am pleased to acknowledge their generous support.

Bob Shapiro, who is the editor of this series, proved to be a sharp critic of my work. His comments helped to strengthen the argument in important ways. I deeply appreciated his advice and support. I should also acknowledge the important empirical work that he and Larry Jacobs have done (and continue to do) in the area of polls and policy-making. Their findings have not only helped to bolster many of my claims, but will also prove important contributions in their own right.

My editor at Columbia University Press, John Michel, deserves thanks too. John showed great support and good cheer as he steered this manuscript through the editorial waters. I hope someday we get the chance to do another book together. The reviewers selected by Shapiro and Michel also were helpful critics. The referees offered detailed comments on the manuscript, which allowed me to improve the manuscript. I greatly appreciate that type of feedback. Finally, Leslie Bialler, my copyeditor at Columbia University Press, helped to fine-tune the manuscript.

Stanley Kelley, my friend and mentor, deserves special mention. It was Stanley who originally urged me to write this book. I had written a conference paper on this general subject that he argued was best expanded into a longer treatise. He saw the need to develop more fully the ideas I had only hinted at in that original paper. I also had the benefit of Stanley's comments on the full manuscript. As always, I owe him a deep debt of gratitude for his counsel and his friendship.

My last acknowledgment goes to Tom Rochon. Tom, more than anyone else, was able to understand what I was trying to say, especially in the early stages of this project. He always managed to look past the uneven prose and the truncated ideas, finding interesting connections that helped to save many a faltering argument. During the midst of this project, Tom and I spent two weekends together in Arizona criticizing each other's written work. One very long exchange in the fall of 1993 literally left me hoarse and unable to talk (much to the relief of Tom). Those exchanges not only served as a fantastic way to improve this manuscript, but they were also great fun. Tom loves ideas and even crazy ones—the latter of which makes him an excellent judge of my work. Simply saying "thanks" does not even begin to do justice to Tom's contribution both as a friend and as a critic. But it is the best I can do in these pages.

The dedication of this book to my parents, James and Jean Geer, and to my children, Megan and James Geer, was an obvious choice for me. My parents have always supported me in any way possible. Or to use a term common to this book, I have had the great fortune to experience their "leadership." Now, I have the joy of "followership," as I watch my children grow and learn. James and Megan are a constant source of pride and fun. It is this kind of leadership and followership that really matters. And I have had the blessings of both.

I could not possibly close without mentioning my wife, Maria. The fact that she tolerates me is enough reason to warrant waiving the five-year waiting period for induction into the Spouse Hall of Fame. But Maria goes beyond putting up with me. She provides support, love, and inspiration. It was Maria who urged me to take a full year off for my sabbatical in 1992–93 so I could have more time to write this book, and then, she provided the financial support that made it possible. I could not ask for more from her. I just hope this book manages to generate enough royalties to take her to Italy again.

It is now commonplace to absolve all these helpful souls from the many faults that line the pages of this book. I shall not break that honorable tradition. Whatever shortcomings exist, the blame lies squarely with me.

John G. Geer
Nashville, Tennessee
February 1996

From Tea Leaves to Opinion Polls

IN THE 1790S, GEORGE WASHINGTON found himself the leader of a struggling nation. The new Constitution had been in place only a few years, and it was far from clear whether that controversial document would provide an enduring foundation for the country. The former general was painfully aware of this situation and took great care to foster the development of the nation. But he was frequently unsure about the best course of action. Washington had lots of advice from individuals in his cabinet, like Alexander Hamilton or Henry Knox, and he had access to the views of political figures in Philadelphia, then the capital. But he had little concrete sense of how the Constitution and his policies were playing with the people. In the end, he knew that the survival of the fledgling republic would rest in the hands of the citizenry. In an effort to lessen his uncertainty about the public's views, Washington toured the country on horseback to assess the "temper and disposition of the people toward the new government."[1] By witnessing firsthand the attitudes and opinions of average citizens, he hoped both to decrease his uncertainty and to undertake actions that would be greeted favorably by the populace.[2]

---

1. These are Washington's own words as quoted in Tulis (1987, 69).

2. For a useful and informative account of Washington's tenure as President, see Smith (1993). Much of the information reported above comes from this recent biography of the nation's first president.

Given Washington's situation, it is fair to say that he was not very well informed about the state of public opinion. Even if his tour was successful, the chances that our first president received honest answers to his questions or that he managed to contact a representative cross section of the citizenry were not great. Moreover, his own predispositions surely influenced his interpretations of the events he witnessed and the answers he received. From the 1700s to the middle part of this century, lack of accurate information about public opinion plagued all politicians who confronted large and diverse electorates. Washington's successors, from John Adams to Herbert Hoover, were in the same situation—all were attempting to read, so to speak, the tea leaves of public opinion. Not all of them took to their horses in pursuit of the electorate's views, but the problems inherent in the various methods they used prevented them from accurately tapping the public's attitudes.

This situation changed dramatically, however, with the introduction of the public opinion poll. The development of survey research made it possible for politicians to have access to precise and accurate readings of the electorate's pulse.[3] So rather than galloping around the countryside trying to get a sense of what their constituents want, elected officials can now rely on polls to provide accurate estimates of public opinion. Bill Clinton, in stark contrast to George Washington, could simply walk to another room in the White House to study one of Stanley Greenberg's latest printouts and get a good sense of the electorate's reactions to his proposal on health care or his efforts to quell concerns about the administration's affirmative action programs. Politicians, in short, are now well-informed about public opinion.

This change is significant. Simply put: well-informed politicians behave differently from their less well-informed counterparts—even when their motivations are exactly the same. The purpose of this book is to construct a theory that develops the link between the quality of information and the behavior of politicians in office. This theory, in turn, provides the basis for developing some of the implications of this transformation for leadership and democratic politics.

---

3. Throughout this book I will talk of surveys and polls, and pollsters and survey researchers. The term *pollster* originally had a negative connotation (Rogers 1949). But here I do not distinguish between pollsters and survey researchers. Moreover, academic surveys, such as the National Election Studies, are far different from the polls run by the news media, and both of these are still different from state political organizations that hire a local pollster to sample voters. Nonetheless, I will use all these terms interchangeably, because the differences are not relevant to the argument of this book.

Early Politicians and Information

Politicians of all stripes, noted V. O. Key (1961, 412), "must concern themselves with public opinion." This statement is true whether we are talking about Machiavelli's prince, Britain's kings, or democratically elected public officials. In the case of the Prince, it would be advantageous to know what his subjects want. Such information might allow the Prince to adopt measures that please citizens, thereby increasing their loyalty to him and, hence, his hold on power. Accurate knowledge about his subjects' views might also provide the Prince a better opportunity to manipulate the citizenry to his advantage, by combining, for instance, popular measures with unpopular ones, or by playing up the views of an intense minority. Furthermore, knowing subjects' preferences might allow the Prince to anticipate negative reactions to particular decisions and hence, be able to prepare a more effective defense against those reactions.

The importance of knowing the preferences of citizens becomes even more critical for politicians in a representative democracy. Coercion, an option open to the Prince, is not a viable choice for a popularly elected politician like Ronald Reagan or Margaret Thatcher.[4] With coercion available, a Prince (or any autocrat) can try to counter, with military force, any mistake in judging the public's preferences. In fact, the mere threat of repressive action by the state will often keep unhappy citizens from expressing their dissatisfaction publicly. But presidents and other elected officials hold power only because a majority (or sometimes a plurality) supported their candidacy at the previous election. This support can be revoked, however, at the next election, leading to their ouster from office. Hence, in democratic regimes, politicians have considerable incentive to uncover the views, preferences, and interests of the public. Or to put the matter another way: politicians, who face periodic elections, want to know with as much accuracy as possible the state of public opinion.

Over the last 300 or so years, democratic politicians[5] have faced different opportunities for and obstacles to gathering good information about the public's views. There is good reason to believe that politicians who faced small electorates were actually pretty well-informed about their constituents'

---

4. Of course, it is possible that an elected politician might use coercion on part of the citizenry, as in the case of the American Civil War. But such examples are exceedingly rare in a democracy. See also Kelley (n.d.) for an interesting and thoughtful discussion of the role of coercion in the development of political parties.

5. By "democratic," I am referring to politicians who face periodic, free elections.

preferences. Stanley Kelley (1983, 134) observes that at the time of Edmund Burke, British electorates were so small, usually fewer than one thousand people, that politicians could in fact know whether their victory in an election constituted a mandate or not. The reason is obvious: with such small numbers, politicians had firsthand knowledge of the preferences of most, if not all, of the voters.[6] Such personal and direct contact surely made officeholders keenly aware of the desires of those they were elected to represent.

In the United States, however, politicians from the first days of the Constitution faced much larger electorates than those of their British counterparts and colonial predecessors. Governors, and especially the president, usually faced large numbers of voters because of the constituencies they represented. The geographic size of many congressional districts, compounded by a lack of good transportation and effective communication, also made it difficult for these representatives to get a good sense of public opinion.[7] Only the most local, urban politicians probably could claim to be well-informed about the views of their constituents. With the expansion of suffrage and the skyrocketing population in the 1800s, politicians (on both sides of the Atlantic) faced increasing numbers of voters and, hence, increasing uncertainty about public opinion.

With a large number of constituents, politicians had to develop ways beyond direct contact to tap public opinion. Politicians built networks of local officials to provide information, paid attention to the claims of various interest groups, and kept tabs on the content of newspapers. But, as I shall argue in Chapter 2, these indicators had a number of biases and problems. The end result was that politicians were not well informed about public opinion throughout most of American history.

---

6. Hirst (1975) reports that British electorates for members of Parliament during the mid-1600s often failed to exceed 200 voters, making it extremely easy for politicians to know personally all voters in the district. The same was apparently true in seventeenth-century America. Only 3 percent of Boston's population voted during this time (Lasswell 1941, 3). And given that the city's total population was 7,000, no more than 250 people cast ballots in the city. This estimate is confirmed by Rossiter (1953, 20). His research suggested that about 1 in 4 white males were eligible to vote in most colonies. And that among the eligible, only 25 percent bothered to go to the polls. In short, only about 1 in 16 white males were active in electoral politics, which is about 6 percent. Given that white males constituted about half of the population, the end result is about 3 percent of the total population voted.

7. In Federalist #9, Hamilton acknowledges the potential problem of politicians' gathering information in the large electorates that were constructed under the Constitution. But he argued that the alternatives of "monarchy or of splitting ourselves into an infinity of little, jealous, clashing, tumultuous commonwealths" were even worse.

The era of poor information came to a quick halt, however, with the advent of the public opinion poll in the 1930s. Survey research has allowed politicians to gather accurate readings of any *large* electorate's preferences, thereby signaling the reemergence of the "well-informed" politician.

The Advent of the Information Age

The development of the public opinion poll, of course, represents only one tiny part of the many gains in information over the last fifty years. Developments in telecommunications and computer technology have provided important changes both in the quality of information and the speed with which it comes to our attention. It took days for many northerners to learn of Abraham Lincoln's assassination in 1865, but today we learn about events in the embattled republics of the former Soviet Union the moment they unfold in the streets. Because of all these changes, it is now common to talk about the dawning of the "information age."

Scholars, of course, have begun to think and to write about the many implications that this surge in information has for society in general, and for politics in particular (e.g., Graber 1988; Dizard 1985; Beniger 1986; Luke 1989; Ferejohn and Kuklinski 1990; Neuman 1991; Ricci 1993). But since this transformation is recent, we still lack a good grasp of its ramifications. As one historian writes, by "bouncing words and images off satellites in space, storing and manipulating undreamed of quantities of information in the twinkling of an eye, we have been creating awesome communications technology that is leading society into many dimensions of unknown territory" (Brown 1989, 3)

Most of the work about the impact of information in the field of political science has focused on citizens. Given that voters can now learn about the debates and discussions in Congress at a touch of a button or find out about the latest events in the world by just switching stations on the radio, there is good reason to determine whether and how the rising tide of information influences citizens. This interest is set against the background that "nothing strikes the student of public opinion and democracy more forcefully than the paucity of information most people possess about politics" (Ferejohn 1990, 3). This focus on voters is also consistent with the belief that any successful democracy requires an electorate capable of making good political decisions. Wise choices, of course, rest, in part, on gathering sound information about the relevant options. With more information available, perhaps citizens are better informed and thus more up to the task required of them in a democratic polity.

Nonetheless, the influence of this surge in information on politicians is probably even greater and more consequential than it is for the mass public. The political survival, as indicated above, of any democratically elected politician hinges in large part on developing accurate readings of public opinion as quickly as possible. So while princes used spies, presidents now employ pollsters to gather information about those they govern. Politicians are always looking for an "edge," and polls provide it. In her book *Processing the News* (1988), which examines the reactions of citizens to the onslaught of information, Doris Graber uses the subtitle *How People Tame the Information Tide*. Politicians, by comparison, want to do more than just tame the tide; they want to conquer it. Elected officials have good reason to digest all relevant data about the public that might help them develop positions and policies that increase their popularity and, hence, their chances for reelection.

In many ways this point is the logical extension of Walter Lippmann's contention that average citizens have too many demands upon their time to be informed participants in the democratic process. Politicians, because politics is their business, *will* make the time to become informed participants. As James Bryce (1921) once observed, elected officials "look incessantly for manifestations of current popular opinion." Consequently, the active players in politics (e.g. politicians) are likely to benefit disproportionately from the surge of information that has accompanied such things as the public opinion poll.

If this observation that politicians are now well informed about the electorate's views is correct, it demands our attention. V. O. Key (1966, 2) once observed that a political system works like an echo chamber, where changes in the inputs invariably affect the outputs. My argument, in one sense, is that the advent of polls has altered an important "input," public opinion, that, in turn, has affected some prominent "outputs," such as public policy, leadership, and political change.

Leadership, Democracy, and Information

If we were to read a textbook account of how representative democracies work, we would learn that elected officials attempt to translate the public's views into governmental action. While much more goes into policy than that simple statement suggests, the basic point is that officeholders represent and act on the interests of the electorate. Many scholars have argued, however, that politicians must often become leaders rather than followers, since the public may be wrong in its judgment about some issues or it may not be informed on the matter. In such instances, it is the task of politicians to lead and to educate public opinion. The tasks of leading and following, of course, have a long and noble tradition. Edmund Burke addressed these two tasks in his famous speech to the Electors of Bristol—which we now label "delegates" and "trustees."[8] In a "trustee" democracy, politicians employ their own judgments and values when making policy, hoping that, if necessary, officeholders can change (or expand) the electorate's thinking on those matters.[9] In contrast, a "delegate" democracy requires politicians to translate directly, without question, the wishes of the electorate into policy. Followership, therefore, is the order of the day. There is an incompatibility between the two ideas in their purest form. Even so, most observers want to balance the two. They see a need for democratic politicians to wear both hats; otherwise, the political system will decay (Key 1961; Wilson 1952; Schattschneider 1942, 1975; Pitkin 1967; Tulis 1987).

Beneath these discussions about the proper relationship between leadership, followership, and democracy lies the assumption that politicians actually know what the preferences and interests of the electorate are. How can any democratic politician lead public opinion without first knowing the views of the citizenry? Without knowing where the public stands, it is quite possible that the electorate already agrees with the politician's position, and so does not need to be led. At the same time, how can any democratic politician follow the electorate's wishes without knowing what those wishes are? Not knowing what the public wants makes following opinion little more than guesswork. No matter how one wants to balance a representative democracy's need for leadership and followership, one confronts the assumption that elected officials need to know the views of the citizenry.

That assumption, as suggested earlier, may have been warranted when electorates were small and was one reason that many political theorists

---

8. Even though Burke usually gets full credit for the terms "delegates" and "trustees," he did not actually use them in that famous speech.

9. If one takes the logic of a trustee to an extreme, politicians need never worry about what the public is thinking. That is, they do what they think is in the best interests of their constituents and ignore the views of the public. Politicians who hold such an attitude better be either lucky or extremely persuasive if they want to be re-elected.

thought that republican government could work only in *small* localities. As Montesquieu (1966, 120) writes, in a small republic "the interest of the public is more obvious" and "better understood. . . . " But for most of this nation's history and that of other democratic nations around the globe, the assumption that officeholders knew public opinion was clearly unwarranted. Politicians, under those conditions, have a difficult time fulfilling the roles required of them *either* as leaders or followers.

Being well-informed, however, guarantees neither good leadership nor effective followership. Even if leaders are sure about the state of public opinion, we cannot assume that they will be the kind of leaders hoped for by many democratic theorists. They may, instead, try to manipulate opinion to their own advantage, rather than the public's. Or politicians seeking support may become slaves to opinion, because popularity matters more to them than policy. Such mechanical reactions to the whims of the public may lead to the pursuit of poorly conceived policies.

In short, how much information politicians have about public opinion plays a central part in understanding how leadership and followership works and whether it works well. This book demonstrates the implications of changes in the amount of information for politicians, in particular, and for leadership and followership, in general.

The Argument

It is not new to argue that polls influence the behavior of politicians. A number of scholars have made just that point (e.g., Ginsberg 1986; Bogart 1972). My purpose here is to develop an explicit theory that explains how information from polls has altered politicians' actions. This theory will be set within an historical context, examining how polls systematically have *changed* the behavior of politicians. The actual looking glass employed in this book will be a rational actor approach that considers the differences in behavior between well-informed and poorly informed politicians while in office, and to a far lesser extent how politicians act while trying to win office. The theoretical underpinnings of the rational choice framework give an explicit role to information, thereby making it a fruitful way to explore this question.

My hope is that this argument represents the first of many volleys in an evermore systematic discussion of politicians, leadership, and public opinion. In an effort to make this first volley an effective one, I will make a strong case that the behavior of politicians has been altered by changes in the quality of information available to them. Toward that end, I adopt a number of assumptions that lead me to ignore important parts of the political process. Most notably, this book will have almost nothing to say about the news media. Yet, it is the fourth estate that often lies at the center of many of our accounts of politics and changes in politics over the last 50 years (see, for example, Beniger 1986; Patterson 1993; Altheide and Snow 1979). To some degree, my single-minded focus on information will help to counterbalance what is surely an over emphasis on the impact of the news media by other scholars. But even more importantly, because the news media work in different ways in the many democracies around the world, this focus allows me to build a general theory that can then be applied to non-American cases. Finally, many of the changes in the methods and actions of the news media have taken place at the same time these shifts in information have occurred, making disentangling these dual effects a theoretical and empirical nightmare. In short, by placing this important institution on the sidelines for this book, I will be able to develop the relationship between information and politicians more clearly and forcefully than if I incorporated, at this point, the complexities of the real world in this argument.[10]

This decision does, however, have its costs. As David Mayhew (1974, 9) warns, "monocausal ventures . . . carry arguments to the point of exaggeration. . . . " Politicians are not as single-minded as I assume, nor is the world as simple as I suggest. But information has always been an important "variable" in the political process, and the emergence of polls represents an important enough shift in its operation to warrant starting with a highly simplistic theory to sort out the potential ramifications of this change.

The specific objectives of this book are four-fold. First, I develop a theory that represents an effort to understand how politicians in representative democracies make decisions on matters of public policy. Second, I apply this theory, arguing that "leadership,"[11] under certain circumstances, can actually be thought of as a *mistake* made by rational politicians. That is, support-maximizing politicians only "lead" opinion on highly salient issues when they misjudge the position of the median voter. This view con-

---

10. Another important "variable" I will not consider is the institutional context of leadership. Skowronek (1993), for instance, documents the importance of such factors in constraining how U.S. Presidents have behaved (see also Rockman 1984). But in an effort to develop a general theory of leadership, I have adopted, as we will see in Chapter 1, a simple institutional setting that faces politicians.

11. This theory rests on an explicit definition of leadership and followership, which I will describe and defend in the next chapter.

stitutes a departure from previous work, since leadership is usually associated with the purposeful acts of politicians trying to improve the condition of a nation. The theory also offers additional guidelines for how leadership and followership work when issues are not very salient to the public.

The <u>third</u> objective is to show how the prospects of "leadership," as defined here, have been fundamentally altered by the rise of public opinion polls. With accurate estimates of the electorate's views, one might expect rational politicians to make fewer mistakes and to "follow" public opinion more effectively than in the past. But, at the same time, polls also permit politicians to identify less pressing issues that provide opportunities for leadership and for educating the electorate about the best course of action. It is this possibility that initially led George Gallup and Saul Rae (1940, 266) to argue that with polls, politicians "will be better able to represent . . . the general public" by avoiding "the kind of distorted picture sent to them by telegram enthusiasts and overzealous pressure groups who claim to speak for all the people, but actually only speak for themselves."

My <u>final</u> goal is to develop the theory's implications for democratic government—from changes in the kinds of politicians who are now elected to how political change works. For example, using this framework, I argue that in an era of polls, political change will unfold differently because polarization on highly salient issues will not occur as often as it did 75 years ago. Rational politicians, knowing the public's views on important issues, will tend to adopt similar positions, thus making critical realignments a thing of the past. That is only part of the story, however. The increase in information also permits politicians to polarize on issues of little importance to the public. With good information, politicians can target those issues that will please activists and not cost much support from the electorate at large. Thus, Republicans can take a non-centrist position on abortion and get away with it, or Democrats can be opposed to the death penalty without many costs in the voting booth. This argument may help explain the episodic change that has been characteristic of the American party system since the New Deal.

Some of these kinds of changes can be viewed as good for democratic politics; others must be treated more cautiously. Regardless of one's interpretation, the argument suggests that we may need to rethink how leadership works in modern democratic societies.

To illustrate my basic argument, let me briefly pose some questions about the actions of two American presidents. More than seventy years ago, Woodrow Wilson worked past the point of collapse trying to get the

Senate to ratify the Versailles Treaty. The exact reasons for the President's behavior have been the subject of much dispute (see, for instance, George and George 1954; Barber 1977; Weinstein 1981). But among the reasons for his actions was his belief that the public supported the treaty (see Heckscher 1991; Merriam 1926).

Suppose for a moment that Wilson had pollster Pat Caddell surveying the American populace. How would that information have changed Wilson's behavior? First, if the findings showed that the public opposed the treaty, Wilson would not have been able to claim that the citizenry supported it, as he often did (Tulis 1987). The opponents of the treaty would have been buoyed by such findings, making them even more willing to scuttle the agreement. On the other hand, if the findings suggested that the public favored the treaty, Wilson's hand would have been greatly strengthened. The opposition would then have had to fly in the face of "public opinion," and Henry Cabot Lodge's coalition might well have collapsed. In addition, Wilson would not have had to undertake a national tour to demonstrate the public's support for the treaty; instead he could have focused his time on convincing the necessary two-thirds of Senators to support the covenant.

Some 60 years later, facing a stagnant economy and low ratings in the polls, Jimmy Carter retreated to Camp David for ten days with business leaders, politicians, journalists, and consultants to discuss what was wrong with his presidency and with the country. Emerging from Camp David after these discussions, Carter delivered the now infamous "Malaise" speech. The speech was designed to address the sense of alienation many Americans felt, touching on themes about the decency of the people and the corruption of powerful interest groups within Washington. One of the major reasons Carter gave this speech was Pat Caddell's polls showed Americans felt alienated and no longer trusted government (Moore 1992, 148–153). Obviously, other factors entered into Carter's decision to make this address, such as a slumping economy; but it is clear that polls were influential.[12]

Assume that instead of relying on Caddell and his polls, Carter had only Colonel House at his side. What might have driven the President's behavior then? Would he have delivered such a speech? Rather than speaking to

---

12. Even though the "Malaise" speech is now viewed as a failure, Caddell notes that following the speech Carter's ratings jumped 15 percentage points. But "it was all lost when Carter demanded mass resignations from his cabinet members and White House senior staff three days later" (Moore 1992, 152). For further debate on the "Malaise" speech see an exchange between Warren E. Miller and Pat Caddell in a 1978 issue of *Public Opinion*.

the alienation of Americans, might he have addressed their economic concerns? Without polls, would Carter even have been aware of his low standing with the American public? It seems hard to argue that the presence of polling data was not an important explanatory variable in this process.

Leo Bogart (1972, 6) raises similar types of questions, noting that Franklin Roosevelt had much better readings of the public mood with regard to World War II than did Lincoln as he embarked on the Civil War. This observation led Bogart to ask the question: "How different would Roosevelt's action have been if he had not had opinion survey data, or Lincoln's if he had?"

At first blush, one might think that the basic line of inquiry behind these questions involves no more than a "what if" scenario. Much speculation, for instance, exists about whether John Kennedy would have curtailed the U.S. military commitment in Vietnam if he had not been assassinated in 1963. Such debates are of interest, but, as Nelson Polsby (1982) suggests, they are "social science fiction." My task in this monograph is much different. I am interested in examining whether a fundamental change in the political environment may have restructured the way politicians behave. Thus, I am not so much interested in whether or not Wilson would have behaved differently with access to polling data, as I am in investigating the differences in behavior between well-informed and poorly informed politicians.

We know that shifts in information can have important effects on behavior. Whether one is coaching a football game or simply deciding which stock to purchase, information matters and it matters a great deal. My purpose, therefore, is to examine theoretically the consequences of this trend toward more and better information for politicians. There has been much work about the role of information and the voter—well represented by a volume edited by John Ferejohn and James Kuklinski (1990). But, as noted earlier, we also need to theorize about politicians. While they are usually well-informed, especially by the definitions offered in this literature about voters, there is good reason to believe that the amount and quality of that information has changed dramatically over the last fifty years. And if the political world operates along the lines of Key's echo chamber, then there is some urgency to study those actors who are making the original sounds.

This argument about the changing nature of leadership also assumes even more importance within the context of the many complaints about the lack of leadership in American politics. The apparent tendency of

George Bush to be blown around by the breezes of public opinion underscores this basic point. Scholars ranging from James MacGregor Burns to Aaron Wildavsky have complained about the lack of leadership.[13] Burns (1984), for instance, argues that the problem is that our institutions need reform to permit more effective leadership. Others argue that there are just not enough good leaders available (Hart 1987; Gardner 1990).

The theory presented here takes a different cut at this issue, predicting that today's politicians will be less likely to engage in the kind of behavior usually associated with leadership. But rather than suggesting that there are too few leaders around or that our political institutions need repair, the interpretation I offer is that we need to rethink what constitutes leadership and, therefore, alter our expectations of democratic politicians.

The Blueprint

Chapter 1 offers a theory of how politicians run government. To start this effort, I discuss some of the shortcomings of previous work on leadership, showing why my approach will shed new light on this age-old question. Next, I define leadership and followership. With the foundation poured, I then construct a theory of how politicians behave in office. This theory rests upon a number of assumptions, among them that politicians seek to maximize their popularity within the electorate so as to ensure re-election. That theory, in turn, allows me to consider explicitly how politicians—both well-informed and poorly informed—will behave in this simple world. By changing the amounts of information available to politicians, new ways of thinking about leadership emerge, as noted earlier.

The second chapter documents how the sample survey has transformed politicians from being poorly informed to being well-informed. I will argue not only that polls have shifted the quality of information available to politicians, but also that this change has led to a conceptual shift in how politicians and other relevant political actors think about the term "public opinion." Prior to polls, public opinion was thought of as amorphous and uncertain; today the concept assumes a scientific air that allows people to think of it as tangible and knowable. This conceptual shift further encourages politicians to believe that they are operating in a much more "certain"

---

13. See also Hart (1987), Ehrenhalt (1991), Miroff (1976), and Gardner (1990). Of course, complaints about the lack of leadership are not new. For one example see Ostrogroski (1921).

world. These changes, given the theory in chapter 1, marks a potential watershed in understanding how leadership works.

Chapter 3 presents a bit of evidence to support the theory developed in the previous two chapters. I start by briefly commenting on a couple of instances of presidential behavior that lend credence to the theory: Lincoln's decision to issue the Emancipation Proclamation and Bush's support of health care reform. These two cases highlight in dramatic form the fundamental difference between the two eras. The chapter continues by documenting the extensive use of polls by recent American presidents. The final section reports on existing scholarly evidence that public opinion polls have affected politicians' behavior in ways that I suggest.

Chapter 4 represents the first of the "implication" chapters. Here I will generate some probabilities for various types of leadership occurring under conditions of "complete" and "incomplete" information. When so doing, I distinguish between the salience of issues to the public and the direction of opinion on them—the two core components of "public opinion"—which allows me to get a more accurate reading about how politicians behave in the two eras.

The fifth chapter tackles the implications of this argument for the types of politicians elected to public office. We tend to attribute a certain set of skills as critical to being a good leader, such as forceful speaking. The growth in the quality of information suggests, however, that politicians will acquire skills different from those of their predecessors. These new skills are at odds with those traditionally associated with leadership. This change indicates that not only have the characteristics of successful politicians shifted, but so too may have the characteristics that constitute a successful leader in the modern era.

The sixth chapter examines what our theory about politicians has to say about political change. Since competing politicians, armed with polls, react to issues differently from their less well-informed counterparts of the past, we can expect a shift in politicians' joint positions on issues. Simply put, well-informed politicians are less likely to take polarized positions on the critical issues that confront the polity. As a result, polls have cast a monkey wrench into our theories of partisan change, requiring us to rethink how old party systems die and how new ones emerge.

The concluding chapter ventures into four larger questions. First, I shall present a richer definition of leadership that moves beyond the confines of my theory. Next, I shall discuss what my argument has to say about the theory of representation. Specifically, I shall carve the study of representation into three distinct eras that follow from the changes in information available to politicians. Third, I shall address the long standing tension between leadership and democracy. By viewing this tension in light of how much information politicians possess, some new perspectives emerge. Finally, I shall speculate about the import of recent developments in information about public opinion, such as the rise of the focus group.

Whether one agrees with my conclusions or not, it is essential that we think explicitly about the ramifications that changes in information have for politics. This discussion takes on greater urgency as we enter an era where the quality of information is likely to increase in ways only imagined at this point. These developments will further alter the relationship between the elected and the electors. These kinds of developments demand a rethinking of how leadership and representation can and should work in modern, information-rich democracies. We must adjust our theories to changes in the political environment; otherwise, we apply outdated ideas to understanding how our world operates.

While this book makes a simple and obvious point—that information matters—these chapters will pinpoint new ways in which information matters to politicians and why we need to take these changes seriously. By so doing, I hope to contribute to a better understanding of the interaction between politicians and information. Chapter 1 begins our journey.

Chapter 1

POLITICIANS, INFORMATION, AND LEADERSHIP:
A THEORY

THE STUDY OF LEADERSHIP HAS
captured the imagination of some of the world's best known political
thinkers. Plato was probably the first to give serious, systematic thought to
the importance of leadership in politics (Tucker 1981).[1] Even though not
framed as a discussion of leadership, Machiavelli's advice to the Medici can
be viewed as a Princes' handbook on effective (and ineffective) leadership.
Of more recent vintage, such noteworthy people as John Stuart Mill,
James Madison, and Woodrow Wilson have given much thought to this
general subject. "Leadership is as old as mankind," writes Jean Blondel
(1987, 1), "it is universal, and inescapable."

The reason for this great and enduring interest in leadership is simple.
Most political systems vest power in a handful of individuals, thereby
making the actions of these few of particular importance for how that system works and whether it works well. Because this power is granted to only
a small set of rulers, most governing arrangements create, by definition,
two general classes of political actors: leaders and followers. While there
are a host of middle-range actors (e.g., activists, journalists), this basic divi-

---

1. Tucker (1981, chapter 1) provides a thoughtful account of leadership and its historical roots.
According to Bernard Bass (1981, 7), "the word 'leadership' did not appear until the first half of
the nineteenth century in writings about political influence and control of the British
Parliament." The word "leader" has a longer history, dating back to at least 1300 in the English
language (Bass 1981, 7).

sion of power lies at the core of any political system or institutional arrangement. With leaders holding the reins of power, their actions draw a tremendous amount of interest. The presumption is that any act, good or bad, undertaken by "leaders" affects the workings of the polity, and often, these acts matter a great deal.

The specific role of leaders varies, however, across different political systems. In any nondemocratic political system, the actions of any leader are absolutely crucial, since their decrees have immediate (and potentially serious) implications for the masses. Some autocrats may pursue their own self-interest or act on behalf of the larger public. But in either case, the ruler shapes and directs the political life of the community. At the other end of the spectrum lies a "delegate" democracy where, as noted in the Introduction, there is little need (theoretically) for formal leadership, since the views of the electorate should be translated directly into public policy. Rather than shaping or directing policy, politicians simply follow the electorate (or act as delegates).

Somewhere in between these two extremes lie representative democracies. In such regimes, elected officials must be *both* leaders and followers. For some issues, politicians need only follow the wishes of the public, ensuring that these concerns find voice in specific policy. But for other issues, politicians need to become "leaders," informing and directing the public debate. This dual role is well represented by Jeffrey Tulis's (1987, 39) observation that in the American case

> the presidency . . . was intended to be representative of the people, but not merely responsive to popular will. Drawn from the people through an election (albeit an indirect one), the president was to be free enough from the daily shifts in public opinion so that he could refine it and, paradoxically, better serve popular interests.

This need for leadership in representative democracies cuts two ways. First, the public, at times, will simply be unaware of some problem or pressing concern. Here it is the responsibility of leaders to inform the public about the best course of action. So Clinton, believing NAFTA was a good thing, took his case to the people in an effort to inform them of what he thought was the best policy for the United States.

Second, citizens will periodically arrive at "bad" judgments; thus it becomes the responsibility of elected officials to move the electorate toward a new and better course of action. So Margaret Thatcher, strongly believing in the merits of conservative thinking, attempted to guide

Britain away from its socialist past. This is a much tougher test of leadership, since politicians are not forming opinion, but changing it. Despite the potential obstacles, many argue that it is sometimes important for leaders to make a case in order to prevent the public from walking down an ill-advised path.

In the face of large and often uninterested and uninformed electorates, the ability of democratic politicians to shift from being scribes to authors is critical to the effective operation of the polity. As James Madison argued in Federalist 10, a key advantage of representative government is that it can "refine and enlarge the public views, by passing them through the medium of a chosen body of citizens, whose wisdom may best discern the true interest of their country, and whose patriotism and love of justice will be least likely to sacrifice it to temporary or partial considerations."[2]

Other astute observers have echoed Madison's theme about the important role that elected officials play in representative governments. John Stuart Mill (1972 [1861], 352), for instance, contended that it was important to have the "very best minds" inspiring those with less talent and information. Woodrow Wilson (1952, 45) is more pointed in his call for leadership, arguing that when the "forces of the public thought" are blind, leaders "must lend them sight"; when these forces "blunder," leaders "must set them right." V. O. Key (1961, 558) continues this basic theme, claiming that when politicians fail to inform and enlighten public opinion, "a democracy tends toward indecision, decay and disaster."

Although we usually want strong leaders at the helm of a representative democracy, there is a delicate balance between leading and following public opinion. On the one hand, we do not want politicians only to lead opinion. Such action could leave important concerns of citizens untended. Moreover, politicians may use their leadership skills to pursue their own agendas, which has led some scholars to worry that excessive leadership could encourage manipulation and demagoguery.[3] But, on the other hand, no leadership at all risks giving an often ill-informed and uninterested electorate too much say on important governmental decisions. Thus,

---

2. Madison also warned that these representatives could work against the interests of the people through intrigue and corruption. Hence, representative governments, he contended, needed to be large so as to ensure that these different interests would be checked and not be allowed to dominate government.

3. The Founding Fathers, for instance, were wary of popular leadership because it might encourage emotional appeals to the masses. See Tulis (1987) for an interesting account of the rise of the "Rhetorical President," where he attempts to document a change from the Founders' view to the modern view of popular leadership.

a representative democracy must walk a tightrope between excessive leadership, which could lead to a less democratic regime, and the absence of leadership, which could allow a nation to pursue ill-conceived policies that might harm the interests of the citizenry.

This tightrope becomes even narrower and more precarious when one considers that the distinction between leadership and followership in a representative democracy is not as clear as some may initially think. James Stimson (1991, 11), for instance, questions the presumption that "leading and following are mutually exclusive activities." Part of good leadership, Stimson and others argue, involves effective followership. Or as Morris Fiorina and Kenneth Shepsle (1989, 36) observe, "*one cannot understand leadership without understanding followership*" (emphasis in original). Politicians must be able to identify those issues on which they can lead; otherwise, they risk rebuke at the next election. "Leadership, for the statesman, is interpretation," Wilson (1952, 42, 43) once argued, "He must read the common thought: he must test and calculate very circumspectly the preparation of the nation for the next move in the progress of politics," while noting later that "the ear of the leader must ring with the voices of the people." Perhaps Martin Luther King, Jr. put it best when he stated: "There go my people. I must catch them, for I am their leader."[4]

In what follows, I shall develop a theory about how elected politicians behave in office. I do so because we can understand how leadership works only in the context of how politicians behave. With this theory in hand, we can address both leadership and followership. First, I shall briefly review past work on leadership in order to identify more clearly the niche of this theory about politicians as well as some of the difficulties that lie ahead.

Narrowing the Focus

Even though a vast amount has been written about leadership, "there seems to be little cumulative advance in our understanding: the empirical regularities are neither robust nor compelling; the theoretical formulations neither precise nor reliable" (Fiorina and Shepsle 1989, 17).[5] The exact reasons for this lack of progress are not entirely clear. Part of the problem may simply be

---

4. Quoted in Chong (1992, 192). Actually, the origin of the passage from King goes back to the French Revolution, where a man sitting in a cafe suddenly sees a mob running past him and exclaims that he must follow those people since he is their leader (see Burns 1978).

5. Fiorina and Shepsle are not alone in this view, see also Jones (1989), Tucker (1981), Paige (1972, 1977), Ellis and Wildavsky (1989).

that since the subject of leadership touches so many political and social arenas, scholars have attempted to capture its full meaning; the result of these inclusive efforts is that the concept often appears amorphous and elusive.

To document this slippery quality, let us consider a few efforts to define leadership. Robert Tucker (1981, 11), for example, views leadership as "a process of human interaction in which some individuals exert, or attempt to exert, a determining influence upon others." For Glenn Paige (1977, 1), leadership is "the behavior of persons in positions of political authority, their competitors, and these both in interaction with other members of society as manifested in the past, present, and probable future throughout the world." Blondel (1987, 2–3) writes that leadership "is manifestly and essentially a phenomenon of power: it is power because it consists of the ability of the one or few who are at the top to make others do a number of things (positively or negatively) that they would not or at least might not have done."

These definitions are not bad. To the contrary, they represent some of the best thinking on this subject. But the problem is that they are very general and discourage the development of a precise understanding of what constitutes leadership. For instance, the phrase "a process of human interaction" casts a wide net, as does the idea that leadership is "a phenomenon of power." In general, these definitions suggest that leadership involves a relationship between an individual (or set of individuals) and a larger group, where the former possesses some influence over the latter. Few would disagree with that basic thrust, but it is not always clearly specified who the leaders and followers are, nor what their exact relationship is to each other. Such ambiguity has led other scholars to offer further definitions of the term in an attempt to rectify the situation. The result is a proliferation of definitions. James MacGregor Burns (1978) found more than 130 different definitions in his seminal work on the subject. Bernard Bass (1981, 7) went a step further, noting that there are "almost as many definitions of leadership as there are persons who have attempted to define the concept." In fact, because of the vast array of definitions some scholars have developed classification schemes as a way to organize previous work on the subject. Roger Stogdill, for instance, places the many definitions in an eleven-part classification scheme (Bass 1981, 7–14). Burns (1978), on the other hand, makes distinctions between different types of leadership, such as transforming or transactional.[6]

The field, in short, lacks conceptual focus. This confusion has not gone unnoticed (Burns 1978; Tucker 1981; Kellerman 1986; Blondel 1987;

---

6. See also Rockman (1984) for a useful discussion of different types of leadership.

Hargrove 1989; Jones 1989; Wildavsky 1989; Sinclair 1993; Moe 1993). In an oft-quoted statement, Burns (1978, 2) wrote that "leadership is one of the most observed and least understood phenomena on earth." Bert Rockman (1984, 19) concurred, observing that while "leadership bedazzles us," it "also befuddles us."

Can we bring the study of political leadership into conceptual focus? Some have suggested that the answer is no. Aaron Wildavsky (1989, 87) observed that leadership, in the final analysis, may be "an amorphous, undefinable subject." Cecil Gibb agreed, arguing that because of leadership's slippery quality, the "concept . . . has largely lost its value for the social sciences."[7] I reject these conclusions. The concept may be messy, but by clearing away some of the underbrush we can move towards greater clarity. The effort needs to be made, since, as Robert Dahl and Deane Nuebauer (1968, 251) once noted, "no question is as central to political discourse as that of political leadership."

The first step in clearing away the "underbrush" is to limit aspirations. I will *not* offer a general theory of political leadership. While the study of leadership has wide applicability, the relationship between leaders and followers changes in important ways across different contexts that make it difficult (if not impossible) to build an overarching theory of how all politicians might lead or follow. In a dictatorship, for instance, politicians hold nearly all the power, and citizens have few opportunities, short of revolution, to shape the behavior of leaders. But in representative democracies, the citizens have much more say in the process, since they can change leaders through elections if they are so inclined. Thus, even though leadership is important to all forms of government, the incentives for a politician in a democracy are vastly different from those in a dictatorship. These different incentives structure the behavior of politicians in such a way that may prevent a generalizable account of political leadership that would capture both situations. As a result, this book attempts to offer only a theory of *democratic* politicians.

Second, I am *not* even offering a theory of how all democratic politicians behave in office. The theory applies only to those politicians (or parties) who lead government (or who seek to lead it).[8] Individual members of legislatures, such as the U.S. Congress, are single players in a larger

---

7. Quoted in Wildavsky (1989, 87).

8. As described in the theory below, there are two sets of politicians who battle for control of government. Hence, this theory addresses the actions of those who win the battle and those who are hoping to win at the next election. This book does not, however, explicitly address the actions of the opposition until the sixth chapter.

game, bargaining with and cajoling other politicians to enact their preferred policies. Under these conditions, they are not the head of government and hence, fall outside of the confines of the theory that follows.[9]
Third, I shall focus solely on the relationship between politicians and the
electorate, shedding light only on how public officials attempt to lead (or
follow) the electorate on issues facing the polity. In so doing, I exclude how
politicians might lead other politicians (see Edwards 1989) or how politicians might lead the bureaucracy (see Hargrove 1994).

Even though I am limiting the terrain, this relationship between elected
officials and public opinion represents a critical aspect of representative
democracies. As suggested above, scholars have placed great importance on
how politicians translate the wishes of the electorate into policy. In addition, the relationship between governors and the governed lies at the center
of democratic government (see Key 1961; Pole 1983; Ferejohn 1990; Stokes
1993). "The open interplay of opinion and policy is," as Harold Lasswell
(1941, 15) once observed, "the distinguishing mark of popular rule."

The final step in clearing away the underbrush is my assumption that
elected politicians engage in purposive behavior. In observing the behavior of politicians and reading scholars' work about how politicians behave,
I believe that by making some simple assumptions about politicians and
their world, one can make headway in understanding how leadership
works. Both Terry Moe (1993) and Barbara Sinclair (1993) recommend this
tack as a useful way to advance the study of leadership in general, and the
presidency in particular.[10]

The rational actor approach has some immediate appeal, since democratically elected officials all have a common incentive: ensuring that at least
a majority of the public will support them in future elections.[11] This common goal has provided the basis for some useful theories about how politi-

9. Of course, if individual legislators join a governing coalition, they fall back into the theory. But in joining that team, they are no longer acting as individuals but as cogs in a political
machine. Hence, the GOP's domination of the 104th Congress is a possible example of members of Congress leading government. Since the Senate did not sign on completely to all parts
of the "Contract with America" and the presidency was in the hands of the Democrats, the case
is not ideal. But the recent behavior of the House Republicans helps to illustrate the point,
nonetheless.

10. Not all would agree with this approach. Fred Greenstein (1982) and Erwin Hargrove
(1966), two leading figures in the study of the presidency, have put personality at the center of
their explanations of presidential behavior.

11. Of course, in some electoral systems winning a plurality of votes ensures victory. In this
theory, there will be only two sets of leaders, making majority support the criterion for victory
in an election.

cians behave.[12] Of course, by making this move, many of the details and ambiguities of the political world disappear, making the theory a simplification of reality. But I am willing to make this tradeoff for a number of reasons. First, the clarity of this framework makes it possible to develop a logically consistent theory of leadership and followership. Second, rational choice theories are parsimonious.[13] These two assets are particularly attractive in light of past work that has tended to lack clarity and parsimony.

A final reason that makes these insights of potential interest is that there have been surprisingly few previous efforts to apply this framework to how politicians may lead (or follow) public opinion (Fiorina and Shepsle 1989).[14] Given that some scholars think that "the public-choice approach offers the possibility of a comprehensive theory of political leadership" (Jones 1989, 12), there is further reason to proceed with this effort.

With this underbrush cleared away, so to speak, I now define leadership and followership.

Leadership of Public Opinion   The requirements of a rational actor approach make an initial definition possible:

Democratic leadership occurs when politicians move the median point of the distribution of public opinion toward their stated position.[15]

There are two things to note about this particular definition. First, it refers to the "stated" position of the politician. The reason for this phrasing is that one can never be sure of a politician's *true* position on an issue. As Max Weber (1946) and others have observed, political life is filled with ambiguity. So, for example, when Clinton advocated health care reform, did he do so because he really cared about improving the medical system

---

12. For a sampling of such theories, see Mayhew (1974), Riker (1982), Tsebelis (1990), and Arnold (1990).

13. For those interested in an extended and useful discussion of the merits of the rational choice approach, see Tsebelis (1990). He also tackles head on many of the complaints leveled against the approach. See also Moe (1993) for a thoughtful argument about why rational choice theories offer an important approach to the study of the presidency.

14. There has been a good deal of work on applying a rational actor framework to leadership in Congress. See Fiorina and Shepsle (1989) for a list of these works. Since the relationship between members of Congress differs dramatically from that of elected official and their constituents, these theories are not of direct interest for this book.

15. Implicit in this definition is that the shift by the electorate is not temporary. If the public moves toward the politicians' position only to return to its previous position a week later, that would not count. The difficulty, of course, is knowing exactly how long the move needs to be in place before it qualifies as leadership. I see little point in offering an arbitrary period of time, noting instead that the shift in opinion must be *durable* before it can be considered "leadership."

or because he wanted to be reelected in 1996 and saw this issue as his ticket to reelection? The answer is probably both. But to avoid any debate about a politician's "true" position, I simply use the phrase "stated." Thus, I treat the *public* pronouncements made by politicians as their "stated" position.

Second, the definition states that "politicians move the median point of the distribution of public opinion." With this statement, I am focusing attention on outcomes, as opposed to inputs. Thus, the *attempt* to move the median point counts as leadership only if it succeeds. This choice of words, like that above, removes the intentions of politicians from the definition.

Followership of Public Opinion   With an initial definition of leadership in hand, I now can define followership:

Democratic followership occurs when politicians' stated positions align with the median point of the distribution of public opinion.[16]

This definition, like the one above, focuses on outputs and avoids trying to sort out the personal views and intentions of politicians. If officeholders shift their stated positions to align with that of the public's, such behavior is an obvious example of followership. At the same time, if a new issue arises and the politician just happens to occupy the same position as the public, that behavior is also treated as followership. Even if an officeholder is extremely committed to that particular policy, the fact that the politician's view matches the public's places it, according to this definition, in the followership camp.

One may be uncomfortable viewing such accidental alignments as examples of followership. Followership, for many observers, does not usually involve a personal commitment to an issue. But here such commitments are not part of the equation. The basic problem is that given the public's view and the politician's position, there is simply no *opportunity* to engage in leadership. Why would any politician try to "lead" a public that already agrees with her? Now, of course, one might respond that by enacting some policy into law a politician is practicing a form of leadership. While true, it is a kind of leadership that I have explicitly set aside in this book. The focus here is the relationship between the politician and

16. The term "followership" has a different meaning here than what we normally associate with the word. Usually followers either follow silently or claim to be taking someone else's lead. Leaders who engage in followership, in contrast, may or may not say the people are on their side, but they will certainly, as Mayhew (1974) has argued, advertise, take positions, and claim credit. Hence, politicians who follow opinion will often try to look as if they are leading it.

the public, not the relationship between different politicians in government. When a president convinces a reluctant Congress to pass some piece of legislation, that is surely leadership—but *not* leadership of public opinion.

Despite the apparent simplicity of these definitions, they are consistent with past work. James Madison and John Stuart Mill, who argued that good leaders should both be able to follow the public's dictates and be able to educate the public about the proper course for the nation, would find some merit in these definitions. These definitions also give voice to the conflicting forces of a representative democracy. That is, politicians must find ways to persuade and be persuaded by public opinion.

The advantage of these definitions, then, is not their novelty, but their clarity. These definitions also fit the observed behavior of politicians. When Franklin Roosevelt moved the electorate toward a greater willingness to support governmental intervention in the economy, that shift represented a genuine change in public opinion and can be reasonably viewed as an example of leadership. On the other hand, President Reagan's support for the social security system in the 1980s, a program that he had often opposed in speeches during the 1970s, provides a good example of followership. Since the time of FDR, the public has been committed to the social security system, and Reagan, fearing reprisal from the electorate, simply followed suit in this matter.

The Theory

With the definitions in hand, I shall now develop a bare bones theory of leadership, which follows directly in the footsteps of Anthony Downs.[17] Downsian logic, of course, has become common in the field of political science. Scholars have presented numerous models that have built upon the original insights offered by Downs and Harold Hotelling (1929). Surprisingly, the basic argument has been rarely applied to the behavior of politicians *in office*. Downs himself dedicated a number of chapters to the logic of how governments make decisions; but he did not explicitly tie his

---

17. My objective here is *not* to present a formal model of how rational officeholders behave. Instead, I want to borrow the theoretical power of these models, but not develop the more complex mathematical formulations that often comprise the best work in this area (see, for instance, Davis and Hinich 1967; Wittman 1983; Aldrich 1983a and b; Enelow and Hinich 1990). By doing so, I hope to keep the ideas presented here accessible to all kinds of scholars, ranging from historians to specialists in formal modeling.

spatial framework to how governments act. Instead, he offered a different framework to examine decisions by parties in government.[18]

But applying wholesale Downs's spatial theory of elections to the study of officeholders ignores the all too obvious point that campaigning is different from governing. Some assumptions, therefore, need modification. These adjustments not only make the theory fit better with the realities of government, but also move the argument into some new, and I think interesting, territory. For instance, this modified theory avoids the Downsian conclusion that incumbents cannot be reelected, showing instead that any officeholder who acts consistently with public opinion will win the next election—a much more sensible prediction.

For some readers, this discussion of the assumptions of the theory will be tedious. But it is essential that I lay the groundwork for this theory or otherwise some may feel that I have built little more than a house of cards. Those who are uninterested in the guts of the theory can skip to the very next subsection titled: "Applying the Theory."

The Assumptions   The assumptions listed below provide the starting point for this theory of how politicians behave in office:

1. There are only two types of actors: politicians[19] and citizens.
2. One set of politicians holds elected office, facing reelection at some point in the future.[20]
3. Only one rival team of politicians exists, but they do not hold office. They also face an election at some point in the future.
4. All politicians seek reelection by maximizing their popularity among citizens.

---

18. There have been other efforts to study the behavior of "rational" governments (see Mueller 1989 for review). This literature treats governments as monopolies, enacting the policies they prefer. This work, by scholars like Buchanan and Tullock, views government as making a series of decisions about taxation and spending. This approach casts the problem in the opposite direction of Downs, since voters have no say in the actual operation of government. In some sense, government for Buchanan and Tullock are the ultimate leaders, shaping and creating the direction of policy. My concern in this book is to examine the interaction between leaders and followers during government, which makes this alternative approach of limited value for the questions I ask.

19. I could refer to parties rather than politicians. However, given that this book concerns leadership—a subject that generally focuses on particular individuals—I have chosen to refer to politicians. But, as we shall see later, this model has implications for parties as well as politicians.

20. I am being unclear about what constitutes "some point in the future." It could be years or months. My point here is simply to provide the context that politicians are governing and not (officially) campaigning.

5. The ability of officeholders to enact policy is tied to their popularity among citizens. Unpopular politicians have a harder time passing legislation than popular ones.[21]
6. Both sets of politicians represent unified teams.
7. Politicians possess complete information about citizens' views on issues.
8. Each issue that faces the polity can be represented by a single, unidimensional continuum.
9. All citizens care about all issues, which makes their preferences on them "sticky."[22]
10. Citizens can estimate the politicians' views on all issues.
11. Citizens evaluate the two sets of politicians by the positions they adopt on all issues.

Those scholars familiar with Downs will recognize most of these basic assumptions. However, three main differences set off this argument from Downs's model; those differences involve the context of the theory, the role of issues, and the behavior of citizens. In what follows, I shall highlight each of the three differences, justifying them and showing some of their implications for the behavior of office-holders.

The Shift from Elections to Government   Assumptions 4 and 5 explicitly shift the political context from elections to government. For starters, officeholders are no longer interested immediately in votes, since they are not engaged in an official campaign. Instead, politicians, according to assumption 4, seek to maximize their popularity among citizens. This goal, of course, is tied closely to their chances for reelection, since we know that unpopular leaders are not kept in office (Tufte 1978; Lewis-Beck and Rice 1982; Finkel 1993).

Assumption 5 goes one step further by explicitly tying the ability of officeholders to enact public policy to their support among the electorate. Neustadt (1990), Brace and Hinckley (1992), and Edwards (1989) demon-

---

21. One could set precise standards about the minimum amount of popularity needed to be an effective governmental leader. For instance, an officeholder needs at least 50 percent support to control policy. While, obviously, more public support helps to strengthen any leader's political hand, I do not want to set any arbitrary standards. My objective is simply to suggest that popular leaders have more clout than unpopular leaders.

22. More will be said later about the term "sticky." For the moment, the key is to understand that the electorate's preferences are not fixed and vary only when good reasons are presented to them.

strate, in varying ways, the importance of popularity for presidential influence in Congress. The objective of assumption 5 is much less specific than
the arguments and ideas presented by these scholars. My point is simply
that the "machinery of government," loosely defined,[23] is more responsive
to a popular leader than to an unpopular leader.

These two assumptions are highly significant, since they address the
institutional constraints that confront politicians. A simple accountability
model, which is a rival theoretical perspective, ignores this constraint,
arguing in effect that the only popularity contest that matters is on election day. That perspective has much appeal (see especially Schattschneider
1942, 1975; Schumpeter 1950). Politicians often make exactly that claim.
Such statements, however, are usually offered by unpopular leaders who
are trying to put a positive spin on a series of bad events. The basic point
here is that politicians have a short-time horizon, especially given the
uncertainty of the future. The rule of thumb I adopt is that it is better to
be popular now than to be unpopular. While any politician would like to
peak at the time of the election, the best predictor of tomorrow's success is
today's and, consequently, politicians need to pay close attention to short-
term considerations. That is why, for instance, it is usually easier for
Congress and the President to adopt tax cuts than enact real deficit reduction, even though nearly all economists agree that reducing the deficit will
be better for the economy in the long run than a tax cut.

By tying the effectiveness of leaders to their popularity, politicians do
not, as a result, possess absolute control over government. The basic point
is that government responds better to the demands of popular leaders than
to unpopular ones. These assumptions, thus, have the advantage of sepa-
rating politicians from the actual institutions of government. In other
words, representative democracies are not under the unfettered control of
elected officials in this theory. In the classic spatial model, the winning
party is government. Now Downs (1957, 24), in his discussion of decision-
making of the government, does talk about the institutional "apparatus"
that politicians seek to control. But this distinction fades as his model
assumes that the governing party controls the action of all other players in
government (Downs 1957, 26). In my theory, however, politicians are in
complete charge of government only when they are extremely popular

---

23. Such machinery could involve a parliamentary system (e.g., Britain, Norway), separated
powers (e.g., United States), or just a sluggish bureaucracy.

with the electorate, and even then government is not the same thing as the politicians who head it.

These assumptions, nevertheless, do greatly simplify the institutional context facing politicians. This theory ignores, for instance, such specifics as "divided" government—a recurring pattern in American politics (Jacobson 1990; Mayhew 1991; Fiorina 1992). Nor does it consider the historical context that confronts leaders (Skowronek 1993; Hargrove 1994). By assuming that only one set of politicians runs government, I am putting aside the details of the political and institutional constraints that often plague (or aid) politicians. These different contexts have been shown to matter greatly for the prospects of leadership (see Burns 1984; Rockman 1984; Ellis and Wildavsky 1989; Skowronek 1993). For the American case, Neustadt (1990) has persuasively argued that because of institutional design, presidents must bargain with politicians from the legislative branch. In fact, Neustadt sees the presidency as an office weak in formal powers that forces its occupant to rely on personal skill to forge successful political alliances. Thus, to ignore such specific constraints may seem problematic to some readers.

Kernell (1993), however, offers a different way to think about the presidency, which focuses on "going public" rather than bargaining. Kernell's theory puts the relationship between the chief executive and the citizenry at its core. The argument presented here, therefore, falls much more in Kernell's camp than in Neustadt's.[24] That is, by limiting the focus to the relationship between politicians and citizens, this theory talks, in a sense, about the prospects of "going public."

This decision to simplify institutional context also keeps the theory as straightforward as possible—an advantage in and of itself. But, more important, the theory can be applied to democratic governments in general, which broadens its potential appeal to scholars in the field of comparative politics. So while I am being unclear here about this "institutional drag," I am hoping that I have provided a general theory that can be applied to other countries besides the United States.

These assumptions, in tandem, not only shape the behavior of officeholders, but also give the opposition incentives to stake out positions that minimize the public support of those who govern. In particular, this competitive environment provides the opportunity to solve one of the nag-

---

24. Tulis (1987) offers additional support for this focus, since he, like Kernell, documents the increased tendency of presidents to engage in popular leadership.

ging problems that Downs (1957, 62) identified in his discussion of incumbent parties:

> the opposition need only follow the policy-*matching* strategy, thus narrowing the election down to some Arrow-problem issue, and wait for the government to commit itself on that issue. Then it merely selects the policy that defeats whatever the government has chosen, and—presto—it is elected [my emphasis].

The Downsian spatial model, as a result, yields the discomforting conclusion that incumbent politicians cannot get reelected. This claim, while logical, rests, in part, on the assumption that matching is a viable strategy.[25] But Downs and others have assumed that every issue confronting parties is a kind of mini-election. Politicians seek to maximize votes, and citizens cast ballots for either set of politicians. In this theory, by contrast, citizens are *not* choosing between parties in an election, but, instead, are approving or disapproving of the incumbent's policies.[26] The electorate is stuck with one set of politicians for a period of time (as specified by a constitution). Thus, rational citizens will want those politicians heading government to succeed. The public has little incentive to see any set of rulers fail, since that failure undermines the quality of their lives. Under such conditions, if the opposition adopts exactly the same position, the leadership can claim ownership of that issue. Being responsible and accountable for the acts of government, they will get credit (or blame) for it. Since the median position, by assumption, is the ideal point for maximizing support, officeholders will get lots of credit.

With this arrangement, the opposition will have an incentive to *differentiate* itself from the governing politicians on each issue, even if it is by a very small amount. Otherwise, incumbent politicians will control each issue and greatly increase their standing with the public. In the health care debate of 1993–94, for example, Republicans supported the concept of health care reform but did not support Clinton's specific plan. Instead, the GOP offered alternatives to the so-called Health Security Act. Thus,

---

25. Another assumption that generates the conclusion that incumbent parties lose their bids for re-election is that voters will have different preference rankings for issues, allowing intense minorities to work together to defeat the party in power (Downs 1957, 55–62).

26. Downs (1957, 43–45) actually hints at this decision rule in his discussion of "performance rating" of incumbents. However, "voters use performance ratings only when their current party differentials are zero," assuming that the rating itself is a non-zero quantity (Downs 1957, 44). In this theory, performance ratings drive the process and are not an auxiliary decision rule.

the opposition tried to prevent Clinton from controlling the issue by carving out a base for its own support. In so doing, the GOP hoped not only to minimize the potential gains Clinton might have secured from health care reform, but, more importantly, block that particular bill from becoming law.

There are two advantages to a move away from the policy of matching—each of which lends credibility to this theory. First, and most important, if those in power always adopt the popular position on each issue, they will ensure themselves of reelection regardless of what the opposition does. Thus, if the opposition is to have a chance in any upcoming election, it must hope for the incumbent party to make a mistake—a proposition consistent with the notion of retrospective voting. Such an outcome for incumbent politicians makes much more sense both theoretically and empirically than the Downsian conclusion that officeholders are doomed to electoral defeat.

The second advantage of this argument is consistent with the empirical results from the presidential approval rankings conducted by Gallup and other polling firms. To begin, we should expect that incumbents should hover just slightly over 50 percent approval. Given that the opposition differentiates itself slightly from the ruling politicians, we should generally see leaders with popularity over 50 percent. George Edwards (1990, 157) has summarized all the Gallup poll data on presidential popularity. While there is, of course, variance, presidents since Eisenhower have averaged about 55 percent approval—a finding consistent with the basic predictions of this theory.

This framework is also consistent with the boost in popularity presidents often get at the beginning of military actions or crises in foreign affairs (see Mueller 1970; Brody 1991; Brace and Hinckley 1992). The opposition, not wishing to be tarred as disloyal, supports the governing politicians on such matters (i.e., perfect matching). Seeing no initial disagreement, the public rallies to the President's side, increasing his popularity. Thus, the inability to differentiate themselves on such matters puts the opposition in a hole. So we can see highly popular leaders within this theory, but only *when* an issue arises that forces consensus among the competing politicians.[27]

[handwritten margin notes: "this is a stretch" and "Unclear how he gets there from his assumptions"]

---

27. If such a scenario unfolds, the surge in popularity of the incumbent could provide some additional flexibility in pursuing future policies. Specifically, a highly popular politician could adopt some non-median positions on issues, since the officeholder could afford to sacrifice some of this accumulated political capital. I will raise this possibility in Chapter 4.

This explicit move to the governmental arena has further implications: officeholders may be *freer* to adopt support-maximizing policies than suggested in the original spatial model. Downs (1957, 55–60) mentions that the positions incumbents adopt when facing reelection are just reflections of their actions in office. In contrast, officeholders in this theory are developing and implementing the policies that *will* constrain them in the upcoming election. Now, elected officials do not have complete mobility, since radical shifts in positions adopted during the previous campaign would undermine their credibility. Moreover, as their term unfolds, previous actions in office will serve as an ever increasing constraint. Nonetheless, elected officials have some additional flexibility when adopting particular policies that can maximize their standing among the public.

This point becomes even clearer if we distinguish between "new" and "old" issues. One can think of *campaign* issues as old issues; that is, issues for which politicians have already staked out positions during the previous election. For these matters, governing politicians will face the constraints placed upon them by their stated positions during that campaign. Of course, politicians may have been vague enough on campaign issues to avoid tagging themselves with a clearly defined position (Stokes 1993; Geer 1993), which gives them some freedom in pursuing a particular course of action once in office. Perhaps even more important, many of the issues confronting any elected official can be considered "new." Not only will there be issues that were ignored during the election, but there will also be a large number of emerging (i.e., brand new) issues that confront officeholders during their terms. When Iraq invaded Kuwait, President Bush was not constrained by any specific campaign promises and instead could forge a position as he saw fit (see Mueller 1994). For these "new" concerns, politicians have much more flexibility.

Finally, let me return briefly to the short-term orientations of the politicians in this theory. Since politicians face an election in the future, why can't they adopt, one might ask, a long-term perspective? That is, why can't politicians undertake unpopular actions in the short term to increase their popularity in the long term? This question becomes even more pressing in light of Douglas Arnold's (1990) work. He builds a powerful theory of congressional behavior on the notion that politicians *anticipate* the behavior of voters at election time, which gives a more long-term cast to the problem.[28] While Arnold's theory has much appeal, members of Congress are much

---

28. Key (1961) develops a very similar idea, calling it "latent opinion."

different actors from the officeholders envisioned in this argument. Specifically, politicians here are executive or parliamentary heads of government, trying to pass legislation as needed for their continued public support. Within this context, a visible opposition exists that would seize on such "far-sightedness," making life as miserable as possible for the politicians in office. The opposition could claim that the governing group is undemocratic and is trying to manipulate public opinion. The opposition in fact lives for such opportunities. In Arnold's world, however, the member of Congress is just one player in a much larger game. The opposition for Arnold *only* appears at the time of next election. So, politicians in that game can look to the future, since there is no official opposition undermining them while they support or oppose legislation. But because my players are running government and always facing a competing set of politicians, these officeholders have a short-term horizon, especially in their attempts to enact as much popularly supported legislation as possible.[29]

The Issues Facing Officeholders   The explicit shift to the context of governing also has implications for the unidimensional assumption (#8), which has been a frequent subject of concern (Stokes 1963). Donald Stokes (1993, 2) in a recent article has once again questioned the applicability of this spatial assumption, reminding readers that

> . . . it was a third . . . axiom, the assumption of *ordered dimensions*, that led me to note the existence of "valence" issues with a structure radically different from the "position" issues that lent themselves to the spatial framework. The frailty of this axiom was the most fundamental critical point I raised about the spatial models.

This very credible and serious attack, however, is aimed at the *campaign*. As Stokes (1993, 20) himself states, valence issues are the stuff of campaigns, but "position issues will face a government in power." Hence, by moving the context of the theory to how politicians govern, one of the major weaknesses of the spatial model is lessened. Bill Clinton can no longer simply claim that increasing the number of jobs requires us "to expand our export base and to expand trade on terms that are fair to us."[30] He must instead propose and adopt specific policies, such as NAFTA,

---

29. See Croley (1994) for additional questions about the distinction Arnold and others make between "short-term" versus "long-run" calculations.

30. This statement comes from an answer Bill Clinton offered during the October 15, 1992 debate in Richmond between himself, Bush, and Perot.

that are designed to solve the problem. In so doing, he acts more consistently with the notion of ordered dimensions associated with the unidimensional assumption. Thus, even what appears to be the same issue often is recast from a valence issue to a position issue, once the politician assumes power.

In addition, I do *not* limit the theory to only one issue, as is usually the case. Here, politicians can focus on a number of issues, but their decisions about what positions to adopt will be taken one at a time. Each decision can be thought of as a separate battle where the officeholder seeks to maximize political support on that issue. Of course, a politician may apply a similar ideological orientation when deciding what position to adopt in each case, but that does not undermine the workings of this assumption.

In the presidency literature, there is a belief that occupants of the Oval Office should limit their attention to a few issues at a time (Neustadt 1990; Kernell 1993). Given this assessment, one way to think of this assumption is that the politicians in this theory face an issue every day (or week) and tackle that issue in a way that best maximizes support. Thus, over the course of the year, the officeholder has addressed numerous issues, but has done so one at a time. The Reagan administration did in fact try to limit the President to one theme per day in an effort to control the content of the news media. This basic point is also consistent with the criticisms Clinton received for not being focused enough.

By allowing multiple issues in the theory, however, I must assume independence among them. That is, as each issue arises, the officeholder treats it as an independent event—much like separate rolls of the dice. Of course, this assumption ignores the fact that politicians may treat particular sets of issues as packages, rather than one at a time. While this assumption simplifies matters, it still allows us to move away from focusing on a single issue.[31]

At first blush, some may be worried about this assumption. But consider the "Contract with America." It was constructed in a manner perfectly consistent with this assumption. As we now know, the GOP relied heavily on the surveys of Frank Luntz and Associates when writing the

---

31. Actually, Downs (1957, 54) at one point in discussing government decision-making assumes that all "choices are independent of each other, i.e., the outcome of each decision has no bearing on the possible choices or outcomes of any other decision." At a later point, Downs (1957, 132) suggests that one can think of party's position as a "weighted average of the positions of all the particular policies it upholds." Under this notion, a rational party can pursue a mix of moderate and extreme positions in order to maximize votes. To pursue such a strategy, Downs also had to assume (implicitly) that the issues were independent of each other.

contract. The issues that garnered very favorable ratings with the public were included in the contract and those that did not were left off. There was little discussion about how these policies fit together, rather the concern was maximizing popularity. This bullet approach did lead to some trouble after the election, as GOP members of Congress realized that some of the planks ran counter to each other. But in the end, 9 of the 10 items passed the House, with only the term limits amendment failing to garner the two-thirds vote necessary.

Citizen's Preferences   The final set of changes involve the assumptions about citizens. Assumption 9 reads that citizens care about all issues and have "sticky" preferences on them. So, unlike most spatial models, I am *not* assuming that voters have fixed views on policy (see Riker 1990). But I am interested in studying leadership, which involves, broadly speaking, the ability of politicians to change the public's thinking on some matter— an idea that runs counter to the notion of *fixed* preferences.

Surprisingly, few efforts have been made to consider explicitly the possibility of changes in the preferences of citizens (see, however, Riker 1990; Dunleavy 1991). It is clear from studies in public opinion that people do change their views on policy, and scholars have made a number of attempts to understand how and why (see Page and Shapiro 1992; Zaller 1992; Iyengar and Kinder 1987). Riker (1986, 1990) has tried to rectify this neglect by studying heresthetics and rhetoric. The former involves politicians trying to alter the political agenda to their benefit while the latter concerns the persuasion of voters. The theory developed here follows Riker's notion of the rhetorical politician although, later, the manipulation of the agenda will also become an important part of our story.

There are a number of reasons to abandon the assumption of fixed preferences. First, politicians may under some conditions fear changing their own positions, given the likely outcries of "flip-flop," and may, instead, attempt to convince the public to move closer toward them (Riker 1990; Dunleavy 1991; Geer 1992). Second, when scholars have assumed fixed preferences, they are really assuming them to be fixed at that given time. It does not preclude the possibility of change down the road—otherwise the distribution of opinion could never be altered, and parties would never adjust their positions (once they found the ideal point). In addition, when making the assumption that voters have fixed views on policy, scholars must assume implicitly that the amount of persuasive information that formed those preferences is constant.[32] But, in this theory politicians may present *new* information (or new arguments) as they try to move the distribution of opinion. These efforts further undermine the notion of fixed preferences, since citizens armed with new information may reconsider their views.

So while abandoning the notion of fixed views on policy makes sense, one may wonder what constitutes a "sticky" preference. The basic idea here is that since citizens care about the issues, they are reasonably committed to their views. It is neither easy nor impossible for politicians to alter the public's views. More important, it is costly for politicians to change these preferences. Because of the commitment citizens have to their "sticky" views, officeholders must expend a good deal of energy to win over a doubtful electorate. Even with such effort, the attempt will not be an overnight success and may well fail. Hence, politicians will be careful before embarking on that kind of endeavor. While the concept of "stickiness" lacks precision, it is closer to the truth. That is, citizens do have stable preferences that will, under some conditions, shift (Page and Shapiro 1992; Stimson 1991; Zaller 1992).

As a final topic, I want to address why this theory speaks to citizens, not voters. This focus may puzzle some, since it is voters that politicians ultimately care about and with turnout hovering around 50 percent, there may a big difference between the preferences of "citizens" and that of "voters." First, since this theory is focussing on how politicians govern, it is important that we talk about citizens rather than voters, because government is suppose to serve the interests of the former. Second, citizens who did not vote in the previous election are still potential voters in the next one, so politicians have interests in trying to mobilize the previously unengaged. Finally, there is little difference empirically between the distribution of aggregated preferences of citizens and voters, which means that the mean, median, and variance of opinion are largely unaffected by which group one addresses.[33]

---

32. At this point, it is important to distinguish between the assumption of "complete" versus "perfect" information. Complete information involves knowing the policy choices of all relevant actors. Perfect information goes one step further, where voters know all the consequences of their actions. Under the latter condition, an actor would be able to anticipate all future arguments and thus there would be *no* new arguments a politician could make to a voter to change his or her mind on a particular policy.

33. Using data from both the 1988 and 1992 National Election Studies, there is almost no difference in the shape of preferences of the two groups: voters and citizens. These questions, 12 in

Further Objections   Even though one may find some of the changes attractive, other parts of the theory are sure to be a source of concern. For instance, by limiting the argument to politicians and citizens, I ignore the important role of party activists and members of the news media. We know, for instance, that the news media influence how citizens think about politics (see Iyengar and Kinder 1987). We also know that activists are important players in the game (see Abramowitz, Rapaport and McGlennon 1986; Jennings and Miller 1986; Miller 1988). Scholars such as Sjoblom (1968) and Aldrich (1983) have shown the theoretical relevance of party activists to the spatial model. Even so, it is reasonable to limit our initial focus to citizens and politicians, since most previous discussions of opinion leadership concern leaders and followers, giving little role to intermediaries. But, as we proceed in this essay, other actors will make (cameo) appearances in the story.

One may also question why politicians in this theory are not motivated by policy, especially since views on policy would provide an obvious incentive for politicians to try to lead public opinion. To compound this potential concern, a number of scholars have constructed theories that assume parties (or politicians) are driven by views on policy (see, for instance, Wittman 1983; Chappell and Keech 1986). Of course, politicians do have policy goals, as implied in the general idea of leadership. I assume, however, that concerns about policy take second place to maximization of public support.[34] The reason for this particular ranking is that politicians need the public's support before they can effectively pursue policy. As one Congressional liaison observed: "when you go up to the Hill and the latest polls show Carter isn't doing well, then there isn't much reason for a member to go along with him" (Kernell 1993, 33). Seymour Sudman (1982, 307), observing the behavior of Richard Nixon and Lyndon Johnson, noted that the "emphasis was on retaining or recovering presidential popularity rather than in making wise policy judgments" (see also Altschuler 1990). More recently, Kernell (1993, 190) has systematically

---

total, all asked respondents to place themselves on a seven-point scale for issues ranging from abortion to government spending. The average difference between the mean position of voters and all respondents was less than .1 (on the 7 point scale). For the standard deviation, the gap was just, on average, .05. The median position was exactly the same for both groups in 10 of the 12 cases. I thank Rick Herrera for making these results available to me.

34. As will be shown later, there are a set of issues in which maximization of support does not figure prominently into the calculations of politicians, allowing policy goals to reemerge.

demonstrated that even "a modest downturn in a president's poll rating" triggered "a flurry of public relations activities from the White House." Clinton was surely aware of the importance of his popularity. As a *New York Times* headline in 1993 read, "Clinton's Plan for Economy May Hinge on His Popularity."[35]

Other assumptions too may trouble readers. Treating both sets of politicians as representing unified teams is an obvious simplification. For some countries, like Britain, it is more reasonable than for the United States. Treating the President as a unitary actor, however, is not a serious problem, since executives tend to be unified—at least by comparison to other actors like political parties or legislatures. The problem is more serious for the opposing set of politicians. The opposition, being out of power, may find to harder to unite. However, the Republican National Committee and visible figures like Robert Dole and Newt Gingrich have organized a coherent opposition to many of Clinton's actions. And, of course, following the 1994 midterm elections, Congressional Republicans became highly unified, especially in the House.

If one likes shooting fish in a barrel, it would prove great sport to attack each and every assumption presented here. But by modifying the assumptions to increase the realism of the theory, one must make the argument "more cumbersome, less elegant, and less parsimonious" (Jones 1989, 44–5). Kelley (n.d., 19) describes this situation well, noting that the "model builder attempts to map the world, not describe it. His gamble is that real-world conditions absent from, or imperfectly related in a model will turn out to be relatively unimportant conditions for the purposes at hand. It is a gamble taken for the sake of simplicity in specifying relationships and the ability to make definite predictions about outcomes." Thus, I ask the reader to suspend judgment about the assumptions and instead see what kinds of insights can be gained by this admittedly crude theory of how politicians behave in office. Or to put it another way, let us wait to see whether the "gamble" pays off.

---

35. David E. Rosenbaum (1993), p. 1. Also an article by Thomas Edsall in the *Washington Post National Weekly Edition* makes a similar point, stating that Clinton's troubles with Congress are largely tied to his declining popularity in the polls (May 10–16, 1993, p. 23).

Applying the Theory

Given the assumptions of our theory, rational officeholders should adopt the position of the median citizen in the distribution of opinion on the issues that face the government (see Figure 1.1).[36] This prediction is, of course, analogous to Downs's famous observation that competitive parties move to the center of the distribution (Downs 1957, 118). Officeholders make this move for two reasons. First, the median position will maximize public support in the short term, providing increased influence in government. Second, this decision takes place in a competitive environment. If officeholders fail to take the median position, the opposition will seize the "center" to maximize their own support so as to increase their chances of winning the next election. Thus, leaders in our theory not only adopt median positions to maximize political support in the short term, but also to increase the prospects for reelection in the long term.

In this theory, leadership, as defined earlier, does *not* exist, since politicians are just reflecting the public's views. Only when the public changes its positions do leaders switch their views, indicating that rational politicians only practice followership. Consequently, the engine of change lies with the citizenry, not elected officials (Downs 1957; Jones 1989). In this simple world, rational politicians do not lead public opinion. They only follow it.[37]

The prediction that leadership never occurs, of course, is at odds with the observed behavior of politicians. A number of scholars have shown that presidents do from time to time lead public opinion (see, for instance, Page and Shapiro 1984, 1992; Edwards 1983, 1989). We need only to search our own memories for examples of leadership. Winston Churchill's actions during World War II or Harry Truman's efforts regarding postwar Europe can be considered examples of "leadership."

---

36. Diagram 1.1 depicts public opinion as normally distributed. Given the theory, I do not need to make any assumptions about the shape of the distribution of opinion. Barry (1970) has shown, for example, that even if the distribution is bimodal, it is still rational for politicians to adopt the median position.

37. Since preferences are not "fixed" in my theory, politicians could, one might argue, lead opinion. But since politicians have a short time-horizon in this argument, any such efforts would lead to an immediate drop in support. And that outcome will be avoided by politicians seeking to maximize public support.

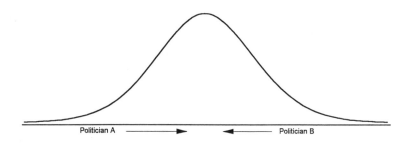

FIGURE I.I Classic Model of Party Competition

But this theory is a "bare bones" approach to how politicians behave in office. Downs (1957), when confronting this same problem in regard to elections, saw an opportunity for rational politicians to lead public opinion. By relaxing the assumption that all citizens care about the issue (i.e., possess "sticky" preferences), opportunities for leadership arise.[38] When citizens do not possess a particular preference (or are unsure about their views), leaders can try to convince them to form (or to shift) positions in an effort to maximize public support. Thus, support-maximizing politicians can "lead" opinion.[39]

This slightly revised theory of how politicians behave is now consistent with many of the ideas of Mill, Madison, Wilson, and Key, despite the simplifying assumptions. That is, politicians lead opinion when the public is unsure about its views, which allows officeholders to shape and to

---

38. Downs's original model relaxed the assumption that voters have fixed preferences. But as noted earlier, I have modified that original assumption to fit this argument to the study of leadership. Even though the assumptions from the two theories are different, the basic idea still stems from Downs and I just want to acknowledge that fact.

39. By relaxing this assumption, some additional modifications to the theory arise. Specifically, the revised assumptions 10 and 11 would read: 10. Citizens can estimate the politicians' views on all issues citizens care about; 11. Citizens evaluate the two sets of politicians by the positions they adopt on those issues citizens care about.

The assumption that citizens evaluate politicians only on those issues they care about fits better with the observed behavior of the electorate (Kelley 1983). In addition, citizens no longer need to estimate politicians' positions on all issues—just those they care about. This move too has empirical support, since Kelley (1983) has shown that voters are much better judges of the candidates' positions on those issues they find salient than those they do not.

define those views. So when Bill Clinton took to the airwaves to generate support for his health care plan, he was trying to mold an uncertain electorate around the proposal he thought best met the needs of the American people. These conclusions about the role of leadership and followership should bolster our faith in the theory, since despite the simplifying assumptions, it provides an account of leadership consistent with many previous theories.

I must, however, issue a word of caution. This theory does not allow politicians, as Woodrow Wilson (1952, 49) once argued, to "defy public opinion." That is, when the electorate cares about an issue deeply and has well-developed (or sticky) preferences on it, rational officeholders will only follow opinion under those conditions. Leaders will not take contrary stands in an effort to persuade the electorate to adopt a new course. This part of the theory may cause concern, since some observers may think that leaders do occasionally try to convince an already committed electorate to change its mind and adopt a new course. In fact, some equate that effort with the ultimate test of leadership (e.g. Burns 1978; Nixon 1982, Wilson 1952). That concern, while important, will be addressed in an orthodox way (within the confines of this theory) in the next section.

Politicians and Information

The chances for leadership, at this point, hinge on what kinds of assumptions we make about citizens. Politicians, the other major players in our game, have not so far been part of these calculations. But once we explicitly consider assumptions about the information politicians possess about public opinion, a new way to think about leadership emerges.[40]

As shown above, support-maximizing officeholders practice followership when the public possesses sticky preferences on an issue. That is, politicians will stake out a position near the median citizen in order to maximize public support. This prediction holds if we assume that politicians possess complete information about the public's views on the issue

---

40. One can, of course, play with other assumptions, such as the number of unified teams of politicians and the absence of political activists. When doing so, it is possible to generate scenarios under which "leadership" would be rational. My goal, however, is to build a simple theory that limits its attention to the two major players in our leadership game: politicians and citizens. In so doing, the argument will be potentially applicable to a variety of political contexts. And once applied to those contexts, like Britain or Japan, one can modify the assumptions so that they better fit those particular situations.

(assumption 7). If we relax that assumption, however, an alternative mechanism arises for leading public opinion. Politicians, not knowing the true median position of the electorate, may pursue a policy that is out of step with the public's views. Thus, a poorly informed officeholder might accidentally stake out position A rather than position B (see Figure 1.2).

But this mistake in judging the electorate's thinking provides politicians, ironically, with an opportunity to "lead" public opinion. Politicians may believe they are explaining their position to an electorate already in agreement with them, when they are actually convincing the public to alter its position (see Figure 1.3). Recall that even though citizens have preferences on this salient issue (assumption 9), the preferences are not fixed. Thus, an effective set of speeches could lead citizens to alter their attitudes. We know that citizens will change their views under certain circumstances, especially if given good reason to do so. As a result, this *mistake* need not cost the politicians the support of the public.

The opposition, of course, could point out the mistake, but they too lack complete information. Under this condition, they may offer a position close to that of the governing politicians, or they may present an alternative view based on their own (flawed?) perception of opinion. If the opposition correctly judges opinion, governing politicians stand to lose support, perhaps contributing to their defeat at the next election. On the other hand, if the opposition follows the judgment of those in power, it may make it easier for the governing officials to influence opinion. Finally,

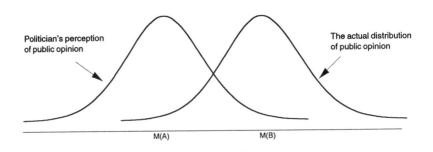

Politician's perception of public opinion

The actual distribution of public opinion

M(A)   M(B)

FIGURE 1.2 Perceived v. Actual Distribution of Public Opinion

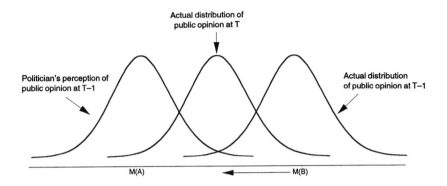

FIGURE 1.3 Leadership by Mistake

if the opposition stakes out a position different from that of the governing politicians *and* it is also flawed, then the issue will become the focus of a leadership contest. The governing politicians or the opposition may move opinion, by accident, toward their "flawed" position, thereby making great gains in the public's eyes. Of course, both attempts may fail, leaving both camps worse off in the public's view.

However one cuts it, leadership of opinion takes on a vastly different meaning within this revised theory. Usually leadership is associated with the purposeful actions of politicians trying to chart a new course for a nation (Burns 1978; Wilson 1952; Rockman 1984). Here we see that rational, poorly informed politicians may "lead" public opinion on highly salient issues as the result of an error in judgment. Thus, rational politicians can become "leaders" by mistake. Such an interpretation goes against the conventional wisdom, which argues that leaders induce "followers to act for certain goals that represent the values and motivations . . . *of both leaders and followers*. And the genius of leadership lies in the manner in which leaders see and act on their own and their followers' values and motivations" (Burns 1978, 19).

Even though unconventional, this alternative view has merit. Do leaders always intentionally move public opinion? Or do they just seek to maximize public support while a chain of events raises them to the status of "leader"? We generally label a politician as a "leader" only *after* the fact. That is, if the outcome is good (e.g., solving an economic crisis or winning a war), we may elevate that individual to the status of leader. But by using the outcomes of policy to establish who the leaders are, we may include politicians who were not leading, as defined by most scholars, but instead were trying to follow public opinion. Although some leadership may be the intended consequence of politicians seeking to steer the nation in new directions,[41] we expect under conditions of incomplete information that some leadership will occur by accident.

Anecdotal evidence suggests that acts, like heroism, have been undertaken without advance understanding of their outcomes. When one considers that a central task of leadership is to gauge correctly the public's aspirations (see Lowell 1913, Wilson 1952, Key 1961), it is reasonable to believe that politicians, from time to time, misjudge the nature of those aspirations. Despite the "error," the public may respond to that course of action, resulting in "leadership by mistake."

An Expanded Account of Leadership

This modified theory leads to a better understanding of how leadership works. Figure 1.4 presents the four types of behavior that arise, depending on whether one assumes that politicians possess complete information or not, and whether citizens possess well-developed preferences or not.[42]

The left-hand side of the diagram presents the two types of "leadership" already envisioned in Downs's original formulation. First, when citizens have sticky preferences and politicians know those preferences, we predict that support-maximizing officeholders will engage in "followership." Second, on issues where the public does not have strongly held preferences, rational politicians can practice what I term *Wilsonian* leadership.[43]

---

41. See, for instance, Wills's (1992) interesting analysis of Lincoln's Gettysburg Address. According to Wills, this speech is an example of a politician trying to lead a nation (or perhaps more appropriately trying to give it "a new birth of freedom.")

42. For the purposes of this argument, I distinguish between citizens who have well-developed and poorly developed preferences. These phrases are designed to capture the idea represented in assumption 9 that citizens care about an issue and hence possess sticky preferences. More will be said about this matter in Chapter 4.

43. I chose this particular phrase because of Wilson's extensive writings on the subject where he argues that an effective leader is one who can give voice to the latent concerns of the public. This view of leadership is best represented in Wilson's (1952) *Leaders of Men*. A careful reading of this interesting little book will find that Wilson also calls for politicians to persuade a committed electorate to change its mind.

Despite the inconsistency, Wilson, for the most part, challenges elected officials to rally an unengaged public to their position.

	Complete Information	Incomplete Information
Well-Developed Preferences	Followership	Leadership by mistake
Poorly Developed Preferences	Wilsonian Leadership	Followership by mistake*

FIGURE 1.4 Differing Types of Leadership and Followership

* This cell will be developed more fully in chapter 4.

That is, politicians attempt to move and to shape the distribution of public opinion toward their stated position. If these attempts are successful, then that behavior counts as "leadership."

The new twist arises when elected officials are uncertain of the public's preferences, as shown on the right side of the diagram. For the issues on which the public has well-developed preferences (i.e., sticky), rational politicians will always try to follow public opinion. Their efforts may, however, be misguided, resulting either in the loss of public support or leadership by accident. A second kind of mistake arises when citizens lack well-formed opinions. Here, politicians can practice Wilsonian leadership, but they are unsure about the public's views. As a result, poorly informed politicians will, at times, miss opportunities to shape public opinion. Thus, they may practice followership when such behavior is unnecessary.[44]

44. Of course, an important irony is that a misguided attempt at followership by a poorly informed politician may still produce an unintended shift in public opinion. This counts as leadership under the definition presented here. I shall set this matter aside, however, until the fourth chapter.

At other times, they will try to rally the electorate to their cause; in such instances, with an impressionable electorate, they may be effective.

Adjusting the Definition of Leadership

With this account of how rational politicians might practice leadership, I want to reconsider the initial definition of leadership posited earlier in this chapter. The original definition read as follows:

Democratic leadership occurs when politicians move the median point of the distribution of opinion toward their stated position.

Given this definition, one might ask whether "leadership by mistake" counts. Can politicians engage in leadership when they did not intend to do so? From a normative point of view, one might prefer that politicians lead by design rather than as an accidental byproduct of incomplete information, since the former may seem more noble and purposive than the latter. But the outcome remains the same in either case; that is, the electorate does shift its position toward the politician's.

Interestingly, a similar question arises in the study of representation—a close cousin to leadership. Philip Converse and Roy Pierce (1986, 630–631), in their award-winning book on France, grapple with these very questions. If a politician accidentally represents the public's interests, does that behavior qualify as representation? By the same token, what if an officeholder intends to represent her constituents but fails in the effort? Does that behavior count as representation? These inquiries led Converse and Pierce to examine the ability of French legislators to judge the sentiment of their districts accurately. Their basic view is that if politicians do not have very good information about the views of constituents, then mistakes are understandable. But if politicians have good information, mistakes *should* not be part of the equation.

The parallel between their argument and mine is obvious. Poorly informed politicians can engage in leadership and representation by mistake. But when politicians are well-informed, leadership by mistake should no longer exist.

The second step in revisiting the initial definition of leadership concerns a small, but important, adjustment. Currently, leadership involves moving the distribution of opinion on an issue, which implicitly assumes that all members of the electorate both care about and possess "sticky" preferences on the issue. But, as we have seen, I have relaxed the assumption about the preferences of citizens, which now permits two types of leadership in the theory. One involves the attempt of an officeholder to change an existing distribution of opinion, which I shall refer to as *Periclean* Leadership.[45] In these instances, the public cares about the issue and has preferences on it. Such examples of leadership are not common, since under the assumption of sticky preferences it is difficult to change an existing distribution of opinion. The second kind of leadership, which I have already labeled *Wilsonian*, involves the attempt by politicians to create a distribution of opinion that favors their stated position. Here most of the public does not initially care about the issue or have clear preferences on it. The task of the leader is to give life to such views. This kind of leadership is more common and since most issues will fall into this camp, I must revise the initial definition:

Democratic leadership occurs either when politicians move an existing distribution of opinion toward their stated position OR when they create a distribution of opinion favoring their stated position.

Conclusion

This chapter has applied the theory of how politicians behave in office to the study of leadership. Despite the strong assumptions that underlie this theory, we have not only an account of leadership consistent with previous work, but we have also derived a new way to think about it. No longer should we consider the acts of "leaders" as only intentional. Instead, it is quite possible that politicians stumble into acts of leadership.

This new wrinkle, as we will see, has much import for the way we think about politicians and how they behave. Specifically, the argument places at its core the role of information for politicians. In what follows, I shall suggest that recent changes in the amount of information available to politicians may have systematically recast how leadership works in modern democracies. If so, then perhaps the "gamble" has paid off. That is, we have a theory that helps us understand the workings of real-world politics and, more important, how those workings have changed over the last 100 years.

45. I borrow this term from Wills's (1994) book on leadership. Wills and others have noted that Thucydides' description of Pericles during Athens' war with Sparta represents a nearly ideal form of leadership—where the hero rallies the people to his side in an epic struggle.

INFORMATION AND OPINION POLLS

ACCORDING TO THE ARGUMENT
developed in the previous chapter, the quality of information that politicians have affects how leadership works. When rational politicians possess complete information about the electorate's views on important issues, they will, according to the theory, engage in followership. But when they have flawed (or incomplete) information on such pressing matters, politicians will periodically make mistakes when judging the views of the electorate. These errors can result in leadership by mistake. Even though it may be interesting theoretically that politicians behave differently under conditions of complete and incomplete information, does this distinction shed any light on how political leadership works empirically? In other words, do we have reason to believe that politicians have had access (at varying times) to "complete" and "incomplete" information about public opinion?

The answer is yes. It is easy to believe that politicians have operated under conditions of incomplete information, which makes the scenario of "leadership by mistake" of immediate interest. But the advent of the public opinion poll represents a significant enough change in the kind of information available to politicians that it becomes reasonable now to distinguish (theoretically) between "complete" and "incomplete" information. If so, the behavior of politicians, in general, and the workings of leadership, in particular, have been altered with the introduction of the sample survey in the 1930s.[1] But before anyone accepts such a strong conclusion, I must demonstrate that polls have in fact altered information about public opinion in such a way as to warrant this important shift in assumptions. With that task complete, I need then to marshal some evidence that supports the actual workings of the theory—but that particular undertaking will have to wait until the next chapter.

Polls and the Assumption of Complete Information

Of course, it is not literally true that information gleaned from public opinion polls constitutes complete information. One need only scan the vast amount of research on public opinion to come across frequent warnings about the errors embedded in the results of survey research (see, for instance, Crespi 1988; Stimson 1991; Page and Shapiro 1992; Zaller 1992; Brehm 1993; Mueller 1994). Nonetheless, the public opinion poll (and the improvements developed since its introduction) make the assumption reasonable and worthy of our consideration.

One way to think about this change is to examine the nature of the assumption itself. Specifically, the distinction between "complete" and "incomplete" is quite crude, covering up some potentially important differences. While complete information concerns one identifiable category, incomplete information involves a vast range of possibilities. Consider the following example about two consumers, Megan and James, who are in the market to purchase a new car. Before making that decision, James, let us assume, has information only from a few friends and neighbors about what are the best automobiles. Clearly, whatever choice he makes, it will be undertaken with "incomplete" information. Megan, by contrast, while aware of the views of friends and family, has also bought all the magazines that rate the new cars, and thus has much more information about the choice before her. Yet even with this additional effort, Megan also lacks complete information. Even so, there are clear differences between the levels of information James and Megan possess. While Megan is less likely to be susceptible to the chance factors associated with relying on the opinions of others, and much less likely to choose (mistakenly) an unpopular car, James,

---

1. There were, of course, polls prior to the 1930s. Perhaps most notable were the "straw" polls that sought to predict the outcome of elections (see Robinson 1932). The first one occurred in the 1824 election (Smith 1990). These "polls" did not, however, use representative samples and they were usually not designed to gauge the public's views on matters of policy. For an excellent history of polling, see Jean Converse (1987).

not dependent on the ratings of the magazines, may be more likely to buy the car he really likes, regardless of whether it is supposed to be reliable or stylish. Hence, James might display more "leadership" than Megan, who may "follow" the advice of these supposedly objective judges of automobiles.

As this example illustrates, the distinction between "incomplete" and "complete" information can be misleading, since it lumps together vastly different situations under a single rubric. My real hope, therefore, is to show that the shift in assumptions is warranted, not because polls represent "complete" information, but because they represent a sufficient departure from the politics of the early part of the this century that we may think of politicians as members of two eras: pre-poll and post-poll.[2]

How Polls Changed Things

This argument that polls have fundamentally changed the kinds of information available to politicians will be conducted on two fronts. First, surveys, despite their flaws, represent a significant improvement in the quality of information available to politicians. At one level this point is obvious, since few would argue that polls do not represent at least a modest increase in the quality of information available to politicians about public opinion. But the amount of increase becomes clearer when we recall explicitly the kinds of information available prior to polls. In so doing, we get a better sense how polling data led to an important shift in politicians' ability to read public opinion. Second, the concept of public opinion itself has shifted with the onset of survey research. As a result, politicians think about "public opinion" differently, which further justifies the idea of distinguishing between these two eras when theorizing about the behavior of public officials.

More Accurate Information   Abraham Lincoln once stated that "what I want to get done is what the people desire to have done, and the question

---

2. The pre-poll era, as defined here, only concerns that period from the extension of mass suffrage in the 1820s to the advent of polls. As noted in the introduction of this book, the situation was probably much different when electorates were small and voting was public. As one may recall, with such a small number of voters, politicians could learn *firsthand* of their constituents' preferences. Thus, there was little need for polls. Only with the expansion of the electorate did politicians lose direct touch with the views of the constituents. Note also that the adoption of the secret ballot further separated politicians from the electorate. But by going into the homes of average citizens and asking them their political views, pollsters have re-established this link. For an interesting and informative historical account of measuring public opinion, see Herbst (1993).

for me is to find that out exactly." But as Lincoln surely knew, finding out what the people desire was rarely exact. For instance, according to James McPherson (1988, 269), Lincoln relied on the tone of newspaper coverage "as signs of northern opinion" when deciding whether to reinforce or evacuate Fort Sumter. While the President may have been able to figure out what the citizenry wanted from such an indicator, it was a tricky enterprise at best. Prior to polls, politicians, for the most part, relied on a wide variety of sources for information. Among those they most commonly used were the results of previous elections, the number of people in attendance at political rallies, content of newspapers, letters from constituents, personal conversations with supporters, views of political allies, and the claims of relevant interest groups (see Bryce 1921; Exline 1922; Smith 1939; Mendelsohn and Crespi 1970; Converse and Pierce 1986; Ginsberg 1986; Herbst 1993).

These sources of information have two basic flaws. First, politicians had to infer the electorate's opinions from *indirect* indicators. So rather than getting readings from a cross-section of citizens, politicians had to weave various bits and pieces of information into some general notion of what the public actually desired. Eric Foner (1988, 315), for instance, reports that the Democratic gains in the 1867 local elections convinced Republican "moderates that issues like disenfranchisement, black voting in the North and impeachment must be avoided at all costs." McPherson (1988, 688) finds that Republicans interpreted the GOP gains in the state and local elections of 1863 "as signs of a transformation of public opinion toward emancipation." But, of course, the connection between the proportion of votes cast for a particular party in any election and the public's thinking on specific issues is tenuous (Kelley 1983; Dahl 1990).

Grover Cleveland, on the other hand, used newspapers as a guide to sorting out the public's views on the possible repeal of the Sherman Silver Purchase Act (Glad 1964, 80). William McKinley was apparently very interested in tracking opinion during his presidency, especially in regard to the Cuban Crisis. To make these judgments, McKinley not only relied on newspapers, but also "consulted men throughout the country" (Hilderbrand 1981, 12). Such sources, while they had merit, did not directly tap the views of average citizens.

The second, and perhaps more important, problem was that these sources of information were (and are) often misleading. Russell Neuman (1986, 3), for instance, comments that prior to scientific surveys the "voice of the people was the voice of those who chose to speak out—those who voted, wrote letters to editors, went to public meetings, wrote to legisla-

tors, or hired professional lobbyists to represent their interests in the corridors of power." Ginsberg (1986) stresses a similar theme, observing that
public opinion at the time was shaped by those who cared most about an
issue. But as we know, the engaged differ systematically from the less
engaged (Zaller 1992; Verba and Nie 1972), thereby yielding a biased
account of public opinion.

Just consider for a moment that if the major source of information
about public opinion for today's officeholders came from interest groups,
an issue like abortion or environmental protection would be treated much
differently by politicians. Or assume that Clinton ignored the polls of Stan
Greenberg and instead relied heavily on the editorial page of *The
Washington Post* as a guide to the public's thinking. Such a change would
surely have put a different cast on what the "public" was thinking on such
matters as affirmative action and welfare reform.

James Bryce (1921, 155) provides an insightful testimony about the difficulty of assessing the public mood, prior to the advent of polls:

> How is the drift of Public Opinion to be ascertained? That is the problem
> which most occupies and perplexes politicians. They usually go for light to
> the press, but the press, though an indispensable, is not a safe guide, since
> the circulation of a journal does not necessarily measure the prevalence of
> the views it advocates . . . .
>
>   Neither are public meetings a sure index, for in populous centres almost
> any energetic group can fill a large hall with its adherents. . . .
>
>   Stray elections . . . are much relied on, yet the result is often due rather
> to local circumstances than to a general movement of political feeling.

Bryce (1921, 156), then, recommended that the best "index" for a politician
was to go into local neighborhoods and talk with people so as to assess
their "attitudes and proclivities." Whether Bryce's reasoning was sound or
not is open to dispute. But the point is that politicians of that era had only
rough guesses about public opinion.

It is highly likely that politicians knew that these guesses were crude, as
Bryce himself suggested. Surely the unfolding political events of their time
would have underscored the inaccuracy with which officials judged mass
opinion. For example, William Gienapp (1987, 441–42) reports that the
results of the 1856 presidential election, won by James Buchanan, stunned
Millard Fillmore, who would prove to be the last Whig candidate, and
pleasantly surprised the Republicans, who had nominated John Frémont.

Both sides had expected, given the information available, a much less favorable outcome for the then fledgling GOP. Teddy Roosevelt also expressed genuine shock at the margin of his victory in the 1904 election (Blum 1977, 70; Cooper 1983, 79). Most indications suggested a closer contest between himself and Judge Alton B. Parker. Such "unexpected" outcomes surely gave politicians reason to believe that their information was often flawed. Woodrow Wilson gave direct testimony that one should be aware of such problems, noting that interest groups often try to "create an artificial opinion to overcome the interests of the public for private profit."[3]

The development of survey research recast the information available to politicians. Public officials no longer have to tease out the views of the public from indirect measures. They now have the means on a large and systematic scale to follow Bryce's recommendation to talk with constituents. This more direct indicator supplies politicians with a much better view of their constituents' opinions. So, for example, rather than trying to sift through newspapers to get a handle on the public's thinking, as Lincoln or Cleveland did, Bill Clinton knew, according to one poll, that 86 percent of the public was willing to support a tax increase in order to expand health insurance.[4]

Thus, polls not only provide a direct link between politicians and citizens, but they also supply an estimate of opinion for specific issues. Because surveys might ask whether respondents favor allowing gays in the military, or whether they support a tax increase, the information they provide speaks directly to particular issues. Before polls, information often had only a loose relationship to the issue in question. Politicians who used the results of an election to sort out the public's willingness to support the Kansas-Nebraska Act had to make a big leap. Or if attendance at a meeting was used as a proxy for public opinion, its connection to the specific issue was uncertain. Of course, some information was tied to particular issues, such as the tone of newspaper editorials that tackled a subject directly. But still such a connection was not as clean as that generated by polls.

Another difference in character of information provided by polls is a less biased reading of the opinions of the mass electorate. By tapping the views of a representative sample of the citizenry, surveys eliminate the bias favor-

---

3. A letter written by Wilson on May 26, 1913 (Link 1966, 27: 473).
4. This specific proportion was reported from a poll conducted by Time/CNN. See *Arizona Republic*, A19, 1/17/93.

ing the engaged over the less engaged.[5] Thus, politicians have a much more accurate reading of what the average citizen thinks about political matters.

A third change that polls initiated is that there is less room for rationalization. With the uncertainty of the measures available prior to polls, predispositions surely influenced the interpretation of the "data." That is, if a politician supported increasing tariffs, there was probably some information about public opinion that could be considered consistent with that view. Polls in contrast provide less room for such interpretations, since a finding that 75 percent of the public disagrees with your position is hard to rationalize.

Despite all these advantages, any one poll can be misleading—as can any one question in a series of polls. The way samples are drawn and the way questions are framed make a big difference in the results. But with the proliferation of polls (and questions) among both candidates and the news media (see Mann and Orren 1992), the multiple indicators provide a sound overall assessment of the direction and intensity of public opinion. For example, when different polls converge on a similar finding, there should be more confidence about what the public thinks. In contrast, if disagreement about public sentiment exists among different polls, politicians should view opinion as more unsettled—important information in itself.

Few disagree that polls provide readings more accurate than what was available prior to the 1930s; indeed, there are some data that provide an estimate of the magnitude of the difference. Claude Robinson (1932) asked a sample of state politicians to predict the outcome of the 1928 presidential elections in their respective states. Robinson (1932) surveyed these politicians, in part, because they had access to local opinion through the various party organizations that would allow them to make accurate judgments about the attitudes of the mass electorate. The actual survey was conducted "3 weeks in advance of election day" (Robinson 1932, 6). With the results in hand, Robinson then compared the predictions with the actual results from the state elections.[6] While some politicians proved to be quite good prognosticators, others were not. Overall, the error across

---

5. Ginsberg (1986) makes a spirited attack on the normative implications that arise from the advent of polls. He finds it troublesome that polls have led to a "pacification" of opinion by sidestepping the views of activists and interest groups that used to define "public opinion." His argument has much appeal, but it hinges on the idea that the less engaged and less informed should have a smaller voice on issues than the more engaged, vocal segments of society. There is certainly reason to fear manipulation of the less engaged by elites, but it is unclear why the more engaged elements of the electorate should carry more weight. On the surface at least, such an argument runs counter to the notion "one person, one vote."

6. It would, of course, be better to see how accurate politicians were in their judgments about

the 16 states in the sample was about 11 percentage points. Republican politicians, however, were much more accurate than the Democrats. In fact, the Democratic politicians correctly predicted the presidential winner of the state only 50 percent of the time—no better than chance.

In contrast, the state-by-state polls conducted about three weeks prior to the 1992 presidential election were much more accurate than Robinson's politicians.[7] These surveys predicted the winner in all but six states—even in the special circumstance of a three-candidate race. And in those six states, the actual proportions reported in the polls were within the margin of error. So one could argue that state polls had an unblemished record in 1992. In addition, the mean difference in the predicted Clinton vote and his actual vote was just 3 percentage points. This simple comparison provides some sense of how much more accurate polls are in judging public opinion than even the best guesses of state politicians.

Largely because polls can provide accurate information, as in the 1992 elections, politicians now trust their results. At first, politicians were generally skeptical about the accuracy of polls (Jacobs 1993; Herbst 1993). But as time has passed, and as the older generation of politicians has faded from the scene, more and more (younger) politicians have accepted polls as reliable and valid indicators of opinion. The generation of Bill Clinton, for instance, grew up with polls, and not only trust them, but also know how to take advantage of these devices. So even if one wants to argue that polls are not accurate indicators of opinion, the fact that politicians *think* they are lessens the impact of such complaints. More will be said about this matter in the next section.

Besides accuracy, there is another informational edge gained by politicians who use polls to judge opinion. Surveys (and other technological changes) allow for quicker feedback and hence quicker reactions to shifts in opinion. Thus, even if an initial error is made in judging opinion, it can be corrected swiftly. Hence, mistakes in the era of polls are short term in nature, which minimizes their potential impact. In contrast, the feedback loop was much longer during the pre-poll era. Politicians lacked the quick access to information provided by surveys, as well as accurate readings showing any

the public's view on specific issues. But the problem is that we lack any standard by which to judge accuracy. But the actual tally of votes in an election provides such a standard.

7. These data are from The American Political Network, which compiled the various polls available for the 50 states at periodic intervals during the 1992 campaign. I secured these data with the kind help of Doug Mills.

sudden shifts in opinion. Thus, when mistakes were made, they were not corrected quickly because no one detected that they were "mistakes."[8]

So far I have treated the development of polls as the turning point in the quality of information available to politicians. While the distinction is analytically useful, the break is not quite so clean as I am suggesting. The history of the public opinion poll itself is an interesting one. At first, pollsters used flawed theories of sampling (Converse 1987; Crespi 1988) and paid little attention initially to the effects of how the questions were phrased (Kahneman and Tversky 1984). Thus, early polls contained lots of errors, as best symbolized by the famous 1948 misprediction of Thomas Dewey's victory over Harry Truman.[9] But over the last 50 years much progress has been made on these fronts (see, for instance, Schuman and Presser 1981; Converse 1987; Moore 1992); so much, in fact, that the leading textbook in the field argues that the results from polls "should inspire trust" (Erikson, Luttbeg, and Tedin 1991, 13).[10]

Besides the advances in polls themselves, other developments further increase the information available to politicians. Focus groups, for instance, provide a way to fill some of the holes in the data supplied by surveys. By asking a small number of people to react in detail to specific issues and ideas, focus groups allow politicians to probe deeper into people's attitudes than the typical poll. In the 1980s, politicians began to make much greater use of focus groups (Polsby and Wildavsky 1991; Delli Carpini and Williams 1994). There has also been an effort to employ additional ways to gain information from focus groups other than just through open-ended discussion among the participants. Richard Wirthlin, for instance, experimented with a device called the "speech pulse" to get people's immediate reactions to some of Reagan's speeches (see Brace and Hinckley 1992, 3).[11] These kinds of devices allow politicians to get even quicker feedback about how different framings of an issue might play with the public. Thus, politicians can explore various ideas to determine which will get the most

8. This general point about the quick feedback provided by polls will enter our story again when we discuss the workings of political change in Chapter 6.

9. Of course, in the case of the 1948 election the real mistake was in Gallup's decision to stop polling before the end of the campaign. Even so, the polling industry's reputation was dealt a serious setback by the widespread perception that the polls were "wrong."

10. In a very useful book, Brehm (1993) argues that the nonresponse rate in polls endangers their accuracy. This point is reasonable and well-defended, highlighting the errors associated with surveys. Brehm does offer, however, some solutions to the problems, suggesting that the errors can be lessened that would enable surveys to continue to produce reasonably accurate readings of opinion.

11. A "speech pulse" is where people use a computerized dial to register positive or negative reactions to parts of speeches as politicians deliver them.

favorable response from the public. There have also been advances that prevent focus groups from being dominated by one or two participants (see Porado 1989).

Thus, the increase in the quality of information about public opinion did not end with the advent of polls, nor is it likely to stop with the focus group. As additional technological advances unfold, the assumption of "complete" information may become increasingly reasonable. But for the purposes of this argument, we shall treat polls as the defining event in the kinds of information politicians gather about the public's views.[12] For all intents and purposes, that development was the most important in recasting the quality of information available to support-seeking politicians.

A Conceptual Shift　　It is reasonable to claim that politicians are now better informed about public opinion than their predecessors were in the early part of this century. But agreeing that politicians are better informed today does not mean that one accepts the assumption of "complete" information. However, accompanying this increase in the quality of information was a conceptual shift in the meaning of "public opinion" that lends additional support to my claim.[13] Perhaps most important, political observers thought of public opinion as uncertain and nebulous prior to polls.[14] But today, "poll results and public opinion are terms used almost synonymously" (Ginsberg 1986, 60). Or as Ronald Hinckley (1992, xvi) comments, "whether one thinks it is appropriate or not to measure public opinion through polls or that such findings should be considered by policy makers, the fact of the matter is that polls are conducted, [and] their results are offered as public opinion."[15]

---

12. I will, however, return to the subject of focus groups in the concluding chapter.

13. For discussions of the early development of the concept of public opinion see Gunn (1989) and Palmer (1936). Both of these studies take a historical look at the concept, largely ignoring the changes during the twentieth century.

14. There have been other conceptual changes in this concept that can be tied to the rise of polls. Price (1992) provides a useful summary of many of these changes. For example, the roots of the term used to be grounded in political science and philosophy, and it now has a home more in sociology and psychology. Other changes in the term (to be noted later in the text) are connected to the shift from "uncertainty" to "certainty." Another shift of some import, but which will not be discussed here, is that public opinion has much more of a national connotation than it did in the past. With mass surveys, politicians can get a handle on the nation's views, where before most indicators had more of a local, state, or regional origin. This change has potentially important ramifications for how politicians tried to represent "public" opinion. But I shall not tackle the matter here.

15. Some encyclopedias (e.g. Grolier's Academic American, 1992), when discussing public opinion, will have a "see polls" reference for those who want to know more about the term. Such thinking documents the conceptual overlap between the two items.

This conceptual shift helps justify the assumption of complete information. If politicians treat the results from polls as equivalent to public opinion, then the estimates derived from survey research become reified into what the public really thinks about issues. So, for instance, if a poll reports that 62 percent of the public favors cuts in military spending and that result is treated as what the public thinks on the defense budget, then politicians, by their own calculation, have "complete" information.[16]

THE PRE-POLL CONCEPT   To document this conceptual shift, let me turn to how scholars prior to polls thought about "public opinion."[17] To start, it is clear that the subject was viewed as something uncertain and mysterious. For instance, Sir Robert Peel, writing in 1820, referred to public opinion as "that great compound of folly, weakness, prejudice, wrong feeling, right feeling, obstinacy, and newspaper paragraphs."[18] Bryce (1895, 270) thought of it as "omnipotent, yet indeterminate, a sovereign to whose voice everyone listens, yet whose words, because he speaks with as many tongues as the waves of a boisterous sea, [are] so hard to catch." More than twenty-five years later, Bryce (1921, 153) continued that theme, noting that "it is confused, incoherent, amorphous, varying from day to day and week to week." In 1914, a German scholar, Herman Oncken, stated that public opinion is like "dealing with a Proteus, a being that appears simultaneously in a thousand guises, both visible and as a phantom. . . . "[19] Or consider Walter Lippmann's (1922, 162) claim that public opinion was something akin to "uncanny forces." Finally, Edward Bernays (1923, 61), one of the leading figures in his field, noted that public opinion is "vague, little-understood and indefinite."[20]

The uncertainty associated with public opinion probably helped fuel the many definitions of the term that existed at the time. In a thorough accounting, Harwood Childs (1965) reports more than fifty different def-

---

16. Philip Converse (1987, S17) bemoans the fact that despite warnings by academics and polling experts, practitioners of politics rarely interpret polls with sufficient caution.

17. This account of what scholars thought of public opinion is not intended to be a representative sample of all views of that day. Even so, it is a fair rendition of those works that I have come across in examining the meaning of public opinion prior to survey research.

18. Quoted in Bryce (1895, 255).

19. Quoted in Noelle-Neumann (1984, 59).

20. Perhaps the most entertaining description comes from H. L. Mencken (1926) who writes that "public opinion, in its raw state, gushes out in the immemorial form of the mob's fears. It is piped to central factories, and there it is flavoured and coloured, and put into cans." What this passage means is open to interpretation. But it does provide a sense of the diversity of perspectives observers of the pre-poll era had about public opinion.

initions. Even though Childs was already writing in the era of polls, the definitions he reported were almost completely drawn from the so-called pre-poll era.[21] To provide a flavor of these different views, I offer a few of them (Childs 1965, 18–24):

> Public Opinion may be said to be that sentiment on any given subject which is entertained by the best informed, most intelligent, and most moral persons in the community. —*W.A. MacKinnon, 1828*

> Public opinion is the social judgment reached upon a question of general or civic import after conscious, rational discussion. —*Clyde King, 1928*

> . . . there is no such thing as a public opinion, and it only requires a moderate understanding of human nature to show that such a thing as an intelligent public opinion is not possible. —*E. Jordan, 1930*

> Those features of the world outside which have to do with the behavior of other human beings, in so far as that behavior crosses ours, is dependent upon us, or is interesting to us, we roughly call public affairs. The pictures inside the heads of these human beings, the pictures of themselves, of others, of their needs, their purposes, and relationships are their public opinions. Those pictures which are acted upon by groups of people or by individuals acting in the name of groups, are Public Opinion with capital letters. —*Walter Lippmann, 1922*

These definitions underscore the numerous ways scholars approached this concept. In one case, Jordan simply rejected the notion of an "intelligent" public opinion. In the others, there is an assumption that opinion exists; but its form is not agreed upon. For example, what are the differences between public opinion being a "social judgment," a "composite expression," or "pictures inside the heads of . . . human beings"? The first two phrases depict public opinion as more of a collective behavior, whereas the third pitches it more as an individual-level phenomenon. In addition, the MacKinnon view connects public opinion to various elites in society, whereas Lippmann and King tie it to the masses. These differences underscore the lack of conceptual clarity that confronted the term "public opinion" in the early part of this century, paralleling in many

---

21. If one uses 1940 as the cut-off, fewer than 5 percent of the definitions presented in Childs were offered in the post poll era.

ways the problems with the definitions of leadership noted in the previous chapter.

THE POST-POLL CONCEPT   The uncertainty associated with the concept of public opinion has lessened. Polls have provided an aura of scientific precision to assessing the public's attitudes.[22] The scientific aspect of polls was actually the product of two technological changes: the advent of sampling and measurement theory (Price 1992). Sampling theory allowed pollsters to get a representative segment of the electorate to participate, thereby greatly lessening the biases of previous indicators. Measurement theory was also important because scales were developed that allowed researchers to ask questions that provided a valid and reliable indicator of the public's views on particular issues. These dual developments gave credibility to the idea of a "scientific" sample survey.

The scientific aspect of polls is also reinforced by the numbers that they generated (Herbst 1993). Prior to polls, politicians rarely thought, for instance, that 56 percent of the public favored a particular position on an issue. Instead, their guesses probably led them to judgments about whether most of the people or a few of the people favored a particular position. As a result, public opinion in the era of polls was no longer a "glorified kind of fortune telling" (Gallup and Rae 1940); it had become something concrete and tangible. For instance, changes in the Gallup Poll approval rating of a president are treated as a real change in the public's judgment of the chief executive (Brody 1991; Brehm 1993).

After the introduction of public opinion polls, the increased precision with which politicians could now measure opinion lessened the conceptual ambiguities. Philip Converse (1987, S13) notes, for instance, that "what the firm establishment of a public opinion polling industry has done is to homogenize the definition and to stabilize it for the foreseeable future." Converse (1987, S14) then goes on to state that "public opinion is what opinion polls try to measure or what they measure with modest error."[23]

---

22. I am not the first to note this change. As early as 1948, Blumer (1948, 554) argued that "by virtue of its sampling procedure, current public opinion polling is forced to regard public opinion as an aggregate of equally weighted opinions of disparate individuals." Bogart (1972, 15) writes that polls give the "form and the appearance of measured precision to what was formerly visceral in origin and nebulous in shape." Most recently, Herbst (1993) has made this point.

23. Note that Converse is being careful about recognizing explicitly that surveys contain errors. This care reflects an attempt to counteract more simplistic definitions that suggest that "public opinion consists of people's reactions to definitely worded statements and questions under interview conditions" (Warner 1939, 377).

The effects polls have had on the concept of public opinion is now reflected in the textbooks in the subfield. Erikson, Luttbeg and Tedin (1991, 13), in the leading textbook, comment that "in the recent era, the meaning of public opinion sometimes seems to evolve into whatever public opinion polls show public opinion to be." This view is implicitly reinforced by the fact that Erikson et al. spend little time trying to define the term.[24] In contrast, earlier textbooks by Childs (1940, 1965), Albig (1939, 1956), and Ogle (1950) spent a good deal of time talking about the meaning of public opinion. But with the "homogenization" of the term, those who seek to provide an overview of the field see little need to tackle this matter.

Perhaps Key (1961, 536) put it best when he observed that:

> In an earlier day public opinion seemed to be pictured as a mysterious vapor that emanated from the undifferentiated citizenry and in some way or another enveloped the apparatus of government to bring it into conformity with the public will. These weird conceptions . . . passed out of style as the technique of the sample survey permitted the determination, with some accuracy, of opinions within the population.

Key's observation is nicely reflected in the titles of two books on this general subject from the respective periods. In the 1920s, Walter Lippmann wrote about *The Phantom Public*; Benjamin Page and Robert Shapiro now write about *The Rational Public*. Such changes highlight the basic thrust of this argument.

The shift from "uncertainty" to "certainty" has additional implications for how politicians think about public opinion. First, there is good reason to believe that the term was often restricted to describe widespread agreement on the issue in question (Childs 1965). Lowell (1914, 15) writes, for instance, that a "majority is not enough" to constitute public opinion, and while "unanimity is not required," there must be widespread agreement. Echoing a comparable theme, Smith (1939, 19) argues that if "individual opinions are not similar enough to flow together, there cannot be a public opinion." In a recent biography of Woodrow Wilson, Heckscher (1991, 276) writes that Wilson usually "saw leadership as being actions taken in conformity to opinions which, though they might not be expressed, were nevertheless *widely held*" (my emphasis).

---

24. This pattern is also true for another recent textbook by Corbett (1991).

This notion that public opinion requires more than a majority but less than total consent fits well with the uncertainty associated with the term at that time. Since politicians (and pundits) were guessing at the state of opinion, only when most (or all) sources pointed in the same direction could one feel confident that the public had a particular view. But with polls providing numerical estimates of opinion, the criterion of a simple majority becomes more reasonable for signalling the direction of opinion. So, for instance, politicians now have an estimate that 59 percent or 55 percent support a particular position on an issue, which lessens the need to wait for a substantial majority to rally behind a particular position.

A second related change in how we *think* about public opinion is that during the pre-poll era "public opinion" was considered a rare thing (Lowell 1914; Exline 1922). This was so for a combination of reasons. To begin, if widespread agreement was required for a "public opinion," as suggested above, then fewer issues could meet that standard than if just a majority were enough. Second, some scholars felt the public had to be informed on the issue before their views could count, as implied by Jordan's earlier definition. Charles Smith (1939, 13), for instance, stated that the "public" was composed of "all the people capable of thought in a particular group or area." Holcombe's (1923, 36) view is that opinions held by the public must be based on "a substantial part of the facts required for a rational decision." Others also agreed that a "rational" discussion of issues was necessary for public opinion to emerge (see Childs 1965).

But with survey researchers probing the public's thinking on a wide range of attitudes, we are now aware of many more public opinions. We know that respondents are willing to answer questions on surveys that may not constitute a real opinion on the matter (Converse 1974; Zaller 1992). But even so, we have an impression that more of the public has a view on some matter than in the past. So, for instance, the fact that 79 percent of those sampled right after Clinton's first State of the Union message liked the speech suggests that the electorate has a view on the matter, even if it is uninformed. Thus, because of the many questions that probe the views of the public, there should be more "public opinions" than in the past. These additional opinions, in turn, should encourage support-seeking politicians to pay more attention to the direction of views than when public opinion was less frequent and less clear. As we shall see in subsequent chapters, these changes have important implications for the behavior of politicians.

Polls v. Newspapers

Because of the demands of elective office, politicians have a vested interest in gaining a quick and reliable handle on the public's thinking. Polls certainly fit that bill, especially with technological advances that allow surveys to provide accurate estimates of opinion on a daily basis. This ability surely contributes to the perception that public opinion and the results from polls are much the same thing. This tendency by politicians to develop useful indexes of public opinion is not new, however. Prior to surveys, politicians often treated public opinion and the content of newspapers as nearly equivalent. This change in indexes, so to speak, underscores not only the conceptual change discussed above, but also the quality of information available to politicians in the two eras.

In surveying the work in political science written prior to the acceptance of polls, the link between newspapers and public opinion is quite clear. Childs (1940, 50) bluntly stated that "the expressions 'press' and 'public opinion' were often used synonymously."[25] The statement noted earlier by Sir Robert Peel tied public opinion to "newspaper paragraphs." Bryce (1895, 270–72) argued that newspapers were the central mechanism to judge opinion, since the content of the press could serve as ways to describe public opinion and to assess changes in it.

Perhaps the most convincing evidence comes from a journal that started publication in the United States in 1886 titled: *Public Opinion, a Comprehensive Summary of the Press throughout the World on all Important Topics*. This journal collected newspaper articles from around the country concerning the pressing issues of the day.[26] For example, in the February 21, 1891 issue, a series of articles from newspapers ranging from the *New York Evening Post* to the *Nashville Independent* commented on Cleveland's position on the coinage of silver.[27] There is reason to believe that at least some politicians used the journal as a guide to public opinion (Nevins 1933). Its attempt to represent public opinion can be

25. An unexpected source of support for Childs's claim come in a 1941 cartoon depicting FDR reading a newspaper with the caption below "Let's see what the people have to say" (Kuklick 1988, 62).

26. The journal did not limit itself to politics. Articles appeared on a variety of topics, such as science, music, and art.

27. See Volume 10, number 20 for the actual articles on this topic. Note that these articles ran, in part, because Cleveland was seen as the likely Democratic nominee for president in 1892 to run against Benjamin Harrison.

seen clearly in the disclaimer that the editors offered on the first page of
each issue:

> The aim of the journal is not to create but to reflect opinion. The utmost
> care is taken to treat each question upon which extracts are given in a per-
> fectly fair non-partisan and unbiased manner. Absolute neutrality may
> therefore be relied upon in these columns.

This journal ran for more than twenty years, merging with the *Literary
Digest* in 1906.

The tendency to equate public opinion with the content of newspapers
was not unique to the United States. The journal *Public Opinion*, started in
England some twenty years earlier, provided British politicians with a reading of public sentiment. In Sweden, politicians and other political actors
also treated newspapers as tantamount to public opinion (Esaiasson 1991).

Given this connection between the press and public opinion, politicians apparently did use newspapers as a frequent guide to opinion. Susan
Herbst (1993, 102) found that over 85 percent of congressmen from the
1930s and 1940s relied on newspapers to judge public sentiment. Kernell
(1993, 18) reported that "before scientific surveys were available, . . . the
editorial stances of the nation's newspapers were routinely reported to
[Franklin] Roosevelt in summary form." Even better evidence of this claim
can be found in the behavior of William McKinley. As President, this
Ohioan wanted to keep close tabs on what the public was thinking.
According to Hilderbrand (1981, 12), "newspapers formed his chief guide
to public opinion and he read several of them daily." To aid in this process,
McKinley "instructed his secretaries to prepare scrapbooks of clippings for
his daily use—entitled 'Current Comment'—that included items from
newspaper in every section of the country." Apparently, McKinley was the
first to use the content of the press in such a systematic way. But the fact
that McKinley gauged the public's mood through a wide range of newspaper articles underscores the conceptual linkage between the press and
public opinion in the minds of politicians.

To give a concrete sense of this change, I shall briefly describe some
information that two presidents actually used to assess public opinion.
The first case, drawn from the pre-poll era, concerns William McKinley.
As noted above, McKinley kept track of "public opinion" by compiling
newspaper articles into a scrapbook entitled "Current Comment." Copies
of the original documents are available through the *Presidential Papers of
William McKinley*. The second comes from a memorandum given to

President Johnson in 1966.[28] These examples are in no way designed to be representative, but they illustrate the shift in the kinds of information presidents had when making decisions about particular policies.

William McKinley and the Tariff Question   McKinley's staff organized "Current Comment" around the issues and personalities of the day. Most of the entries began with a crude table of contents that provided a guide to the material. So, for instance, articles concerning William Jennings Bryan got separate billing, as did articles on currency reform or the tariff, which were issues often noted in these outlines. In reading samples of these pages, it becomes clear that efforts were made to get a range of newspapers. For instance, in 1900 debate surfaced over the Tariff—a long-running issue in American politics—and, in particular, whether we should extend the tariff to newly acquired Puerto Rico. The press's response to this action was recorded in the pages of "Current Comment." The range of opinion is represented reasonably well in the passages below:[29]

Free trade with Porto Rico[30] and for Porto Rico would be better than any tariff on its products at all. It might not be better for the makers of sugar and tobacco products in the United States, but it would be better for the buyers and users of them, and the Eagle is not only for the principle of free trade between all peoples within the jurisdiction of the United States, but it also prefers the welfare of buyers and users of commodities to that of the makers of them, because the former are more than the latter. We would like to have the Democratic view of the tariff question adopted and we hope it will be, although we do not believe an everlasting smash will come from the temporary provision of a moderate duty in this case.

—*Brooklyn Daily Eagle, February 20, 1900*

Those members of the Ways and Means Committee who did not and do not agree with the explicit and statesmanlike declaration of President McKinley that "our plain duty is to abolish all customs tariffs between the United States and Puerto Rico," and who insist upon fastening the Dingley

28. This memorandum was collected by Larry Jacobs, who kindly gave me access to it.

29. These passages were not drawn randomly, I chose them to convey a feeling for the range of opinion.

30. "Porto Rico" was the spelling often used at the time for this island.

Tariff law upon the distressed people of that island, invited the Republican members of the House to a conference on Saturday night last for the purpose of securing "harmony" in the matter of the pending measure to levy duties on Puerto Rican products. The plan of "harmony" proposed by these opponents of the President's policy for unanimous adoption was that those Republican Representatives who differed from them should compromise or surrender their principles. The supporters of the honest and constitutional policy of the President were urged to a cowardly and wicked abandonment of their principles and to the acceptance of the mercenary policy represented by Mr. Grosvenor, which he embodied in his speech to the House last week to the effect that, having wrested the country's new possessions from Spain, "We are going to make all the money out of the transaction we can." —*Public Ledger and Daily Transcript, February 27, 1900*

[Republicans] see that the best interests of the people of Puerto Rico and those of the people of the rest of the Untied States demand that there shall be free trade throughout the entire range of our territory.

—*Journal of Commerce and Commercial Bulletin, March 24, 1900*

If it were possible for our free trade neighbors to consider with minds not blinded with prejudice any question affecting a tariff of any sort, they surely might so regard the question of duties on imports from Puerto Rico. Repeatedly it has been shown by this journal that such duties would be of no consequence whatever from a protective point of view. Competition from that island would not in the least affect any industry which it has been the object of protective duties to defend and develop.

—*New York Daily Tribune, March 20, 1900*

In reading these passages, the partisan tone of the press rings clearly, making the detection of the *public's* feelings difficult. One can see what the editors of these newspapers felt, but the electorate's views are another matter. Given McKinley's effort to get the range of opinion, it is reasonable to believe that politicians might have tried to weight the overall reaction among the press. Such a balancing act might have given a sense of general opinion among the press. But as Ginsberg (1986) has observed, the more engaged elements of society are the voices here, masking any reading one might get of public opinion. Moreover, reading these passages is unwieldy, making it hard to figure out what the public wanted. Politicians surely developed a knack for interpreting newspapers, but those judgments still would have been filled with guesses and uncertainty.

Lyndon Johnson and the War   While McKinley may have had to use tea leaves to read public opinion in 1900, Johnson had concrete numbers to work with. As the Vietnam War raged, LBJ became concerned with how the American public was reacting to the conflict. So, for instance, on September 7th, 1966, among Johnson's night reading was a memo that contained the information about the war's popularity (see table 2.1).

In stark contrast to the data used by McKinley, Johnson's gauges of public opinion provided two clear patterns. First, that the vast majority of the public supported the war in some fashion, although within that "support" some wanted more negotiations and others wanted a greater military presence. The second is that there was little change in opinion between January and July. Both findings would be very useful to any politician trying to consider how best to proceed with the war.

A Final Detour

In this discussion of how polls have increased the quality of information available to politicians, I have implicitly assumed that the quantification of the views of average citizens provides a better reading of public opinion than the more qualitative readings prior to polls. In a provocative book, Herbst (1993) talks about how polls have made public opinion more "ratio-

Table 2.1. *President Johnson's Night Reading, September 7, 1966*

Question	July	January
I disagree with present policy; we are not going far enough. We should go further, such as carrying the war more into North Vietnam.	10%	11%
I agree with what we are doing, but we should increase our military effort to win a clear military victory.	28%	24%
I agree with what we are doing, but we should do more to bring about negotiations, such as a cease-fire request.	49%	46%
I disagree with present policy; we shouldn't be there. We shouldn't be bombing North vietnam and should pull our troops out now.	9%	12%
Not sure	4%	7%

SOURCE: Larry Jacobs

nalized" and "structured." Among other things, Herbst argues that numbers associated with polls make the measurement of public opinion more precise than it really is. Hence, one could argue that I have fallen prey to this very problem by assuming that public opinion is in fact a measurable entity. If I instead adopted the old conception of public opinion as uncertain and nebulous, then it becomes doubtful whether polls can provide a handle on "public opinion" that could even approximate the notion of complete information.

I plead guilty. But the penalty for my offense should be quite minor. First, believing that public opinion is something that can be measured does not mean that one believes it is measured with 100 percent accuracy by polls. My point is simply that the views of the public exist and that there are ways to detect them. Polls represent just one "way" to tap opinion. But that way is dramatically different from and much more accurate than those in the past.

The second reason that my crime is minor concerns politicians themselves. Those who seek elective office have a great need to get an accurate reading of what the public wants—their jobs depend on it. As Herbst (1993) notes, there has been a general tendency in society toward quantification of various aspects of life. Numbers give the impression of a more objective and accurate assessment on matters. While that impression may be overblown, from politicians' points of view, numbers are a way of life. That is, getting elected depends on gathering a majority of votes at election time. So, when they hear that 62 percent oppose a policy of theirs, that datum resonates with how they think about politics in general. Politicians, as a result, may be especially prone to buying into the artificial precision offered by polls. But since politicians' perceptions lie at the heart of this theory, someone else's "reality" becomes less pressing.

Whether this move toward precision and scientific thinking is bad or good for society is not a debate for this book. My point is much simpler: the increased precision in the measurement of public opinion, as reported by polls, has given politicians a better handle on what average citizens want. And that fact has changed politics in important ways.

Conclusion

While it is obvious that polls have had an impact on public opinion, I am not sure that most observers have appreciated the extent of the change. Polls have not only increased the quality of information available to politicians, but have also reshaped how we think about the term itself. Because of these changes it becomes useful to think of politicians over the last 150 years as falling into two eras: well-informed and poorly informed.[31]

The idea that there are important differences in the operation of democratic regimes when politicians are well-informed and poorly informed is not altogether new. Bryce (1895, 258–59) talked about four stages in the evolution of public opinion that have some similarity to the argument presented in this essay. The first two stages are not of immediate importance. The initial stage concerns the time when citizens had to obey the wishes of the ruler, which made opinion "unconscious and passive." In the second, "conflicts arise between the ruling person or class, backed by those who are still disposed to obedience, on the one hand, and the more independent or progressive spirits on the other; and these conflicts are settled by arms." The next stage arises when the will of the people is expressed at the ballot box, with voters entrusting the winner of the elections to carry out the "popular mandate." This stage approximates my label of politicians as "poorly" informed. The fourth stage arises when the "will of the majority of citizens [becomes] ascertainable at all times." Or to use the terms of this book, politicians are "well" informed.

Bryce did not, however, anticipate that the fourth stage was reachable, noting that the "machinery for weighing or measuring the popular will from week to week or month to month has not been, and is not likely to be, invented." That judgment, as we know, was in error. Bryce did not foresee the development of the public opinion poll that makes it possible for us to enter this fourth stage in the evolution of public opinion.

This fourth stage, Bryce argues, would be one in which public opinion would "not only reign but govern," hence making it an important step in the process of democratic rule. The argument developed earlier also suggests that the change is important. But before we develop these kinds of implications, our next task is to see whether this theory about politicians has any empirical support.

---

31. I have not labeled the two eras as "complete" and "incomplete" information. The theory presented in the previous chapter makes that distinction the official one. But I prefer the labels "well" and "poorly" informed. The reason is simple: it is more accurate. I shall explicitly relax the assumption of complete information in a subsequent chapter when assessing the prospects of leadership within the two eras.

Chapter 3

MARSHALLING A BIT OF EVIDENCE

THE PREVIOUS CHAPTER ARGUED, IN effect, that the introduction of public opinion polls has altered the relationship between politicians and citizens. Prior to polls, politicians operated in conditions of great uncertainty in regard to public opinion. While elected officials had access to information about the electorate's views, the data usually lacked precision and often contained systematic flaws, leading politicians to view public opinion as something uncertain and nebulous. But with the development of the sample survey, politicians began to have access to much more precise and accurate estimates of what average citizens were thinking on a wide variety of political issues. Given the theory of politicians developed in Chapter 1, this significant improvement in the quality of available information predicts that officeholders will act in systematically different ways in the two eras.

The basic argument has intuitive appeal, but does it have any empirical support? That is, does the theory provide an account of the behavior of politicians that corresponds, even roughly, to what we in fact observe? Given the claim that the actions of well-informed politicians are different from those who are poorly informed, I need (ideally) to control the level of information officeholders possess under various decision-making situations. So, for instance, one would like to see what Washington would have done with Richard Wirthlin at his side or what Clinton would have done had he had Colonel House's advice rather than Stan Greenberg's. But such tests, of course, are not possible.

Despite the difficulty of testing the empirical merits of this theory, there are ways to support it. The evidence offered here is not in any way conclusive. But it is sufficient enough to warrant the consideration of implications that arise from this argument.

I shall start by briefly examining two specific examples of presidential behavior—one from each era—that not only bolster the core tenets of this theory, but also underscore its potential significance in rather dramatic ways. Following these cases, I shall present additional evidence that supports this theory. To begin, I shall document the extent to which politicians who hold office use polls and how that use has grown. Such evidence serves as a necessary, but certainly not a sufficient, condition for assessing the theory. To move toward a "sufficient" test, I shall report existing work that documents how information from polls has apparently affected the decisions of politicians.

Information and Presidential Behavior: Two Cases

When asked about the leadership qualities of all American presidents, most observers would rate Abraham Lincoln at the top for his ability to make and to justify momentous decisions that often flew in the face of public opinion. Because of his political skill in navigating the treacherous waters of the Civil War, scholars long have ranked him as the greatest president (Schlesinger 1962; Murray and Blessing 1988). As evidence of the esteem in which Lincoln is held, politicians often cloak themselves in the Lincoln mantle—especially around election time. Our sixteenth president, in short, was the quintessential American leader.

The pedestal on which we have placed Lincoln frequently serves as a way to deride the skills and talents of modern presidents who seem so willing to forgo principle and eschew unpopular stands. Consider George Bush. In many ways he is the classic example of a politician who, rather than standing up for his beliefs, reacted like a weathervane to any shifts in public opinion. In the 1964 Texas senatorial election, Bush ran as a Goldwater conservative, opposing, for instance, civil rights legislation. But just a few years later in a bid for Congress, he ran as a moderate Republican. Bush's ability to change his political stripes was most visible during the 1980 presidential campaign. In the primaries, he opposed "voodoo" economics and was largely pro-choice on abortion. But when picked by Ronald Reagan to be the GOP's Vice Presidential nominee, Bush altered his views on Reagan's plan for the economy and began an "evolution" in his thinking on abortion. In short, Bush's image as a leader stands in sharp contrast to our general perception of Lincoln.

The theory of leadership presented here, however, suggests that this house is not so divided. That is, the difference between Lincoln and Bush lies not so much in their willingness to make courageous decisions nor in their political motivations, but rather in the fact that the latter had access to poll data and the former did not. Those who are fans of Lincoln will be appalled by such a statement. And as we shall see in Chapter 5, my theory does suggest that some real and important differences will develop between politicians from these two eras. But this claim that Bush and Lincoln are political "cousins" underscores in a stark manner the import of my thesis.

To illustrate the claim that the availability of polls is a critical difference between the governing tactics of George Bush and Abraham Lincoln, I will look at an example of the behavior of each in office. The first case involves Abraham Lincoln's decision to issue the Emancipation Proclamation. The second concerns George Bush's decision to tackle health care.[1]

Lincoln and the Emancipation Proclamation   There is little doubt that Abraham Lincoln viewed public opinion as not only an important force in government, but as something that all politicians must grapple with when making decisions. Lincoln on many occasions talked about the central role of public opinion in representative government. In a speech on December 10, 1856, Lincoln observed, for instance, that "our government rests in public opinion. Whoever can change public opinion, can change the government."[2] During the famous Lincoln-Douglas debates, the then senatorial contender continued this theme, arguing that in "this and like communities public sentiment is everything." And without it, politicians cannot succeed.[3]

Just prior to assuming the Presidency, Lincoln made a statement indicating that he viewed public opinion as a driving force in the policies of

1. I make no claim about the representativeness of these cases. I chose these two examples because they illustrate the core tenets of the argument and because of the widely available information about them.

2. Passage taken from Balser (1953 7:385).

3. Quoted in Jaffa (1959, 309–310).

government: "I deem it due to myself and the whole country, in the present extraordinary condition of the country and of public opinion, that I should wait and see the last development of public opinion before I give my views or express myself at the time of the inauguration."[4] Such deference to public opinion was not new for the soon-to-be president. As a candidate for the legislature years earlier, Lincoln promised potential supporters that "while acting as their representative, I shall be governed by their will, on all subjects upon which I have the means of knowing what their will is."[5] Richard Hofstadter (1974, 170), in reviewing Lincoln's political life, suggested that he tended to be "a follower and not a leader of public opinion."

Lincoln's concern for tapping public opinion was reflected in his actions as President. Each day, for example, Lincoln had his assistants provide him with copies of three newspapers from Washington—*Morning Chronicle*, *National Republican*, and the *Evening Star*—and relevant articles from the Southern press (Trefousse 1975, 10). He also made sure that the articles were from both supportive and hostile newspapers so that he could keep "well informed about the changing currents of thought" (Trefousse 1975, 10). In addition, Lincoln read many of the letters sent to him by citizens so that he could "feel the pulse of the nation" (Trefousse 1975, 10). Members of Congress, as well as representatives from his own administration, were important sources of information about the mood of the public (McPherson 1964; Trefousse 1975).

As the Civil War pressed on, the demands for his already scarce time increased. Despite that lack of free time, Lincoln still sought to get a sense of the currents and eddies in the opinions of the citizenry. This concern is captured well by a statement Lincoln made about three weeks after the Battle of Gettysburg:

> . . . I feel—though the tax on my time is heavy—that no hours of my day are better employed than those which thus bring me again within the direct contact and atmosphere of the average of our whole people. Men moving only in an official circle are apt to become merely official—not to say arbitrary—in their ideas, and are apter and apter, with each passing day, to forget that they only hold power in a representative capacity. Now this is all wrong. I go into these promiscuous receptions of all who claim to have

4. Lincoln made this statement on February 13th, 1861. The quotation is taken from Basler (1953, 4:203).

5. Quoted in Miroff (1993, 95).

business with me twice each week and every applicant for audience has to take his turn, as if waiting to be shaved in a barber's shop. Many of the matters brought to my notice are utterly frivolous, but others are of more or less importance, and all serve to renew in me a clearer and more vivid image of that great popular assemblage out of which I sprung, and to which at the end of two years I must return. I tell you . . . that I call these receptions my "public-opinion baths;" for I have but little time to read the papers and other public opinion that way; and though they may not be pleasant in all their particulars, the effect, as a whole, is renovating and invigorating to my perceptions of responsibility and duty (Cuomo 1990, 285).[6]

As we know, Lincoln made some of the most fateful decisions of any chief executive in American history. Nearly all important decisions appeared to be weighed carefully by this thoughtful individual, and his judgment is credited by most historians as crucial to saving the Union. My purpose here is to look at one of those decisions and to try to place it in the context of public opinion as well as what Lincoln knew of the citizenry's views at the time.

Historians have long disagreed over the reasons for Lincoln's decision to issue the Proclamation that freed the slaves in those states "in rebellion against the United States."[7] One thing seems very clear: Lincoln was extremely cautious in making this move, in large part because of the stakes involved and the great uncertainty associated with the impact of that decision. Trefousse (1975, 28), for instance, writes that even though "favorably disposed towards emancipation, [Lincoln] nevertheless knew that he still had to be very careful. Any untoward move, any premature step, might precipitate such calamities in the border states and among Northern Democrats that the consequences would be incalculable. Given the widespread anti-Negro prejudice, the problem of sustaining the North's will to fight could not be disregarded."

---

6. Jaffa (1959, 309–310) argues that Lincoln's conception of public opinion is something different from what can be gleaned from a public opinion poll. For Lincoln, public opinion involved some central current underlying a political regime—not specific views on specific issues. The problem with Jaffa's interpretation is that Lincoln did show interest in finding out the public's views on various matters, as indicated by his occasional "public opinion baths." My point, however, is not to claim that Jaffa is wrong in this matter. I simply contend that Lincoln was concerned about the public's views on specific matters when making many of his decisions during those fractious years.

7. The amount of research is impressive in this debate. Some of the best work includes Sandburg (1939), Donovan (1964), Donald (1947), McPherson (1964, 1988). Many historians seem to view Franklin's (1963) work on the subject as the standard in the field.

The uncertainty facing Lincoln, as suggested above, cut at least three ways. First, he was worried about the reactions to such a move by the all-important border states. A sudden move to eliminate slavery throughout the land might move these states into the Confederacy. The second concern was the reaction by the Northern troops to such a proclamation. How would they react? They were willing to fight to save the Union. Would they fight to free the slaves? Many thought that the answer was no (McPherson 1988, 497). Finally, how would the general public react to such a move? The abolitionists had been calling for the elimination of slavery for a long time and were very upset over what they viewed as cowardly inaction by Lincoln (McPherson 1964).

While historians have offered a number of reasons for why and when Lincoln issued the Emancipation Proclamation, one thread that runs through most of these discussions was Lincoln's view of public opinion. For instance, in the early part of 1862, Lincoln did not think the public would support emancipation because "the great masses of the people . . . cared comparatively little about the Negro" (Gilder 1909, 46). Carl Sandburg (1939 1:564), in his extensive account of Lincoln's life, reported that in March of 1862 the President felt that the North was not yet ready for the end of slavery. Lincoln himself stated in 1864, fifteen months after the proclamation had taken effect, that "many of my strongest supporters urged *Emancipation* before I thought it indispensable, and, I may say, before I thought the country ready for it. It is my conviction that, had the proclamation been issued even six months earlier than it was, public sentiment would not have sustained it."[8]

Why did Lincoln's view about public opinion change? Why did he put an end to slavery in the Confederate states? Apparently, the decision was a mix of military, political, and personal calculations. The objective here is not, however, to provide a thorough account of this momentous decision; rather, it is to suggest that a perceived change in public opinion was necessary before Lincoln would act.

According to most historical analyses and statements by Lincoln himself, many observers of the time felt that during the latter part of 1861 and the first half of 1862 public support for emancipation was growing (McPherson 1964, 1988; Donald 1947; Trefousse 1975). There were a number of sources of evidence that were used to document this perceived shift in public sentiment. First, attendance at abolitionist rallies was growing

8. Quote in Cuomo (1990), 319–320.

noticeably during this time, indicating greater popularity for the cause (McPherson 1964, 82–90). For example, as 1862 approached, "Frederick Douglass and several other abolitionist speakers were welcomed enthusiastically when they spoke in Syracuse, a city that had mobbed them ten months before" (McPherson 1964, 82). Second, some important changes in major newspapers, such as the *New York Tribune*, took place; namely the emergence of an abolitionist, Sydney Howard Gay, as editor (McPherson 1964, 86). A change in editors may not strike one as very important, but because of the centrality newspapers played in gauging public opinion, such shifts were highly consequential. Lincoln also found on his desk numerous petitions calling for the end of slavery (Trefousse 1975, 32)—yet another sign that the abolitionist movement was gaining public support.

Each of these indicators, of course, speaks to the intensity with which some people viewed the abolitionist cause, but it says little about what the views of most northerners were in regard to the "peculiar" institution. Interestingly, James McPherson (1964) dedicates a whole chapter to "Emancipation and Public Opinion: 1861–1862" in *The Struggle for Equality*, and nowhere does he present any direct evidence detailing what the average citizen in the North thought about slavery and emancipation. This observation is not a criticism of McPherson. Instead, it underscores the difficulty Lincoln (and McPherson) faced in trying to get a handle on public sentiment. Given these kinds of measures and the uncertainty that confronted Lincoln about the reactions to such a move, it is no wonder that he moved slowly on this issue.

But assume, instead, that Lincoln had access to polling information about the views of the North, the border states, and the troops. Such knowledge would have surely altered Lincoln's calculations, since his uncertainty about the reactions from various segments of the public would have dwindled. If Lincoln were truly reacting to a perceived, but not a genuine, shift in public opinion when he issued the Emancipation Proclamation, he may well have been practicing "leadership by mistake." That is, the public may not have been initially supportive of such a proclamation, but after it was presented, and after the debate which followed, Lincoln might have been able to lead (mistakenly) the public toward an abolitionist stand.

It is important to note that Lincoln's "leadership" on this issue was not unqualified. *After* issuing the Emancipation in September, he urged, much to the outrage of abolitionists, "the adoption of a constitutional amendment granting compensation to any state that undertook to abolish slavery by 1900. Slaves freed 'by the chances of the war' would remain 'forever free'; but all others would remain slaves until they were gradually emancipated by the respective states or individual owners" (McPherson 1964, 119–120). Such action represents Lincoln's attempt to find some middle ground on this matter that might be acceptable to most participants.

He was, in short, trying to steer a course with not very good radar, which led him to adopt slow and often halting steps as he moved through the obstacle course surrounding the issue of slavery.

George Bush, "Reactive" President   While Lincoln surely would have loved to have a few polls to lessen his uncertainty about the public's views on the pressing issues of the day, George Bush was awash in information about the opinions of average citizens. This information often figured into his political calculations. When the Los Angeles riots erupted, for example, Bush decided to address the nation about this crisis. But what should he say? Should he express concern for the poverty that helped fuel this uprising, or should he condemn the rampant violations of local, state, and national laws? Kenneth Walsh (1992, 11) writes that "his staff gave him a clear choice between two finished versions of that first speech—one tough, the other conciliatory. Driven by the polls, Bush went Macho in his defining moment."

Bush's ability to adjust his views to the public's thinking is, of course, a tribute to his political skills. But it is also consistent with the behavior of well-informed, rational politicians. While Bush was not solely driven by shifts in public opinion, as represented by surveys, there was an image of him as a politician who was highly influenced by the results of polls.[9] Below I will briefly describe Bush's handling of one issue during his presidency: health care.[10]

In 1991, the issue of health care began to get increasing attention from the news media and politicians as an important problem facing the United States. A Gallup Poll conducted in early August reported that 91 percent of the public felt that there was a "crisis in healthcare." Just 9 per-

9. During Bush's presidency a number of cartoons emerged depicting him as someone driven by polls. Such cartoons reflect the perception of many political observers that Bush did rely on polls in many instances of his political life. While hardly conclusive "evidence," cartoons often capture the conventional wisdom of the day.

10. Since I do not have access to Bush's personal papers or his polls, I have turned to the news media's account of Bush. For the most part, I tried to make sure that the journalists' accounts of the former President's behavior were consistent.

cent believed that no crisis existed, and a meager 1 percent had no opinion on the subject.[11] Such information, in conjunction with Bush's tendency "to sound concerned but do nothing," gave observers reason to
think that this issue might help the Democrats win some votes in the
upcoming 1992 elections.[12]

But given Bush's option of using the "bully pulpit," he could have taken
the lead on this issue. By offering a responsible plan to the electorate, the
President could have rallied a concerned citizenry to support his particular initiative and thus undercut one of the potential Democratic issues in
1992. Even though the electorate cared about the issue, they had not
formed any clear preferences about what to do, giving Bush a golden
opportunity to engage in leadership. But during the summer and the fall
of 1991, Bush chose to duck the issue, except to promise to lessen governmental regulation on the health care industry. His general posture is well
represented by a headline on the front page of the *Washington Post* on
September 26, 1991: "Bush on Health Care: Case Study in Caution."

Harris Wofford, the Democratic nominee for a 1991 special election to
the U.S. Senate from Pennsylvania, was not so cautious. Trailing badly in
the polls against a well-known Republican, Wofford had to try something
to shake up the race. His polls, like those noted above, clearly demonstrated that the issue of health care was highly salient. In July, 1991,
Wofford's campaign conducted a private survey to assess the political clout
of the health-care debate. They surveyed "about 600 registered voters
across the state, and it had included a presentation of the three most powerful concerns people had about national health insurance: that it would
lead to higher taxes, would create massive Government bureaucracies, and
would take away people's ability to choose their own doctor. 'We lumped
the three horribles together and, by a 63 to 30 percent margin, people said
they still wanted national health insurance,' Mr. [Paul] Begala said"
(Hinds 1991, A11).

With such evidence in hand, Wofford, in a nearly single-minded fashion, trumpeted in every corner of the state that the "Constitution says if
you are charged with a crime, you have a right to a lawyer; but it's even
more fundamental that if you are sick, you should have a right to a doc-

---

11. See *Gallup Poll Monthly*, August 1991, p. 4. In addition, a *Wall Street Journal*/NBC News
Poll yielded similar findings, as reported on June 28, 1991, A14). Perhaps even more important,
both Democratic and Republican pollsters found similar trends in public opinion (see *Christian
Science Monitor*, 1991, 1).

12. *The Lancet* 1991, 561.

tor" (Kramer 1991, 51). This tactic apparently worked. Wofford closed a 44-point gap in the polls by election day and won the race. This comeback gave Bush (and all other politicians) reason to pay attention to the issue of health care. As Paula Dwyer and Susan Garland (1991, 28) wrote,

> The seismic tremors started registering about a year ago. In survey after survey, pollsters began picking up distress signals from middle class voters worried about health care costs. . . . These rumblings triggered a political earthquake on Nov. 5, when lightly regarded Democrat Harris Wofford upset former Attorney General Richard Thornburgh in Pennsylvania's U.S. Senate race.[13]

Wofford's surprise victory served as a "wake up call" to Bush. Now one might say that it was election results, not polls, that was the key piece of information. Certainly the outcome was important. But the polling done around this contest had confirmed the importance of the issue to the voters in Pennsylvania. In one survey, 50 percent of the electorate in the Keystone state viewed health care as the most important issue. Taxes, a long-time Republican theme, trailed with 29 percent (Dwyer and Garland 1991, 29). Moreover, it *was* the information from polls that had led Wofford to stress this issue in the first place. Hence, the election results simply confirmed in stunning fashion the findings conveyed by those surveys.

Bush had hoped to postpone taking action on the so-called health care crisis until after the 1992 election.[14] But that option no longer seemed viable. He had to react. As Susan Garland (1992, 43) wrote, "with poll after poll finding that health care has become a top voter concern, President Bush knows he had to offer an election year response to Democratic cries for action."

Part of Bush's dilemma on this matter may have been polls that indicated *both* that Americans viewed health care as a "right that should be guaranteed by the government" and that a solid majority would pay higher taxes to ensure that right (Kramer 1991, 51). Consequently, Bush could not just oppose government-sponsored health care on the grounds that it would require higher taxes.

Bush did finally join the debate, announcing a "comprehensive" health care reform program on February 6, 1992. He had been hinting about pre-

---

13. November 25, 1991, p. 28.
14. This hope of delaying the issue was reflected in a number of commentaries. See, for instance, Dentzer (1992, 22) and Dwyer and Garland (1991, 28).

senting a plan since mid-December. But this program, as some were quick
to point out, was quite vague (Pear 1992, A15). The political realities, partly
a function of public opinion, forced such a hollow response. On the one
hand, the available information from polls demonstrated that a large
majority wanted the government to provide health care.[15] Yet, on the
other hand, such a plan would invite claims that Bush favored "big government"—something that the public did not support. Moreover, he did
not want to give Pat Buchanan any more ammunition, as this conservative
"pit bull" toured New Hampshire hammering the President at every turn
on exactly these issues. Finally, it was not clear what the public wanted
done about health care. As Julie Kosterlitz (1991, 2806) wrote in the
National Journal, "different polls and even successive questions in the same
polls turn up seemingly contradictory responses." Thus, if politicians are
truly driven by polls, a confused electorate should give elected officials no
clear guidance on what to do—other than to do something.

This brief story, cobbled together from various accounts among the
news media, paints Bush as a reactive President who, rather than practicing leadership on this issue, waited until the last moment to respond to
growing public pressure (usually reflected in the polls). Even though there
is no "smoking gun," this story fits with Adam Clymer's (1991b, E5) observation in September that Bush started to tackle issues like health care only
after the President's pollster "reported that the public was tiring of Mr.
Bush's concentration on foreign policy and wanted him to pay more attention to domestic issues."

Discussion   The presentation of these two cases is not designed to argue
that George Bush and Abraham Lincoln were identical, except for differences in the type of information that had about public opinion. Such a claim
would be foolish. My point is that politicians have the same ends, and when
the means to those ends change, behavior is altered. Thus, both Lincoln and
Bush wanted to pursue policies that would be supported by the public. The
difference, however, is that Lincoln adopted his particular course of action
with questionable information about what the public wanted. Bush, on the
other hand, possessed much better information, allowing him to react to the
electorate's opinions. And because the electorate in this case did not speak
with a clear voice, Bush reacted slowly and cautiously.

---

15. A CBS/*New York Times* Polls published in early February 1992 suggested that 75 percent
of the adults sampled favored a government-sponsored health-care plan.

By considering changes in information politicians possess, we can develop (and have developed) new interpretations of behavior. The notion that Lincoln paid close attention to public opinion and sought to stay within its constraints paints a picture of this president that is different from conventional portraits. I do not seek to denigrate the achievements of Lincoln. He did govern the nation during its greatest trial and was able to hold it together despite the many hurdles put in front of him. My point is simply that we should not let good outcomes (i.e., saving the union and ending slavery) dictate our interpretation and assessment of politicians' actions. In the end, Bush and Lincoln both needed public support and tried to understand it and work within its constraints.

Marshaling More Evidence

The stories of Lincoln and Bush offer a few hints about the impact of information on presidential decision-making. Even though these cases fit the tenets of this theory, they cannot stand by themselves. In what follows, I shall describe more systematically the impact of polls on presidents and their actions in office.

The Use of Polls   Polls have become part of everyday life. "There is," as John Brehm (1993, 3) writes, "hardly an aspect of American political life untouched by polling and survey research." One need only scan the pages of the morning newspaper to find an article reporting the findings from a recent survey. Pollsters ask questions on topics ranging from our sex lives to whether we believe in UFOs. As *U.S. News and World Report* notes,

> The poll data pour in daily on everything a person could conceivably have an opinion about—and some things it's hard to imagine anyone having an opinion about. One recent survey reports that by a narrow 42–40 margin, American women believe the First Lady should be active in "all" as opposed to "just some" aspects of presidential business (Budiansky et. al. 1988, 24).

While polling of some sort has been going on since the 1930s, the last few decades have witnessed a proliferation of surveys. The major media organizations make extensive use of polls, averaging about 25 polls per year in 1988 and 1989. Michael Kagay (1991, 19) reports that *The New York Times* and CBS News alone conducted 31 surveys during 1988, contacting more than eighty thousand respondents. A decade earlier, the *Los Angeles Times* sponsored just a single poll (Lewis 1991, 79). The frequency of polling done by the news media hit a new high in 1992 when CNN and ABC conducted nightly tracking polls of the Bush-Clinton-Perot battle. This interest in polls is not just a national phenomenon. Ladd and Benson (1992, 23) find that *local* television stations during 1989 conducted, on average, seven polls per year. Twenty years earlier, the local media almost never conducted polls.

This onslaught of publicly available information does not even consider the massive amount of private polling that politicians themselves have conducted. Franklin Roosevelt was the first president to use polls while in office. But since Kennedy, occupants of the Oval Office have come increasingly to rely on polls during their tenure (Jacobs 1993; Jacobs and Shapiro 1993b; Jacobs and Shapiro 1995b). In fact, Clinton had his pollster, Stanley Greenberg, conduct polls immediately *following* the 1992 election to test the political viability of various policies as he made plans for the early days of the new administration.

Even though the United States is more poll crazy than other countries, politicians in other nations have much access to polling results when making decisions (Butler and Ranney 1992; see also Worcester 1983). According to some data collected in an edited volume by Butler and Ranney (1992, 287), polls are highly important to 75 percent of the sixteen democratic nations examined in their study. In only one country—Italy—did they judge polls to be of little importance. By contrast, local governments in Japan sponsored around 900 polls during 1980 alone (Nisihira 1983). The major parties in Norway take advantage of monthly polling data.[16] Their Swedish counterparts have been conducting their own surveys since the 1960s (Esaiasson 1991). In France, local legislators rarely have access to polling data regarding their constituents (Pierce and Rochon 1991), but numerous national surveys tap the pulse of the larger electorate (Stoetzel 1983).[17] Finally, Jacobs (1993) documents how post-war governments in Britain made polling a central part of their decision-making process.

Even though politicians in most industrialized democracies have easy access to some sort of polling data, I shall focus my attention on the use of polls by American presidents. This detailed look at the American case

---

16. I owe this observation to Gunnar Vogt who is the survey director for Gallup's organization in Norway.

17. Fysh (1992) reports that the Gaullist party resisted using polls as a guide when forming the positions of the party. While this fact shows that not all politicians make use of polls, it should also be noted that this party did not fare well in most French elections during the decade of the 1980s and that general policy was being reconsidered.

will document more thoroughly their potential importance in shaping decision-making.

American Presidents   Given the rise of polls during the 1930s, FDR had the first opportunity to take advantage of them. While he did not make widespread use of surveys, Roosevelt apparently had access to polling data when forging parts of the New Deal, especially social security (Cornwall 1965, 136; Burns 1978, 281). In 1935, the year in which both the Gallup and *Fortune* polls were started, FDR knew of a survey by Emil Hurja indicating a Republican victory was possible in 1936 if Huey Long ran as a strong third party candidate (Barone 1988, 2). It is unclear whether these data helped shape his actions as the election approached, but FDR did try to placate some of Long's supporters during 1935. Roosevelt made much greater and more systematic use of polls between 1940 and 1945 (Steele 1974). In a recent biography, Frank Freidel (1990, 422) observes that throughout "the war Roosevelt closely watched public opinion polls." Cantril (1967) concurs, documenting that Roosevelt did use polls as a way to get a handle on the public's thinking, especially as he tried to steer the nation toward supporting the Allied cause in 1940 and 1941.

Roosevelt held a unique position, since his presidency spanned the two eras of information. How did Roosevelt react to this development? He made some use of polls, but how much? Steele (1975, 205) argues that FDR in fact moved away from most of the measures he had used in his early years as president (e.g., newspapers and mail) and increasingly relied on polls as a way to get "scientific" and "certain" estimates of the entire public's thinking on particular matters of policy (see also Eisinger 1994a). Betty Winfield (1990) and James MacGregor Burns (1970) also contend that Roosevelt increasingly turned to polls to develop a more accurate reading on the public's thinking.[18]

Truman, in contrast, made little use of this information (Jacobs 1993) and was actually distrustful of it (McCullough 1992). "I never paid any attention," wrote Harry Truman (1956, 177), "to the polls myself because in my judgment they did not represent a true cross section of American opinion." Herbst (1993, 91) argues that in the early years of scientific polling many politicians remained skeptical of their value and accuracy.

18. Roosevelt was a natural fan of systematic data on public opinion. Early in his tenure as president, he had his staff carefully analyze the letters sent to him for information about public opinion (Greer 1958). So the rise of polls fit his penchant for precision about what the electorate was thinking.

This skepticism, of course, was fueled by Gallup's prediction in October 1948 that Dewey would be sworn in as president in January 1949.

Usually scholars place Eisenhower in the Truman camp. Recent archival work by Robert Eisinger (1994b, 9) suggests, however, that "previous descriptions and analyses of the Eisenhower presidency significantly understate the Eisenhower administration's poll usage." The extent of Eisenhower's direct involvement with these data is not clear. But Eisinger's work does indicate that we have probably underestimated the import of polls during Ike's tenure.

Regardless of where Eisenhower falls in this discussion, it is the Kennedy and Johnson presidencies that clearly signaled the beginning of a new era. These chief executives were the first to integrate survey research into the daily operations of the White House (Jacobs 1992b; 1992a; 1993; Jacobs and Shapiro 1992a; Altschuler 1990). Kennedy relied heavily on Lou Harris's polls during the 1960 campaign (Jacobs and Shapiro 1994b), and this reliance continued once he was in office (Jacobs 1992; Jacobs and Shapiro 1992a). Jacobs (1993, 35) summarizes this change:

> the Kennedy and Johnson administrations . . . revamped the White House's intelligence gathering capacity. Following his election, Kennedy's relationship with private pollsters became a regular, routine part of the process of making decisions in the White House.
>
> After 1961, then, the White House became a veritable warehouse stocked with the latest public opinion data. . . . The regular flow of these private opinion surveys into the white House provided data on the president's popularity as well as on public preferences for policy issues and for candidates in congressional and gubernatorial races.

The subsequent occupant of the Oval Office continued and developed this pattern further. While Johnson commissioned 130 private polls from 1963 to 1968, Nixon sponsored 233 during his first term alone. Nixon in fact was instrumental in building an separate institutional apparatus within the White House to monitor public opinion (Jacobs and Shapiro 1995b).

Nixon was fascinated by polls, despite protests from himself and his aides to the contrary. "Within three months of coming into office," write Jacobs and Shapiro (1994a, 4), "the President approved a 'policy to stay on top of public attitudes,' instructing his aides to 'work out a place' with private pollsters to give him a 'quick reading [of public opinion] now, overall and on specific issues.' " Other scholars too have argued that Nixon used polls while in office (Bogart 1972), and that he paid close attention to his standing in the Gallup Poll (Sudman 1982; Katz 1993). Kernell (1993, 30) reports that a Nixon aide stated that the president "had all kinds of polls all the time; he sometimes had a couple of pollsters doing the same kind of survey at the same time. He really studied them. He wanted to find the thing that would give them an advantage." This pattern was especially true as the 1972 election approached.[19] Nixon gave Robert Teeter, one of his pollsters, a central role in keeping him abreast of how Nixon might fare against McGovern or Humphrey in the 1972 election. While Teeter was an important player for Nixon, his role grew under Ford. David Moore (1992, 225) notes that Teeter became one of four key strategists for Ford as he tried to climb his way out of the electoral hole created by Watergate.

Jimmy Carter extended further the importance of polling by giving his pollster, Pat Caddell, office space in the White House (Barone 1988). Ronald Reagan continued this practice by making his pollster, Richard Wirthlin, part of the President's inner circle. As Beal and Hinckley (1984, 72) observe, during "the first 29 months of the Reagan administration the President's long time pollster, Richard Wirthlin, met with Ronald Reagan more than 25 times to discuss politics and polls, and he delivered memoranda on the results of over 40 public opinion studies to the President's top three aides: Jim Baker, Mike Deaver, and Ed Meese." Wirthlin confirmed this contact, commenting recently that he met with Reagan 26 times in Reagan's first year in office (Berke 1993, A17).

Bush was no different from his immediate predecessors. For starters, Bush selected Teeter—the former Ford and Nixon pollster—to head his reelection team, highlighting the central role experts on public opinion now play in politics. Bush also had lots of access to polling data while in the White House. Paul Brace and Barbara Hinkley (1992, 4) note, for instance, that prior to the Gulf War, the Bush people were receiving daily reports of the public's views about the struggle with Iraq. John Mueller (1994) confirms the heavy use of polls by the Bush administration during this crisis and subsequent war. Bush also used polls when it came to domestic politics—a topic considered earlier in the chapter. Recent reports also suggest that Bush not only used polls but also was an avid consumer of them, especially in regard to his personal popularity.[20]

19. Jacobs and Shapiro (1994a, 6) report that during 1972 Nixon conducted 153 polls, which represents two-thirds of his total polling between 1969 and 1972.

20. Brace and Hinkley (1992, 19) and *Arizona Republic* January 24, 1992, A17.

President Clinton has certainly proven to be no exception to this rule—he too has paid close attention to polls. Jacobs and Shapiro (1995a) observed that the President's early moves were quite consistent with public opinion: he rescinded the "gag order" on government sponsored abortion clinics, he signed both the family leave bill and the "motor voter" bill. One might counter, of course, with Clinton's call to lift the ban on homosexuals in the military. Here the President misjudged public opinion and the move represented a clear setback for him. However, once the public outcry ensued, Clinton backed down and looked for a compromise—behavior that is consistent with the tenets of my theory. Following the 1994 midterm elections, Clinton's calls for an increase in defense spending, elimination of many federal programs, a middle class tax cut and voluntary prayer in school were all consistent with a president responsive to the wishes of the electorate—as represented by public opinion polls. Of course, Clinton's actions come on the heels of the "Contract with America," which was a poll-driven document, where Frank Luntz, as mentioned in Chapter 1, provided hard data to Republicans about which promises should be included in the Contract and which should be avoided.

Interestingly, Clinton's pollster, Stanley Greenberg, may represent an important change, since he was a much more visible political figure than previous presidential pollsters. In May 1993, for instance, Greenberg delivered an address in which he commented that Clinton had lost control of the agenda in regard to his economic package. In so doing, Greenberg acknowledged that he met regularly with the President.[21] Seven months, later Greenberg talked about the importance of polls in Clinton's White House and how "he meets at least once a week with the President to discuss the latest polling information. He also said Mr. Clinton can recite minute details about survey data, including his popularity ratings, off the top of his head" (Berke 1993, A17).

This degree of openness about the import of polls suggests that Clinton thought of Greenberg as part of his staff and that there was little reason to hide the fact. This pattern of openness stands in contrast to Kennedy, who made considerable efforts to hide Harris's role in his administration.[22] Nixon and his staff also frequently denied that polls were ever part of the

---

21. An Associated Press report published in the *Tempe Tribune*, May 23, 1993, p. A3.

22. The observation that recent presidents are more open about the role of their pollsters I owe to Larry Jacobs—a keen commentator on this general subject.

decision-making process, although "before adopting a policy course, they [had] assessed its costs in public support" (Kernell 1993, 31). Perhaps the public may now expect pollsters to be at center stage in presidential politics, or perhaps politicians, regardless of public reaction, are now more comfortable with the central role pollsters now play in government.

Polls and the Decisions of Politicians

Even though politicians have access to polling data, it does not mean that the information drives their decisions. Of course, the choices politicians make on matters of policy have complex origins (Kingdon 1968, 1984; Putnam 1973), but the task here is simply to show whether it is reasonable to believe that polling data represent a new variable that shapes those decisions. Such evidence is essential to lend credibility to the theory developed here. Let me start with a few suggestive stories about Franklin Roosevelt, and then move into a discussion of relevant findings from recent research on this topic.

As noted earlier, FDR increased his use of polls during World War II. Apparently there are a number of instances where the results from polls directly affected his actions during this titanic struggle. For instance, FDR knew from polling data that the public, as of July 1940, wanted to stay out of the war. Thus, Roosevelt believed that he would have to be careful in his efforts to support the Allies—any explicit effort to involve us in the war might create a serious backlash among the electorate. So, before preceding with the Lend-Lease Act, for instance, he made sure that the public supported such action to help Britain. Cantril (1967, 36) reports in fact that FDR knew in February 1941 that 65 percent of the electorate supported lend lease, providing that Britain paid us back after the war. While it is possible that he might still have advocated such a program without the public's approval, it probably would have been carried out in a different fashion.[23] Much later in the war, FDR used polls to shape his policies in regard to the bombing of Rome. Roosevelt feared that dropping bombs on the Eternal City might lead to a steep decline in support for the war by Catholics. But a poll on March 1, 1944 indicated that a solid majority (66 percent) of Catholics supported such action, if efforts were taken to protect the religious shrines. Two days later Rome was bombed (Cantril 1967, 54).

---

23. For more details on FDR and the polls, see chapters 6 and 8 of Cantril (1967) and Steele (1974).

Presidential Approval and Behavior   With the advent of polls came the Presidential approval rating, made famous by the Gallup organization, which asks a sample of Americans whether they "approve or disapprove of the way" the President is handling his job. The resulting proportion has been hailed as an indicator of whether the president has or does not have public support. Brehm (1993, 6) aptly refers to this survey question as the "Dow Jones Index for Politics." The news media and other political observers spend a great deal of time tracking this rating. As Clinton reached the 100-day mark of his administration, the news media were filled with comparisons of Clinton's standing to that of other presidents at the same point in their tenure. Scholars too have spent much time analyzing this important variable (see Mueller 1970; Edwards 1980, 1983; Rivers and Rose 1985; Ostrom and Simon 1985; Lanoue 1988; Brace and Hinckley 1992).

While pundits and academics study this rating, so do presidents. Surely the most famous example of a president's interest in popularity is LBJ's habit of keeping his approval rating in his pocket (when his ratings were high) to show anyone who might be interested. LBJ may have been more open about it, but other presidents too have paid much attention to this rating. Kernell (1993, 104), when discussing Ronald Reagan's behavior, noted that "because the polls were showing a drop in the president's popularity—which made him vulnerable in Washington—his advisers decided that conferring on location with European heads of state would be good for his image as a leader." Nixon also would engage in a series of public relations moves if his popularity dropped at all in the Gallup polls (Sudman 1982). Clinton too has been very interested in his standing with the public (Woodward 1994). Given the importance that the news media attach to this indicator, presidents must take their poll standings into account, especially as they try to get Congress to enact legislation (Rivers and Rose 1985; Kernell 1993).

Within the context of the theory presented here, we should find that the policies and actions of presidents *respond* to changes in their polls ratings. If it turns out that presidents behave in systematically different ways (i.e., change positions on policies) as a reaction to shifts in their poll ratings, such findings would suggest a causal connection between their behavior and the results of polls. We, of course, cannot be sure of a direct causal link, but the findings would at least be consistent with the tenets of this theory.

When examining the correlates of presidential speechmaking, Lyn Ragsdale (1984) found that changes in approval ratings often prompt a president to deliver a major address to the nation. Using data from 1949 to 1980, Ragsdale (1984, 976) argues that the "greater the change in presidential popularity, the greater the likelihood of presidential speechmaking." She uncovers other explanatory variables underlying the decision to make a speech. But the fact that behavior follows shifts in public approval suggests that presidents use these indicators when making decisions. Brace and Hinckley (1993, 396) offer additional support for this thesis, finding that presidents "make *reactive* choices, taking foreign trips and making major addresses when their approval has fallen" (my emphasis).

These scholars also determined that such action by presidents can boost their standings with the public (Ragsdale 1984; Brace and Hinckley 1992, 1993). These results suggest a dynamic relationship between polls and behavior and might well encourage politicians to pay closer attention to polls, since they can affect, to some extent, their popularity with the electorate. And popularity with the electorate is a powerful commodity within the corridors of Washington.

Policy and Polls   While approval ratings matter to presidents, one cannot conclude that polls directly influence how presidents deal with specific issues. The general view has been that information from surveys provides only a general guideline to politicians—there is no direct correspondence between polls and the decisions that politicians make. There is, however, mounting evidence to suggest that public opinion frequently *leads* policy (see, for instance, Monroe 1979; Page and Shapiro 1983; Farkus, Shapiro, and Page 1990; Russett 1990; Jacobs and Shapiro 1992a; Stimson, MacKuen, and Erikson 1995). This pattern is not limited to the domestic arena (see Russett 1990; Hartley and Russett 1992; Wlezien 1995). There are, of course, exceptions, but as James Stimson and colleagues (1995, 559) have recently observed, "when the public asks for a more conservative government, politicians oblige." And if the public swings back to the left down the road, we can also expect politicians to follow suit.

Even though this research supports my general argument, one still must be cautious about implying a causal relationship from the many statistical relationships uncovered by these scholars. Ideally, one would want to have access to the information that the politician had, not rough proxies of it (see, for instance, Jacobs 1993; Jacobs and Shapiro 1994b). Recent scholarship has started to overcome this hurdle through an examination of the correspondence between the *private* polls of presidents and their actions in office (Altschuler 1990; Jacobs 1992a, 1992b, 1993; Jacobs and

Shapiro 1992a, 1992b, 1993a, 1993b, 1994a, 1994b; Hinckley 1992; Eisinger 1994a, 1994b)

Of immediate relevance is work by Lawrence Jacobs (1992a, 1992b, 1993). Jacobs takes a detailed and careful look at the emergence of polling as an institution within government. As suggested earlier, polls have become an important part of the governmental process. But, of course, it is possible that the information from these surveys is used instead to *manipulate* rather than to respond to opinion. Jacobs (1992a, 212) explicitly investigates this possibility, concluding that while the development of a governmental polling apparatus "initially emerged as an attempt to outwardly affect and manage public opinion," its creation had a "recoil" effect. That is, by becoming more aware of the public's preferences, politicians have become responsive to those preferences.

The "recoil" effect, as Jacobs terms it, makes good sense given the theory presented in this book. Support-maximizing politicians should be constantly searching for clues about public opinion in their efforts to maintain and to increase power. When they uncover a device that provides such a wealth of information about the views of average citizens, one should expect politicians to pay close attention. When seeking to maximize support, they have sufficient incentive to respond to the data from polls, but that incentive increases further within the context of a competitive environment. Politicians would constantly fear that if they failed to take advantage of the information from polls, the opposition might. And like players in a prisoner's dilemma, that fear would help generate such a "recoil" effect.

Jacobs's argument is set within a larger empirical study examining the role of public opinion in the reform of health policy in the United States and Great Britain. In that study, Jacobs (1993, 222) finds that "pivotal policy shifts occurred *after* politicians and specialists reached a new and more accurate assessment of public opinion. . . . This sequence provides support for arguing that the opinion-policy relationship is neither spurious nor manipulated outright." Jacobs (1993, 20) finely tunes his point, contending that "it is not tenable . . . to argue that the public's role is limited to identifying broad policy goals while elite experts have free rein to fashion the means to achieve those goals. In both the U.S. and Britain public sentiment was critical in shaping the administrative means."

Jacobs's work does not have to stand by itself, however. He and Robert Shapiro have pursued this general topic further, looking at the behavior of Kennedy and Johnson during their presidencies and their campaigns for the office. Using the private polls of Kennedy and Johnson, combined with some careful archival work, Jacobs and Shapiro (1992a, 3) show that "polls had a strong effect on Kennedy's selection of particular issues and policy directions." Of course, not all of the policies that Kennedy pursued were a function of Lou Harris's polling data. But "the evidence indicates that . . . polls were a determinative factor in Kennedy's selection of specific policy areas and particular alternatives" (Jacobs and Shapiro 1992a, 44). Consider, for instance, that in Kennedy's first State of the Union speech, the chief executive took positions on issues that were consistent with the findings of Harris's polls in 19 out of 20 instances—the lone exception was foreign aid. In January 1962, the President offered positions that were consistent with public opinion 14 of 17 times. Kennedy's initial resistance to tackling Civil Rights can also be tied to a less than supportive public (Giglio 1991; Stern 1992); it was only when the Civil Rights movement forced his hand that the President chose to act. Of course, by the time of his famous speech on June 11, 1963, which made civil rights a moral issue, public opinion was becoming less tolerant of discrimination against blacks (Schuman, Steeh and Bobo 1985).[24]

Kennedy may, however, have been more sensitive to public opinion than most Presidents, given his narrow electoral victory (Jacobs and Shapiro 1992a). Thus, it is important to consider other cases. Jacobs and Shapiro (1992b, 1993a) have extended their analysis to Johnson's behavior in office.

There is no doubt that Johnson was an avid consumer of polling information (see also Altschuler 1990). According to Jacobs and Shapiro, Johnson used published polls "often before they were publicly released" and relied on 119 privately conducted polls by Oliver Quayle between November 1963, and November 1966. These polls not only went to the White House, but Johnson actually saw their results. "During one period between September, 1965 and September, 1966," write Jacobs and Shapiro (1993a, 5), "the White House received over 70 polls, most of them by Oliver Quayle; over 90% of these polls were analyzed by a staff member and sent along to Bill Moyers, who typically forwarded them to the President."

---

24. The so-called "race" issue has had a long and tortured past (Carmines and Stimson 1989). It clearly has been (and continues to be) important in American politics, generating all sorts of divisions in the country. And measuring the public's preferences on the matter is exceedingly difficult. My point here is not to enter the debate over race, but simply to suggest that Kennedy's decision to support civil rights was not inconsistent with trends in national opinion and that some minimum level of public support was probably a necessary condition for him to proceed forward with his efforts on civil rights.

The effects of these polls on Johnson's actions varied in interesting ways during his term, according to these scholars. The results of the polls had their greatest impact of LBJ's behavior during 1964 and 1966. In 1964, for example, Johnson's positions on Civil Rights and Medicare were fueled in part by Quayle's polls. In 1965, however, after Johnson's electoral landslide, the President's behavior did not respond strongly to the findings of Quayle's polls. This twist suggests that popular presidents have more flexibility in pursuing policies, which fits well with my theory. Politicians are support-maximizers, as assumed earlier, but when their support is at a peak, there would be less need to advocate policies that increase it further—especially if one introduces the notion of diminishing returns. It is quite possible that politicians turn to secondary goals once their popularity reaches a certain level.

As a result, under some circumstances, politicians like Johnson can engage in Wilsonian leadership when using polls. During 1965, Jacobs and Shapiro (1993a) find that it was not public opinion that was driving Johnson's positions on issues; rather the President, with his mandate in hand, tried to alter what the public considered important issues. Altschuler (1990, 36) makes a similar claim about Johnson following the 1964 election, observing that he "used polls not to learn of public opinion but to try to manipulate both that opinion and their perception of it."[25]

While Johnson may have been less driven by poll results after 1964, he still paid some attention to them. John Burke and Fred Greenstein (1989, 193–94) argue that the "inclination of Johnson and his associates in 1965 was to pay heed to the hawkish findings yielded by the Gallup question that asked the public to affirm its support for the popular president and his policies. Thus, Johnson appears to have been attentive to responses to the fixed choice question asked in the same May 12 poll, 'Do you think the United States is handling affairs in South Vietnam as well as could be expected, or do you think we are handling affairs there badly.' "

This dynamic relationship between polls and presidential behavior is interesting and fits within the context of my theory, since Wilsonian leadership should occur for those issues on which the public does not have

---

25. Altschuler (1990, xiv) also finds that during Johnson's administration "polls provided useful information about how to tailor . . . appeals." LBJ, however, appears to have been more concerned with his popularity, limiting the influence of polling data on what specific policies the administration pursued (Altschuler 1990, 107).

well-developed preferences. Much more will be said about the implications for leadership in Chapter 4.

Even though Johnson and Kennedy were the first presidents to place polling at the center of their administrations, what about subsequent occupants of the Oval Office? Did polls influence their decisions? We have already come across some examples that suggest that the answer is yes. Further instances can be found in Jacobs's and Shapiro's (1994a, 1995b) most recent work, which now includes the Nixon presidency. Even though their research is in its early stages, they find "a strong connection" between Nixon's polls and his policies (Jacobs and Shapiro 1994a, 30). Andrew Katz (1993) made a similar claim about Nixon, arguing that "public opinion surveys conducted for the White House during the administration's first year gave some impetus for American assertiveness in Vietnam." In the case of George Bush, Mueller (1994, 116) concluded that during the Gulf War "public opinion polls seem to have importantly influenced Bush's decision-making in several notable respects." Apparently, the Bush people decided to stress the hostage problem in Iraq and Saddam Hussein's nuclear capabilities *after* polling data showed that the public was concerned about these problems (Mueller 1994, 118). Hinckley (1992) finds much the same pattern when examining the impact of polls on the specifics of Reagan's and Bush's foreign policy. He was in a unique position to undertake such a project, since Hinckley worked on the White House policy staff. His study showed that foreign policy decisions were often made within the context of polling data. In fact, there was only one instance where the Reagan administration pursued a policy that was opposed by a majority of the public—the stance toward Central America. But even here, Reagan's advisers knew that citizens did not care much about the actions of the "Freedom Fighters," giving the President freedom to pursue such a policy.

Conclusion

Whether one is persuaded by the evidence presented in this chapter will depend, in part, on whether one tends to view a glass with some water in it "as half full or half empty." While there are many instances where polls have had the kinds of effects on politicians' behavior that are predicted by this theory, officeholders also have ignored (and will continue to ignore) polls. But often when behavior conflicted with poll results, the issues involved were not highly salient. Such action *is not* at odds with the theory, since low-salience issues provide opportunities for leadership.

For the purpose of supporting this theory, it is too bad that Congressmen John Porter's observation in May, 1989 is not true: "Politicians didn't get into office without being pretty good at marketing themselves. They know how to keep people happy too. So we seem to be making public policy in American the same way: take a poll and give them what they want."[26]

Even though Porter is obviously overstating the point (and also probably kidding), the theory here does *not* require a one-to-one correspondence between the results of polls and behavior by politicians. Instead, the central idea is that the information now available to politicians through survey research is different from that available seventy-five years ago, and that difference leads to a systematic change in the behavior of officeholders. This fundamental point is believable in light of the evidence presented in this chapter. Politicians have paid attention to polls, and as with any decision, information often affects the final choice. How often that information has affected the outcome is unclear, but it has almost surely been often enough to believe that politicians now behave differently from the way they did in the past.

The task now is to sort out the political implications of this change, which is the objective of the next three chapters.

---

26. Quoted in Brehm (1993, 8).

Chapter 4

THE CHANGING PROSPECTS FOR LEADERSHIP

> "The longer public opinion has ruled, . . .
>
> the more are politicians likely to occupy
>
> themselves, not in forming opinion, but in
>
> discovering and hastening to obey it."

JAMES BRYCE (1895, 262) PENNED THIS
observation at the very end of a chapter in *The American Commonwealth*
titled "Government by Public Opinion." With the rise of polls and the
increased ability of elected officials to discover and hence to "obey" public
opinion, Bryce's concern has even greater relevance today. The tenor of
this observation has found its way into recent commentaries by political
observers. Russell Baker (1991, A15), for example, argues rather bluntly that
"our rulers never make a move without taking a public-opinion poll."
George Will (1992a, A11) echoes that theme, stating that "government
today involves minute measurement of public appetites by servile politicians worshipful of those measurements." Former Connecticut Governor
Lowell Weicker had perhaps the most amusing observation when he
asserted that most politicians' idea of leadership was to dial the "1–800 line
to their pollster" (Specter 1991, 42). Some concerned groups have even
tried to reward acts of bold leadership as a way to stem the tide of what
they see as pandering to public opinion. The Kennedy Library at Harvard
University, for instance, initiated in 1990 the Profile in Courage award to

a "public official who follows judgment or conscience rather than opinion polls" (Oreskes and Toner 1990, A12).

What does this theory have to say about the prospects of leadership in an era of good information? How do those prospects compare with those of the era prior to polls? At first blush, one might think that the information from polls promotes more followership than leadership. Support-maximizing politicians are now better equipped to react to shifts in public opinion than were their counterparts one hundred years ago, which allows them to follow the electorate's preferences—just as Bryce feared. If so, leadership today may well involve something close to a toll-free call to a pollster. However, this theory's implications for leadership are much more complicated and consequential than a simple prediction of increased followership (or a decline in leadership). While it is true that politicians have a better reading of public opinion, they are also better able to identify issues that provide opportunities for leadership. That is, the advent of polls, at least within our theoretical world, may provide expanded opportunities for *Wilsonian* leadership, rather than just an increased tendency for politicians to follow public opinion.

To get a handle on this matter, we need to determine how the prospects for leadership and followership have changed within our two eras. How often did "leadership by mistake" actually occur prior to polls? How often does it occur now? What about followership? Is it more likely now? To answer these kinds of questions, I make some assumptions about the conditions that faced politicians during the eras of good and bad information. These assumptions then permit me to generate estimates of the probabilities for leadership and followership. With these estimates in hand, I shall compare and then draw implications from them.

This discussion about the changing prospects for leadership also provides the opportunity to address what my theory has to say about the agendas of officeholders. The argument so far has focused on how politicians tackle a single issue. But the theory can accommodate multiple issues, if they are taken one at a time. Given that the tasks normally associated with leadership often involve the selection of issues on which to lead, this topic is of obvious importance. As I shall show, the theory suggests that well-informed politicians will forge different agendas from those of their less well-informed counterparts. These different agendas, of course, have further implications for how leadership and followership work in the era of polls.

Expanding the Theory of Leadership and Followership

The central point of my argument is that the rise of polls has altered the ability of politicians to judge accurately the state of "public opinion." Up to this point, I have assumed public opinion to be a single entity.[1] But in fact for a politician (or anyone else) to estimate public opinion on a particular issue correctly, judgments must be made about both the *direction*[2] of opinion on that issue and its *salience*[3] to the electorate. These two components of public opinion have a long history (see, for instance, Lane and Sears 1964; Zaller 1992).[4] Thus, to provide a more complete account of leadership within our two eras, I shall recognize explicitly these two components of public opinion.[5] This expansion, in turn, will provide the

[1]. The specific assumption in the theory reads that "politicians have complete information about citizens' views on issues" (see Chapter 1).

[2]. Just for the record, the "direction" of opinion constitutes the position the electorate holds on a particular issue.

[3]. An issue is salient when the electorate finds some problem to be of concern or worry. That claim is hardly controversial. But it is incomplete. The salience of an issue is also a function of the politicians' positions on it. Consider the impact of the Democratic party proposing that we amend the Constitution so that the United States can become a "Catholic" nation. That issue, which was not salient to the public prior to this decision, would immediately capture the electorate's attention. In short, politicians themselves can affect the salience of issues. The basic notion of Wilsonian leadership is for a politician to tackle an issue that is not very important to the public and rally the country around it. Of course, if the opposition offers the exact same view on the issue, then it will be harder to rally the public since there is no real choice available.

I raise this point only to note that salience of an issue during the course of its life is not exogenous to the actions of politicians. It may well gain or lose importance to the electorate in response to the actions of politicians. However, an issue's *initial* salience, I shall assume, is solely a function of the public's preferences on the matter. That initial salience, in turn, shapes the behavior of politicians. And from that point on the importance of the issue for the public will be a function of events, politicians' actions, and the electorate's level of concern about the general problem.

[4]. This distinction actually fits will well with a spatial theory, since the unidimensional assumption that underlies the Downsian model captures both the salience of an issue and direction of opinion. The position of the median voter, obviously, captures the latter concept. And when the distribution of opinion includes the preferences of *all* citizens, the issue can be thought of as salient to the entire electorate. In contrast, a nonsalient issue involves only part of the electorate. Thus, the distribution of opinion for nonsalient issues would include only those citizens who care about the issue. Thus, by relaxing the assumption that all citizens possess preferences, the simple spatial model can accommodate these two core concepts of public opinion.

[5]. In the original assumptions of this theory, public opinion was treated as "sticky." That is, citizens exhibited stable preferences that would change when confronted with a very good set of reasons. With public opinion now treated as a function of salience and direction, stickiness is now associated with salience.

That is, issues that are important to citizens will, on average, be "stickier." The presumption is that for important issues the public will be more likely to be informed about the issue, and hence, more committed to their views. It is, of course, possible for a nonsalient issue to exhibit stickiness. The public may not care very much about the issue (which in itself shows stickiness), and their preferences about it may also be difficult to move.

opportunity to generate credible estimates of the chances for leadership and followership within these two eras.

The separation of public opinion into these two core components expands the account of leadership for poorly informed politicians. The reason is simple: poorly informed officeholders can now make two kinds of errors—they can misjudge the salience of an issue and the direction of opinion on it. In contrast, the distinction between salience and direction of opinion has few immediate implications for "completely" informed politicians. Such politicians know, by assumption, both components of public opinion. Thus, for salient issues officeholders can practice followership, and for nonsalient issues they can consider pursuing Wilsonian leadership—just as described in Chapter 1.

Let me briefly discuss these two errors. When estimating the direction of opinion (i.e., the median position) for a spatial issue, a politician either judges it correctly or not. Of course, some miscalculations are larger than others, and hence more costly to the politician. But in trying to sort out the various *types* of leadership, the size of the error is not at issue. In contrast, misjudging the salience of an issue can cut two ways.[6] Officeholders can believe incorrectly that a salient issue is unimportant; they also can perceive a nonsalient issue to be very important. These two errors have different consequences, as we shall see.

There is another matter regarding the direction of opinion that requires attention. In order for us to detect the position of the median voter for an *entire* electorate (i.e., the direction of opinion), the issue must be salient to all citizens. For issues that are not salient to the complete public, no median position technically exists for the whole electorate. One can determine the preferences for those citizens who care about the issue, but a large fraction of the citizenry will not be part of the calculation. Figure 4.1 seeks to capture this point. The top part of the diagram shows the typical spatial distribution, with the median position identified (M). But the lower portion of the graph shows a distribution that includes only those citizens who find the issue salient. There is a median position for that subset (m). But it is *not* the median point for the entire electorate. By assuming that all those who find the issue important are a random sample of the entire electorate, one could argue that "m" is a good predictor of the median point for all citizens. But such an assumption is problematic. Citizens who care about a particular issue usually differ from those who do not, which

---

6. I shall treat issues as "salient" or "nonsalient." That simple distinction will allow me to make my arguments with greater clarity.

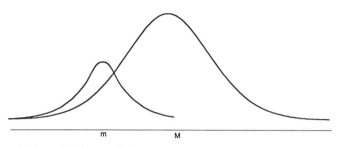

m: Median position for non-salient issue

M: Median position for salient issue

FIGURE 4.1 Median Positions for Salient and Non-Salient Issues

suggests a bias in such an indicator. Few would argue that people who consider gun control or abortion an important issue possess views on it similar to those who do not find either issue pressing. In short, any indicator of the direction of opinion for *non*-salient issues cannot be treated as the position of the median voter for all citizens.

This point has direct import for the discussion here. For issues that are not salient to the public, it is not possible to judge correctly the median position of the electorate, since, strictly speaking, there is no such point for nonsalient issues. Now this claim does not mean that knowing the direction of existing preferences for nonsalient issues is not of value. It is possible that those views would be predictors of what the complete electorate thinks and, at minimum, those views are part of the final distribution of opinion and influence the location of the median position. As we shall see later, knowing how a part of the public views nonsalient issues has a number of potential uses. My objective here, however, is simply to argue that the direction of opinion for the electorate is unsettled for nonsalient issues—which, of course, is one reason that Wilsonian leadership is an option in such instances.

In sum, poorly informed politicians can make *three* kinds of mistakes when judging public opinion, not just two, as originally described in Chapter 1. The additional error surfaces when we consider the possibility of misjudging a salient issue as not salient. Let me briefly describe these errors; the first two are old friends.

Leadership by Mistake: Politicians determine correctly that the issue is salient to the public, but they misjudge the direction of opinion. The misguided attempt at followership may lead to a change in the public's median position (i.e., Periclean leadership).

Followership by Mistake: Politicians incorrectly judge an issue to be salient, which leads them to attempt to follow opinion. But since the issue is not salient, they miss an opportunity to practice Wilsonian leadership.[7]

Wilsonian Leadership by Mistake: Politicians incorrectly judge a salient issue to be nonsalient, giving them the perceived flexibility to attempt to rally the public toward their position or to ignore the issue.

This last (and newest) category is the most risky of all for support-maximizing politicians. Office-holders who think a salient issue is not salient may practice Wilsonian leadership (by mistake). But given the actual importance of the issue to the public, they *should be* trying to follow opinion in order to maximize support. Such an error carries serious risks, since rather than confronting an electorate that does not care about the issue, politicians in fact face a public that has preferences that they do care about. Thus, politicians attempting to rally the public to a new position may confront stiff and unexpected resistance. The level of risk varies depending on how close the politician's adopted position is to the actual median view. The politician may get lucky, playing to the existing preferences, and thereby avoid a loss of political support. And even if the gap is wide, an effort to rally the public may work. Since preferences are not absolutely fixed, there is some chance of success, and hence, leadership might emerge within this scenario. But because of the risks, this scenario should strike fear into the hearts of support-conscious politicians.

Estimating the Probabilities

Even though politicians, both poorly and well informed, *can* theoretically engage in various forms of leadership and followership, how often do they? Do we have any reason to believe that "leadership by mistake" occurred in

---

7. It should also be noted that because the issue is actually not salient, there is no median position for the electorate, as noted earlier. By definition, therefore, politicians in this box are also mistaken about the direction of opinion. One might note that if politicians are wrong about the direction of opinion, could they end up leading by mistake too? It is possible. However, the chances are slim that officeholders would be able to rally (by mistake) the public toward their position. Because politicians are "following," they will undertake little effort to engage the electorate (it would be assumed that they already care). And an uninterested citizenry is unlikely to pay much attention to a politician's position on what is a minor issue to the public.

the pre-poll era? And has its frequency changed because of polls? What about followership? Is it a common event now? Is it more common than it was prior to polls? In the previous chapter, I offered some empirical support for the theory, demonstrating that politicians do pay attention to polls and that some of their decisions are apparently influenced by that information. But nowhere did I estimate the frequency of these various types of behavior. It is possible that the particular types of leadership presented here are rare or nonexistent events. If so, then the relevance of this theory declines. But by estimating these probabilities for the respective eras, I will be able to determine (with some precision) how the introduction of polls may have altered the way that leadership unfolds. This result is of obvious importance.

There is, of course, no set of data that permits us to generate empirical estimates of the chances that leaders practice these various types of behavior. To determine, even crudely, these probabilities, we must know how often politicians of the pre-poll era correctly estimated opinion. But how can we accomplish this task? There are no clear standards available to assess the accuracy of politicians' judgments. While politicians made mistakes, we cannot be sure, for instance, whether Lincoln was right or wrong in his belief that the electorate was supportive of freeing the slaves.

We can, nonetheless, make progress in this matter by simulating the conditions that faced politicians. By making a series of reasonable guesses about the accuracy of politicians' judgments about public opinion and the ratio of salient to nonsalient issues, one can generate hypothetical probabilities. These guesses will, of course, be tied to the particular assumptions we make. But one can always go back and adjust the initial guesses to see how the results change. The comparison of probabilities in the two eras can shed light on *change* in the frequency of leadership and followership even if the absolute indicators may be flawed.

To begin, I must first decide what constitutes an "accurate" estimate of the direction of opinion. If there are, for instance, seven different positions that a politician can adopt on an issue and the electorate's median position is "4," must the politician choose exactly "4" for it to count as an accurate estimate? Or could a "3" be close enough to count as "accurate"? What if an issue cuts ten different ways? With more options, the chances for an error increases. But some of these errors will be very inconsequential, especially as politicians try to cover a number of positions through ambiguity (Page 1978). The assumption that the issue can be presented spatially suggests that the number of different positions is very large, and hence the prospect of making an error, even a slight one, is quite high. But let us, for the purposes of this simulation, view issues in an agree-disagree format (see Rabinowitz and MacDonald 1989).[8] This change allows us to get a manageable grasp of the probabilities. Perhaps more important, treating issues along an extended continuum would, given the numerous positions, greatly (and artificially) inflate the number of errors that politicians make. As a result, this move will supply *conservative* estimates of error, minimizing the possibility that I will overstate the frequency of such behaviors as "leadership by mistake."

This conservative move is also consistent with an implicit part of most conceptions of leadership. As stated in Chapter 1, leadership involves moving (or forming) the distribution of opinion toward the stated view of the politician. Under a strict interpretation of that definition, a very small move by the public toward the politician would count as leadership. But such a small shift is not consistent with the spirit of the concept. Usually only "significant" changes in opinion would count as leadership. Hence, the adoption of an agree-disagree format would make it easier to identify significant moves, since a change in the direction of opinion usually involves that kind of shift.

Using this agree-disagree format, the probability of being "right" on a single issue should be reasonably high. Simple chance suggests a politician would be correct 50 percent of the time for a given issue. But, of course, officeholders, even poorly informed ones, would be more skilled in estimating opinion than just through chance, especially given that these players were talented enough to win office in the first place. Recall that politicians prior to polls were not completely *un*informed. Officeholders in the nineteenth century had some useful information about public opinion, suggesting that they often avoided the errors described above. The data from Claude Robinson (1932) certainly suggest that while errors were made by politicians when judging the outcomes of elections, many did quite well in their predictions.

I shall assume that politicians correctly gauged the direction of opinion 75 percent of the time. This proportion squares with findings reported by Hedlund and Friesma (1972). In a study of Iowa state legislators, they found that only 33 percent of these politicians judged public opinion correctly on *all four* issues that they examined. Under my

---

8. A shift to the agree-disagree format is not as large a departure from the spatial assumption as one may think. For instance, the agree-disagree format gives a rank order to preferences, which allows them to be aligned along a (very short) continuum.

assumption, 32 percent of politicians would get *all four* issues "right."[9] Since Iowa legislators in 1967 did not have access to polling data from their districts, these almost identical proportions give credence to this starting assumption.

But, of course, politicians must also estimate the salience of an issue. Again, one can think of salience along a continuum, offering numerous degrees of importance. If so, there is great potential for misjudging the salience of an issue. But to simplify matters and to avoid inflating the number of errors, I will treat issues as salient or not salient. This move is consistent with the previous discussion about the importance of issues. As in the case of the agree-disagree format, this simplification permits me to make progress in uncovering the probabilities of the various types of leadership.

I shall assume that poorly informed politicians judged the salience of an issue correctly 85 percent of the time. The rate of accuracy is higher than when assessing the direction of opinion, which reflects the kinds of information available to politicians prior to polls. As indicated in Chapter 2, politicians used such things as newspapers, letters, and claims by interest groups in their assessments of public opinion. These sources gave a better indication of the salience of the issue than the direction of public opinion, since they contained more systematic biases of the latter than the former (see Ginsberg 1986). Thus, in an effort to make the starting points as realistic as possible, I have adopted differing probabilities.

Now, of course, one can quibble with the particular rates of accuracy that I selected. But the objective here is to establish the probabilities of the various types of leadership; one can easily adjust the proportions later, yielding different estimates. At this time, I just want to start with a few reasonable (and conservative) guesses about the skill of politicians in judging opinion. For those interested, an appendix at the end of the chapter lays out two alternative scenarios. Those estimates do not tell a different story from that reported below.

Poorly Informed Politicians   Using the two proportions above, the chances of a politician, without access to polls, correctly assessing "public opinion" for any issue is (was) 64 percent:[10]

---

9. If one assumes that calculating the direction of opinion for each issue is an independent event for politicians, then one just multiplies the starting point of 75 percent by itself four times (32% = 75% × 75% × 75% × 75%).

10. I will round to two decimal places when calculating all hypothetical probabilities.

The formula would be

$$p = d \times s,$$

or, substituting,

$$.64 = .75 \times .85,$$

where p = probability of correctly judging public opinion on a given issue, d = direction, and s = salience.

This particular probability assumes that the two judgments about salience and direction are independent of each other. This assumption may come under attack, since, as noted in Chapter 2, typical sources of information used by politicians contained both indicators of salience and direction of opinion. It is possible, therefore, that the two estimates were dependent.[11]

Politicians were, however, aware of this problem, leading them to discount the evidence about the "true" direction of opinion that these sources might promote (Bryce 1895; Ginsberg 1986). So, for instance, if a farmers' group organized a protest against the gold standard in the mid-1880s, politicians might have used that behavior as an indicator of the salience of the issue. But it is unlikely that a skilled politician would believe that the public shared the farmers' exact view of what position was optimal, given farmers' vested interest in making credit cheaper. In addition, politicians may have used different sources of information to estimate salience and direction. By reporting the views and attitudes of relevant actors, newspapers may have provided a better sense of the direction of opinion than would a large, noisy crowd. On the other hand, the size and intensity of a crowd may have given politicians a better reading of the salience of an issue than that which could be found on the pages of the newspaper. In any case, the probability of correctly assessing public opinion (.64) provides a starting point for estimating the relative frequency of the various types of leadership.[12]

---

11. I could calculate the joint probability of politicians knowing the "direction" (D) and "salience" (S) of an issue as a *dependent* event. To do so, I would need to estimate either P(D and S) = P(D|S)×P(S) or P(D and S) = P(S|D)×P(D). In each instance I would have to present a reasonable guess for either of the two conditional probabilities {P(D|S) or P(S|D)}. I could make such guesses, but what constitutes a reasonable judgment for these two probabilities is far from clear. By comparison, the assumption that a politician can accurately estimate the salience of an issue 85 percent of the time has more intuitive feel.

12. On the surface, this probability does not seem unreasonable. I asked a number of colleagues about how often politicians in the 1800s might have correctly estimated the direction of

The next step in the process is to determine the relative frequency of "salient" and "nonsalient" issues. To begin, there should be more non-salient than salient issues. Carmines and Stimson (1989) make a convincing case, as does Riker (1982), that the marketplace of issues offers many more that fail to capture the public's attention than those that do. But given the crudeness of the distinction between "salient" and "nonsalient" issues, there should be a reasonable number of the former.[13] Here, I shall assume that one-third of all issues are salient to the public.

At this point, let me list the probabilities, as defined so far:

$$P \text{ (Correctly judging the } Salience \text{ of an Issue)} = .85$$
$$P \text{ (Incorrectly judging the } Salience \text{ of an Issue)} = .15$$

$$P \text{ (Correctly judging the } direction \text{ of opinion)} = .75$$
$$P \text{ (Incorrectly judging the } direction \text{ of opinion)} = .25$$

$$P \text{ (The Issue is Salient)} = .33$$
$$P \text{ (The Issue is Not-Salient)} = .67$$

These probabilities provide the basis for estimating the chances of leadership and followership.

The estimates that appear in table 4.1 provide a sense of the chances for various types of behavior. The entries in the table indicate the probabilities of the various scenarios when an issue confronts a politician. Given the frequency of nonsalient issues, the opportunities for Wilsonian leadership are great. Of all issues that face this hypothetical world, nearly

---

opinion on an issue and its salience. The answers usually fell anywhere from 60 percent to 80 percent of the time for *each* of the two components, yielding a range of 36 percent (.6 × .6) to 64 percent (.8 × .8) accuracy. In general, most colleagues thought I was being generous in my estimates.

13. What exactly constitutes a "salient" issue, of course, is open to interpretation. Strictly speaking, the issue needs to be important to *all* citizens, according to the theory offered here. Such a standard would mean that empirically no issue is ever salient, since there will always be at least a handful of people who probably do not think the issue is very pressing. The key, therefore, is to find some ratio of important to nonimportant issues that roughly corresponds to the *perceptions* of politicians. So one way to think of this ratio is the frequency with which office-holders judged an issue to be important to the electorate.

To compound problems, the salience of an issue is also a function of how it is measured. For instance, open-ended questions in surveys have often been used to tap salience of issues (RePass 1971; Kelley 1983; Geer 1991). But rarely do more than 50 or 60 percent of respondents mention any one issue as salient. On the other hand, if one asks citizens directly about the importance of an issue, issues often appear more salient to the public. Jacobs, Shapiro and Schuman (1993), for instance, report that around 95 percent of the electorate found health care to be a "very important" or "somewhat important" issue. Hence, the choice of one instrument or another might affect the ratio of salient to nonsalient issues.

Table 4.1 *Probabilities of Leadership and Followership For Poorly Informed Politicians*

P(Followership)	=	P(Issue is Salient)	×	P(Correctly judges Opinion)
	=	.3	×	(.75 x .85)
	=	.33	×	.64
	=	.21		
P(Leadership by Mistake)	=	P(Issue is Salient)	×	P(Correctly judges Salience, but not Direction)
	=	.33	×	(.85 x .25)
		.33	×	.21
	=	.07		
P(Wilsonian Leadership by Mistake)	=	P(Issue is Salient)	×	P(Incorrectly judges Salience)
	=	.33	×	.15
	=	.05		
P(Wilsonian Leadership)	=	P(Issue is not Salient)	×	P(Correctly judges Salience)
	=	.67	×	.85
	=	.57		
P(Followership by Mistake)	=	P(Issue is not Salient)	×	P(Incorrectly judges Salience)
	=	.67	×	.15
	=	.10		

These calculations all follow the guidelines established in the text.

60 percent present the option to practice Wilsonian leadership. Followership, on the other hand, constitutes about a fifth of the moves made by poorly informed politicians. Missed opportunities for leadership (i.e., followership by mistake) occurs once in every 10 issues. The categories of leadership by mistake and Wilsonian leadership by mistake constitute 7 and 5 percent, respectively, of the five kinds of behavior. Even though these three types of errors are not large individually, collectively one error of some sort is made in *one* of every *five* issues. Given the large number of issues that confront any political system, such a rate of error is sizable.

One of the core parts of this theory involves the idea of leadership by mistake. Under the above assumptions, for every 14 issues that enter the political arena, leadership by mistake unfolds once. One may question that claim. But regardless of the initial probabilities one wants to assume, the chances of leadership by mistake are actually quite simple to calculate. When a highly salient issue confronted the country 100 years ago, the chance that any politician would engage in "leadership by mistake" was a function of how often politicians could accurately detect the direction of opinion. Thus, unless one thinks that salient issues are exceedingly rare and that politicians were extremely gifted in judging the direction of opinion, the practice should have been a reasonably common one.[14]

Well-Informed Politicians   Estimating the chances of leadership and followership under the assumption of complete information is, by comparison, much easier than when politicians possess incomplete information. The probabilities are as follows (recall formula used in table 4.1):

$$P \text{ (Followership)} = .33 \times 1 \times 1 = .33$$
$$P \text{ (Wilsonian Leadership)} = .67 \times 1 \times 1 = .67$$

In other words, the chances of either followership or Wilsonian leadership are a function of how often salient and nonsalient issues arise. With complete information, politicians know the salience of an issue ($P = 1$) and the direction of opinion on it ($P = 1$), thus eliminating the various types of errors that could be committed prior to polls.

This shift in assumptions about the quality of information has some immediate effects. First, followership is more common among completely informed politicians than among those who are poorly informed—just as some pundits suggest. But at the same time the option to practice *Wilsonian* leadership increases with the shift to the assumption of complete information. As a result, one cannot just claim that any type of leadership is less likely when politicians become better informed: certain types *increase*, certain types *decrease*.

But before considering the implications of these findings for leadership, I shall relax the assumption of complete information, arguing instead that polls provide much better information than in the past. This assumption,

---

14. Let me add a caveat to the discussion above. Even though a politician might have engaged in leadership by mistake, it does not mean that every effort led to a shift in opinion. That is, the electorate may be stubborn, as apparently they were when William Jennings Bryan tried to get the country to follow bimetallism. Thus, it is important to realize that the probabilities noted above just describe the chances for a particular scenario—not the chances that the actions of the politician actually lead to a shift in the distribution of public opinion.

I could, of course, factor this complication into my probabilities. I see, however, little gain in doing so unless one believes that the electorates in one of these eras were more susceptible to leadership than in the other or that politicians were more skilled in leadership in one of the two periods. One could easily muster arguments in support of such changes for *either* side. Hence, I set this matter aside, assuming that the chances of moving opinion had the same probability of success in both eras.

of course, is more accurate and truer to the spirit of my argument. Given that polls are thought of as "scientific," I adopt the .05 cutoff. That is, the chance of estimating correctly either the direction of opinion on an issue or the salience of that issue is 95 percent. Note that since polls are supposedly able to measure accurately the opinions of citizens, politicians should no longer be better able to detect the salience of an issue than they are the direction of opinion on it.

Under these assumptions, politicians judge "public opinion" correctly 90 percent of the time,[15] a 26 percentage-point increase over their poorly informed counterparts. Such a change in and of itself underscores the potential impact polls have had on politicians' judgments.

Using the same formula as above, I have recalculated the specific probabilities underlying the various scenarios (see table 4.2). As one can see, followership and Wilsonian leadership constitute the bulk of the actions of well-informed politicians (94 percent). The three types of errors now arise only once in every seventeen issues—not once in five. "Leadership by mistake" unfolds only once in every 50 issues—a rare event by comparison to the pre-poll era. Given that these estimates are derived under the claim that access to polls enables politicians to have *more* accurate information, not complete information, the comparison with table 4.1 provides a useful indicator of how polls may have changed the way that politicians act. It should be noted, however, that the basic conclusions hold from when I assumed "complete" information; that is, the potential for Wilsonian leadership is on the rise, while for salient issues, leadership by mistake will be less common.

Implications for Leadership

These results have a number of implications for the workings of leadership in the two eras of information. First, the simulation indicates that the prospects of leadership in the cases of highly salient issues does indeed depend on the quality of information available to politicians. Leadership as defined in Chapter 1 disappears when politicians possess complete information about such issues, since they will practice only followership. Even if we introduce some uncertainty, the frequency of leadership by mistake declines from 7 percent to less than 2 percent—a drop of about 70 percent within that category.

---

15. The estimate of 90 percent is arrived at by multiplying 95 percent by 95 percent.

Table 4.2 *Probabilities of Leadership and Followership for Well-Informed Politicians*

P(Followership)	=	P(Issue is Salience)	×	P(Correctly judges Opinion)
	=	.33	×	(.95 x .95)
	=	.33	×	.90
	=	.30		
P(Leadership by Mistake)	=	P(Issue is Salient)	×	P(Correctly judges Salience but not Direction)
	=	.33	×	(.95 × .05)
		.33	×	.05
	=	.02		
P(Wilsonian Leadership by Mistake)	=	P(Issue is Salient)	×	P(Incorrectly judges Salience)
	=	.33	×	.05
	=	.02		
P(Wilsonian Leadership)	=	P(Issue is not Salient)	×	P(Correctly judges Salience)
	=	.67	×	.95
	=	.64		
P(Followership by Mistake	=	P(Issue is not Salient)	×	P(Incorrectly judges Salience)
	=	.67	×	.05
	=	.03		

These calculations all follow the guidelines established in the text.

This decline in "leadership" for highly salient issues, as predicted by this theory, may help explain why many observers complain about the current lack of leadership among our politicians. For many, the ultimate test of leadership is to challenge the public to shift an already existing set of preferences (i.e., Periclean). Yet that kind of leadership is extremely uncommon in the era of polls, since rational politicians are better able to practice effective followership.

Even though the prospects of leadership decline dramatically for highly salient issues, the situation is different for the less pressing concerns facing the polity. Rational, well-informed politicians are better able than their predecessors to identify those issues as possible arenas in which to provide leadership.

This change can be interpreted as good news, since officeholders have more chances to practice leadership. Under the assumption of complete information, there should be no more missed opportunities to provide leadership. Even when we move to the less restrictive assumption of just "better" information, the proportion of missed chances to provide leadership declines from 10 percent to 3 percent. In turn, the prospects for supplying Wilsonian leadership jump. This change can be heralded as promising for the polity, since politicians will be able to rally the public. But that claim may be premature.

There are at least two reasons to be cautious about the claim that polls increase the chances for Wilsonian leadership. The first concerns the potential implications of changes in the concept of public opinion associated with the advent of polls. The second deals with how multiple issues will figure into the calculations of politicians. This latter discussion moves us into considering the agendas of officeholders.

Conceptual Shifts   First, the chances that politicians will practice followership may be even *greater* with polls than suggested by these results. In Chapter 2, I argued that one of the conceptual changes in the notion of public opinion involved a greater frequency of "public opinions." That is, in the era before polls, public opinion was viewed as a rare thing.[16] But with the ability to tap the views of average Americans *and* the tendency of polls to elicit nonattitudes (Converse 1974), there now may be more "public opinions." As a result, politicians in the era of polls may be engaged in followership at an even higher rate than suggested by the simulated probabilities presented in table 4.2. In other words, issues may appear more salient than in the past because of how politicians are measuring opinion.

If so, the increase in the prospects for Wilsonian leadership might evaporate in light of this conceptual change, since the tendency to follow opinion comes at the expense of Wilsonian leadership. Thus, one *could* argue that leadership of all types is in decline during this era of polling. Table 4.3 attempts to give some feel for how the chances of leadership might be affected by this conceptual change. For poorly informed politicians, I lowered the proportion of salient issues from 33 percent to 20 percent. In the second column for well-informed politicians, the share of salient issues increases from 33 percent to 40 percent. These new starting points for proportion of salient issues in the two eras provides the opportunity to examine the potential effects of this conceptual shift.

As indicated above, these different assumptions introduce significant changes to the prospects of leadership and followership in the two eras.

16. Recall that Lowell (1914) viewed public opinion as an infrequent event, since citizens would not only have to be informed on the matter but also exhibit a general consensus on what position to take on it.

Table 4.3 *Probabilities of Leadership and Followership*

	Poorly Informed Politicians Under Old Conception of Public Opinion[*]	Well-Informed Politicians Under New Conception of Public Opinion[**]
Followership	.13	.36
Leadership by Mistake	.04	.02
Wilsonian Leadership by Mistake	.03	.02
Wilsonian Leadership	.68	.57
Followership by Mistake	.12	.03

These probabilities were calculated using the same formulae as presented in Tables 4.1 and 4.2.

[*]The proportion of salient issues is 20 and the proportion of non-salient is 80.

[**]The proportion of salient issues is 40 and the proportion of non-salient is 60.

Followership is now almost three times more common among well-informed than poorly informed politicians. At the same time, the chance of leadership by mistake drops by half in the era of polls and the probability of Wilsonian leadership also declines from 68 percent to 57 percent.[17]

These results should be even more disconcerting for those who see leadership as critical to the proper functioning of a democracy. Where before the prospects for Wilsonian leadership were greater with polls, now even that gain may be lost. Whether in fact politicians perceive more "public opinions" than in the past is still open to dispute. But given the argument earlier, there is some reason to believe that politicians do think that there are now more salient issues than in the past.

Given that politicians are support-maximizers in this theory, office-holders must adopt public positions on all highly salient issues. If they do otherwise, politicians risk giving the opposition a chance to make deep inroads into their political standings. And if in fact politicians do perceive a greater number of salient issues than in the past, we should see an increase in the frequency that officeholders, like the President, adopt posi-

17. One could argue that this shift in the perception/conception of public opinion is a sign that polls create *new* kinds of errors and hence do not increase the quality of information as much as I suggest. But that position hinges on the assumption that the old concept of public opinion was the right one, that is, that public opinion is not very common. But it is quite possible that the public does have more opinions than originally thought and that polls are better able to detect them. There is no way to settle this issue, except to alert the reader to the fact that the conclusion about the prospects of leadership hinges, in part, on one's conception of public opinion.

tions on issues. This hypothesis is well represented by Kernell's (1993) phrase "going public," which he has used to describe presidential behavior since FDR. Tulis (1987) also argues that presidents in the twentieth century have made more direct appeals to the public than those in the nineteenth century. These scholars tie this change to institutional shifts in the presidency. This theory suggests that part of that "institutional shift" might be attributable to the rise of polls.

Wilsonian Leadership, the Strategic Politician, and the Agenda   The second reason to worry about claims that polls provide greater chances for Wilsonian leadership concerns the actual choices that face politicians. For the most part, I have looked at leadership and followership within the context of a single issue. But at any one time, numerous nonsalient issues confront officeholders, allowing them to *choose* which of them to pursue. This obvious point moves us into a discussion of how polls affect the operation of Wilsonian leadership *and* the crafting of political agendas.

It is tempting to argue that well-informed politicians can become very skilled in the art of Wilsonian leadership. Since politicians know the public's feelings on particular issues, they can present a case explaining why an issue is important and why their position is optimal for the nation. These issues, therefore, represent opportunities to raise the conscience of the American public and to move the nation forward. It was such rosy scenarios that surely fueled the initial optimism of many observers that polls would provide politicians with enough information to serve the needs of the public.

While it appears true that well-informed politicians *can* practice effectively the art of Wilsonian leadership, this optimism may be unwarranted. When a nonsalient issue enters the political world, politicians have three options.

1. They can try to rally the public to their preferred position (i.e., Wilsonian leadership).
2. They can anticipate what the public's position will be and adopt it, so as to maximize public support. So rather than pursuing what they think is the best policy, politicians try to play to where public opinion will be down the road.
3. They can ignore the issue. Since the issue is not of great concern to the electorate, the public's support of politicians does not hinge on their action regarding that issue.

What does this theory say about the agendas of well-informed and poorly informed politicians? For starters, all "salient" issues in this theory draw a response from well-informed, rational politicians. To ignore such an issue, as noted briefly above, a politician would risk allowing the opposition to take all the credit for it and thereby greatly undermine the officeholder's political capital.[18] Hence, salient issues are part of the agenda of any rational politician. So in 1994 Bill Clinton gave priority to anti-crime legislation in his State of the Union address (as did nearly all of the fifty governors) This focus was surely not because of the President's inherent interest in the issue; instead, Clinton addressed the matter in response to the public's heightened concern about it.[19]

But the story changes with nonsalient issues; politicians must not only adopt a position but also publicize it and attempt to convince the public to agree. Yet, such behavior is costly for politicians, since it requires an expenditure of time, energy, and credibility to rally the public. Rational politicians, therefore, will be judicious in choosing nonsalient issues to place on their agendas—unless one is willing to assume that politicians have unlimited time and resources. The early phases of the Clinton presidency underscore the need for politicians to pick and choose with care what issues they will promote. The new President, according to even his staunchest supporters, tried to do too much, lessening his effectiveness on all issues. In a candid assessment after his first 100 days in office, the President acknowledged the need to focus and limit his attention on a few central issues (Ifill 1993).

In short, rational politicians will be strategic when choosing what *nonsalient* issues to promote.[20] This claim about strategic behavior, of course, moves us into a discussion of politicians' agendas. For the most part, we

18. Even though politicians may be forced to respond to a highly salient issue, they can still try to down play it by talking up other issues that favor them (Kelley n.d.).

19. In a survey reported in *Time*, the share of Americans mentioning crime as an important problem rose fourfold from February 1993, to January 1994 (Lacayo 1994, 50–53).

20. If a large number of highly salient issues arose at a particular time, strategic calculations might enter into how politicians deal with them. Assume that the electorate can concentrate on just a limited number of very important issues (e.g. two or three) at any one time. Officeholders, under those conditions, would attempt to stress only those highly salient issues where their stated positions are in alignment with the median citizen. By so doing, politicians can maximize support more effectively than by dealing with less favorable issues. But the opposition is likely to point out these other issues, making such strategic moves difficult. For the purposes of this manuscript, I shall avoid these complicated scenarios and assume that all highly salient issues draw the attention of the candidates.

have treated leadership as solely a function of what positions politicians adopt on issues and whether the public moves toward those positions. But the positions that politicians adopt on issues are really the second step in the process; the first step is to decide on which issues to focus. That is, what set of issues (i.e., agenda) do politicians address while in office? Given that there are hundreds of issues facing any country and that leaders can tackle only a subset of them, the question of their agendas matters greatly. This point has drawn much notice from scholars. One need only scan the literature to detect the increasing focus on the agendas politicians pursue (see Riker 1982, 1986, 1993; Robertson 1976; Budge et al. 1987).

How do rational politicians select what issues are best for Wilsonian leadership? Can we expect a change in how this process worked between the pre- and post-poll eras? The answer, unsurprisingly, to the second question is yes, because well-informed politicians are likely to have a better reading than those who are poorly informed of the *potential* direction of opinion for the less pressing concerns of the public. Officeholders would know from polling data what are the tentative preferences of part of the electorate. These views are unsettled and subject to change, but this information would serve as a guide to the final distribution of opinion. Even though current preferences are usually not a good predictor of the final direction of opinion, the information would supply politicians with a handle on the potential difficulty of rallying the entire electorate toward their stated positions.

Consider the two scenarios represented in Figure 4.2. Even though only part of the electorate holds preferences on the issue, it is clear that politicians will have to work harder to rally opinion on Issue 1 than on Issue 2. The reason is twofold. First, those citizens with existing preferences will be part of the final distribution of opinion, affecting the final median position of the whole electorate. So politicians will have to get many more citizens to agree with them for Issue 1 than with Issue 2 to generate a median position near their own view. The second reason is that the opposition will see the gap between C_1 and P_1 and will attempt to offer a competing position that will raise the hurdle even higher for the officeholder.

Rational politicians thus have reason to select as rallying points those issues where their views correspond well with the existing preferences of the "partial" public. I call such action "easy" Wilsonian leadership. If this behavior occurs, then politicians would not be practicing the kind of leadership often envisioned by scholars. That is, a leader attempts to educate

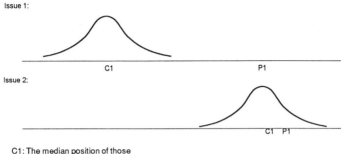

C1: The median position of those
citizens who find the issue salient

P1: Politician's position on issue

FIGURE 4.2 "Easy" v. "Hard" Wilsonian Leadership

the public on the best course of action for "important" issues, as judged *by* the politician. One of the important functions of a leader is to identify future problems and to guide the electorate through those troubled waters. Yet if the proximity between the politicians' and the public's likely position is a guide to what issues officeholders will address, then that aspect of leadership is undermined. No longer do politicians rely on their own assessments of the critical issues facing the country, but they now look for those "easy" issues that will most likely maximize their popularity.

Now, poorly informed politicians would have had the same instincts as their well-informed siblings, but these actors lacked the information to engage in such strategic behavior. That is, politicians would have been less able to identify the "easy" issues to raise. As a result, poorly informed politicians probably accidentally chose more "hard" issues than their current counterparts. (Of course, poorly informed politicians would also try to practice [by mistake] leadership on salient issues—which represents an even "harder" issue.) If so, politicians prior to polls focused on those issues that they thought needed to be addressed as opposed to those that increased their support. This kind of change suggests a possible shift in the balance of "trustees" to "delegates." Prior to polls, politicians used their own skills to make judgments about what issues to pursue, while now public opinion plays a more direct role in the process. Hence, we should now see more delegates and fewer trustees than in previous generations. Or to use far less favorable terms, we shall see more demagogues and fewer leaders.

Thus, even if the prospects for Wilsonian leadership have increased with polls, the *types* of issues around which politicians attempt to rally the public may have changed. This claim undermines the hope that polls could lead to an increase in the chances for Wilsonian leadership.

This hypothesis has a ring of truth to it when we consider concerns that politicians avoid the difficult and thorny issues of government and instead address symbolic issues. Now, of course, it would be silly to argue that politicians of yesterday tackled the hard issues, while today's practitioners avoid such matters. The point instead is that the information from polls may make it easier for politicians to avoid the land mines inherent in tough issues and to spot the easier ones. As a result, this theory predicts a subtle, but important, shift in the behavior of politicians.

The "Ignored" Issues

Are the issues ignored by officeholders of any value to them? Yes. In the simple theory, nonsalient issues that are *off* the agenda have little effect on politicians' popularity, which makes those issues of limited concern to them.[21] But if an issue does not affect a politician's popularity, we can introduce secondary goals for officeholders. Under these modified conditions, such issues can be put to good use by politicians.

For those nonsalient issues where disagreement exists between the potential direction of opinion and the politician's *personal* view, the officeholder could maintain that position, and by *not* publicizing the issue, that position would cost no public support. This issue would not be on the public's agenda and hence would not be part of their assessments of politicians. By so doing, officeholders could satisfy their own policy objectives—and perhaps even enact some small piece of legislation on the matter. Wittman (1983) provides a hint of this kind of behavior, arguing that as the

---

21. A nonsalient issue may still matter to some part of the electorate. If so, then support-maximizing politicians should still pay some attention to them. However, an "ignored" issue is one where both sets of politicians drop the matter from their plates. As a result, this issue falls from sight, decreasing its relevance to the point where rational politicians can ignore it.

Now if either side takes up the issue, the opposing camp will be forced to do so also. In many ways, this particular process can be thought of as an iterated prisoner's dilemma. That game predicts the players will work together on some issues, since keeping them off the agenda since it is in their mutual interests (See Ordeshook 1986).

Chapter 6 explores this possibility further by suggesting that across a large number of nonsalient issues, politicians can adopt extreme positions that in the aggregate will result in little net change in public support for either side.

salience of an issue declines, parties have more flexibility to adopt positions closer to their own preferred points and farther away from that the median voter. As a result, politicians can pursue some personal policy objectives while trying to maximize political support. Thus, in a world of multiple issues, rational politicians can turn to secondary goals. Under this scenario, the oft cited tension between policy and support maximization declines.

Of course, the opposition's role in this matter must be taken into account. Those in control of government would not want to pursue some issue privately that would then provide fuel for the opposition's public attacks. Thus, officeholders must be judicious in such matters. But recall that the opposition too must be careful when raising an issue. They also face limited resources and must be sure to pick favorable issues when challenging the positions of the officeholders. But in a world of many issues and limited resources, politicians should be able to use some nonsalient issues to satisfy their own views on matters of policy.

Issues of little importance to the electorate can also be used to placate special interests or party activists. Up until this point, our theory has not included such actors. But well-informed politicians could make strategic use of such issues to buy support from these players. Aldrich (1983a, 1983b) has made a convincing argument that the views of party activists create a tension in the choices of rational politicians, since the views of activists tend to be more extreme than those of the typical voter. But here the tension is reduced. By selecting some nonsalient issues to garner the support of activists, politicians can avoid that tension. Politicians can adopt a position away from the potential median of the electorate and toward that of the activists. By keeping this issue off the public agenda, politicians can gain political support with little loss in approval from the citizenry.[22]

Figure 4.3 provides a schematic of the potential advantage of not placing an issue on the public agenda. For Issue 1, a politician might not raise the issue publicly, using it instead to draw the support of activists. In the case of Issue 2, the officeholder would have to change positions to draw enthusiastic support from activists. Such a move might be attractive, depending on how the opposition might respond. They might try to publicize that issue, hoping to embarrass the officeholder. But, as noted above, the opposition must be careful about which issues to raise, in part because

22. Another way to think about this point involves Robert Dahl's (1956) discussion of "intense minorities." Activists and special interest groups usually represent such interests. I do not want to dwell on this important and thorny issue except to draw the connection between activists, special interest, and intense minorities.

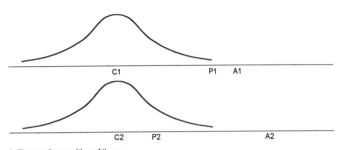

C: The median position of those
   citizens who find the issue salient

P: Politician's position on issue

A: Activist's position on issue

FIGURE 4.3 Activist's, Citizen's, and Politician's Views

of the costs involved and also because they too may be using issues to placate their own activists. If the opposition tries to undo the officeholders' efforts on this front, then the governing politicians could do the same to them. So perhaps some sort of implicit bargain can be struck, keeping some issues off the agenda in an attempt to satisfy the demands of the politicians' respective activists.

Poorly informed politicians would want to use issues to accomplish these goals also. But without accurate information about public opinion, they would be less able to do so. As a result, issues designed to placate party activists might come back to haunt the politicians, because of possible miscalculations about the salience of those issues. Given the uncertainty associated with trying to judge public opinion, poorly informed politicians may take a different tack. Namely, officeholders tend to avoid offering positions on issues, because of the risks associated with such behavior. By comparison, well-informed politicians should be more willing to do so. We should, therefore, see an increase in position-taking by well-informed officeholders. As mentioned earlier, Kernell (1993) and Tulis (1987) present evidence that modern presidents do in fact engage in more position-taking than their counterparts in the past.

Conclusion

This chapter has accomplished two tasks. First, using some simple assumptions, we have developed an account of how polls may have altered the prospects of leadership and followership. These estimates are not designed to provide absolute indicators of the frequency of these various sorts of behavior, but they do supply a useful reading of the *change* in the chances of these scenarios' unfolding within our two eras. This discussion, in turn, moved us into a discussion of how politicians build agendas. As one might expect, the information from surveys may well affect the way politicians go about choosing which issues to promote.

If we hark back to the opening statement by Bryce, we can see that there is merit to his basic position. Rational politicians do increasingly become slaves to public opinion as they secure more accurate readings of it. The claim, however, is not quite as simple as Bryce suggested. First, it is possible that Wilsonian leadership is on the rise during the era of polls. This outcome can be viewed as a good thing. But even here, there are different types of Wilsonian leadership that temper such optimism.

The underlying point is that the self-interest of politicians dictates that they react to changes in public opinion. These interests are common to any political system that places free elections at its center. The drive for support, and ultimately votes, forces responses from officeholders. With information from polls, politicians are simply better able to react; better-informed reactions lead to different behavioral outcomes.

The next chapter extends this general discussion in new ways. Rather than just considering the changes in the actions of politicians, it will examine possible shifts in the skills and talents of politicians. That is, not only have the chances of leadership changed, but also who will actually become the leaders may have changed as well.

Appendix: Additional Estimates for Probabilities of Leadership

The probabilities presented in table 4.4 use higher and lower estimates for the accuracy with which poorly informed politicians judged public opinion. One way to think of these estimates is as a kind of standard error. So while the estimate for the chance of followership presented in the main text stands at 21 percent, the possible (likely?) range falls somewhere between 16 percent and 24 percent. As the table shows, the specific starting points do not dramatically alter the chances that these various scenarios will or will not unfold. These additional estimates add credibility to the argument presented above.

Table 4.4 *Additional Estimates of Leadership and Followership for Poorly-Informed Politicians*

	Original Estimates[*]	"Higher" Estimates[**]	"Lower" Estimates[***]
Followership	.21	.16	.24
Leadership by Mistake	.07	.09	.06
Wilsonian Leadership by Mistake	.05	.09	.03
Wilsonian Leadership	.57	.50	.60
Followership by Mistake	.10	.17	.07

These probabilities were calculated using the same formulae as presented in tables 4.2 and 4.3.

[*]Original estimates appear in table 4.1

[**]The "higher" estimates assume that politicians gauged the salience of an issue correctly 90% of the time and direction of opinion 80% of the time.

[***]The "lower" estimates assume that politicians gauged the salience of an issue correctly 75% of the time and direction of opinion 65% of the time.

THE CHANGING CHARACTERISTICS
OF DEMOCRATIC POLITICIANS

"Never Argue with the Gallup Poll"

Thomas Dewey[1]

PRIOR TO THE INVENTION OF THE
microphone, a useful characteristic for any politician was a booming voice
that could be heard in the back rows of any large gathering. Political
speeches could not be delivered in normal tones: they had to be shouted.
But when it became possible to amplify one's voice, even the soft-spoken
could hold the attention of a crowd.[2] The subsequent development of
radio stirred the pot once more, giving an edge to politicians who, like
Franklin Roosevelt, possessed a compelling voice. Now, of course, rapport
with the TV camera is a valuable asset for any public figure. Ronald
Reagan's success in politics is perhaps the best testimony to the importance
of mastering television. And today, as Ross Perot has demonstrated, the
ability to do well on talk shows like *Larry King Live* may be essential to any
aspiring politician competing for a place on the national stage.

It is, of course, not novel to argue that changes in the environment lead
to changes in who survives and even thrives in that environment. More
than 125 years ago, Charles Darwin presented the theory of natural selection, contending that the survival of any species depended on its ability to

1. Maney (1992, 181).

2. The ability to reach the backrows also meant that parties could sponsor bigger public
meetings, since all attendees could now hear what was being said. Peter Esaiasson (1991, 264), in
a careful study of Swedish campaigns over the last 120 years, has made exactly this point.

adapt successfully to an always changing environment. Practitioners and students of politics have long understood the powerful logic behind Darwin's theory. Much of the debate in the Constitutional Convention over the workings of the presidency, for example, centered on how the proposed selection systems might affect the types of public officials chosen. Some members of the Convention favored the direct election of the executive by the people. The people would be incorruptible, a few founders argued, thereby increasing the chances that honest and well-respected individuals would be chosen. But others feared that such an arrangement would yield public servants who would appeal to the base partisan interests of the electorate. If the country sought qualified officials who would govern above the partisan instincts of the masses, it would be better to let members of Congress make such a decision. In short, Hamilton, Madison, and other founders understood, like Darwin, that different contexts would favor certain kinds of politicians over others.

To use Darwin's terms, politicians can be thought of as a unique species, possessing a variety of traits, characteristics, and skills. It is hard to imagine that politicians like Boss Tweed or Frank Hague[3] would survive very well in today's political environment. They might well have adapted to the requirements of television and declining patronage, but they would not have been Boss Tweed or Frank Hague, or at least not as we know them from history.

A number of political observers have in fact discussed how recent changes in politics have altered the kinds of politicians elected to office. Burdett Loomis (1988) writes of the "new breed" of politician that entered Congress after the 1974 elections. This new breed was more independent than its predecessors, trying to carve out a niche in the policy process upon its arrival in Washington. Alan Ehrenhalt (1991) addressed a similar concern, commenting that the decline of the parties' control over nominations gave rise to politicians who were more willing to pursue their own private ambitions. Morris Fiorina (1994) argued that the professionalization of state legislatures has expanded the pool of available candidates, allowing individuals with less personal wealth a chance to seek those positions.

In short, the workings of the political system, like the structure of an ecological (or economic) system, affects the types of politicians elected to office. One can point to numerous changes in the political world, such as

---

3. Frank Hague was Mayor of Jersey City from 1917 to 1948. He was one of the worst and ablest of the old style political bosses. See MacKean (1940) for an account of Hague's tactics.

radio or television, that have influenced the kinds of public officials that tend to secure elective office. A great deal of attention in fact has been given to how television has altered the fabric of American politics (Jamieson 1988; Entman 1989; Ranney 1983). The purpose of this chapter is to tease out the kinds of changes in the characteristics of officeholders that we can expect within our two theoretical worlds of poorly informed and well-informed politicians.

The changes described below are important in and of themselves. But they become even more consequential once one realizes that the particular characteristics involved are part of the traditional conception of a leader. If so, then fewer politicians than in the past will have the characteristics typically associated with leaders. Now that does not mean that we no longer have any "leaders." That conclusion goes beyond what I will argue. Instead, the criteria we usually apply to identify leaders were forged out of experiences prior to the rise of polls, and we may need to revise them. And by revising them, we will be in better position to determine among our many politicians who are and who are not good leaders in the modern information-rich era.

Politicians v. Leaders

Being a good politician is not necessarily the same thing as being a good leader. It is, for instance, possible for a highly successful politician to be a bad leader. Consider the following people: Richard Daley Sr., Jim Wright, or Richard Nixon. Conventional wisdom treats these individuals as skilled politicians, but we do not usually think of them as great leaders. Because of this general assessment, these individuals are not held in high regard by the public or by most political observers. On the other hand, great (democratic) leaders are usually thought of as great politicians. Consider individuals like George Washington, Abraham Lincoln, Franklin Roosevelt, Winston Churchill, and Charles de Gaulle. These highly regarded figures are typically viewed as extremely talented politicians who were able to lead their democratic nations to new heights.

The point of this brief discussion is that even though there is not a one-to-one correspondence between being a politician and a leader, we tend to evaluate the former by the standards of the latter. We label most elected officials "politicians," while holding aside the term "leader" for a selected handful. Bill Clinton and John Major in fact have often been judged by their skills as leaders, not their skills as politicians. Journalists and pundits frequently attacked Clinton for changing his positions on issues. Yet depending on the circumstance, such moves can be essential for a politician to be successful—even though they run counter to our normal expectations for a leader. In the same way, John Major has been seen by many observers as a poor speaker, which undermined citizens' perception of him as a leader. Although such skills are valuable, it may be more important to Britain that he exercise political clout within the cabinet than speak forcefully in public.

But what if there have been systematic changes in the talents and skills of the average politician that make it less likely that officeholders will meet these standards of a leader? In other words, what if we as a society are applying criteria that are out of date? The widening gap between expectations and reality, in turn, may generate negative attacks from the news media and pundits that could undermine our politicians' ability to govern effectively. Certainly, politicians today are under fire. The typical view is that politicians themselves are to blame for these attacks. Perhaps. But what if we are using unfair standards to judge today's officeholders?

But before we answer such questions, I need first to show what skills are normally associated with leadership and then suggest what changes this theory predicts in the average characteristics of politicians.

The Characteristics of Democratic Leaders

What kinds of characteristics are usually associated with leaders in democracies?[4] When I personally think of the ideal democratic leader, a number of qualities spring to mind. Leaders are tough, forceful, and intelligent— just to name a few. But rather than simply listing various traits that I associated with leaders, I wanted to develop a broader and more systematic sense of the matter. As a starting point, I asked forty undergraduates to write about what skills they thought political leaders *should* possess. Students, of course, are hardly representative of the general public. But their ideas are certainly more likely to capture conventional wisdom about what constitutes a good leader than my own personal ruminations.

For them, good leaders needed to be smart, determined, ethical, committed, unafraid to take tough stands on issues, and able to communicate

---

4. By "characteristics," I mean a number of things, such as traits, skills, and talents. While each of these terms have a slightly different meaning, there is also a good deal of overlap. And because of this commonality, I shall speak of characteristics.

with followers.[5] On the surface these criteria seem reasonable. In fact, respondents to surveys administered by the National Election Studies (NES) mention very similar things when saying what they like and dislike about presidential candidates. The NES asks a series of open-ended questions in their quadrennial national surveys. While these questions do not directly tap issues of leadership, the NES does code those responses that mention related themes. The responses, which include "inspiring," "independent," "good at communicating," and "humble," not only give a few hints about the broader public's thinking, but the results also square with that of the students.

For a very different reading of the traits associated with good leadership, I turned to another source in the NES. In the 1980s, this academic survey organization started to ask specific questions about politicians' traits. The actual questions adopted by this group of political scientists provide some clues about what talents *they* associated with leadership. The NES has included questions about whether politicians are honest, moral, inspirational, intelligent, and compassionate. Again, these items have much in common with the judgments of the students and the general public, providing further confirmation that these traits are useful guides for leaders and leadership.

As a final check, I turned to an essay by Bernard Bass (1981). His edited volume on leadership, *Stogdill's Handbook of Leadership*, summarizes the findings from a vast array of previous research that discuss the traits attributed to good leaders. In this thorough review, he mentions such characteristics as intelligence, knowledge, judgment, insight, originality, adaptability, ambition, self-confidence, and optimism. As before, these topics have much in common with those noted above, further bolstering the claims made above.

While I could refine this list, it is not crucial that there be "the" list. Rather, it is important to understand that the origins of these general perceptions lie in *pre*-poll era. This observation is critical because our basis for judging politicians as leaders today reflect expectations developed in the past and may not, therefore, represent the realities of the current political context.

---

5. Specifically, I ask students "What kinds of skills do you think leaders should have?" On this brief survey, I ask them to respond in an open-ended form. About 20 percent of the responses were highly idiosyncratic. But the remaining responses fell into the categories just noted. I had an advanced undergraduate check my coding decisions. We agreed in nearly every case.

There is, of course, no way to be certain about when exactly these ideas about leaders first surfaced. Surely the ideas of theorists such as Socrates and Machiavelli have been influential. Fortunately, it is not essential that I know the exact time of birth. Instead, I need only to show that these ideas about leadership have a history *prior* to the public opinion poll. To demonstrate that these notions have intellectual roots in the pre-poll era, I examined what scholars before World War II said about the characteristics associated with good leaders. Below is a sample of what a few highly regarded experts had to say.

Max Weber (1918), in his famous essay "Politics as a Vocation," argues that national leaders needed to be able to deliver good speeches, have a passion for the issues of the day, and be detached from political events.[6] Pendleton Herring (1940, 65) took a different tack, believing that leadership required individuals to possess "integrity," and "principles." Robert Michels (1915, 72), on the other hand, viewed good leaders as being smart, possessing "force of will," and "strength of conviction." Like Weber, he also viewed "oratorical skill" as important to leadership (Michels 1915, 69). Merriam (1926, xii) called this general trait "facility in dramatic expression." Bryce (1921, 553) joined the chorus, arguing that "eloquence" was an important trait for leaders. These observations not only represent the various works of that era, but also possess much similarity to those noted earlier, lending credence to my claim that these views have ties to an era prior to polls.

These scholars did, however, add a new (and important) skill to this list. Nearly all argued that good leaders had to be able to judge the state of public opinion accurately. This talent was not mentioned explicitly by Bass, the undergraduates,[7] or the NES. Bryce (1921, 553), for starters, thought that effective leaders had to be able "to comprehend exactly the forces that affect the mind of the people and to discern what they desire and will support." Lowell (1914, 62) develops a similar theme, arguing that "the success of a public man depends very much on his ability to gauge public sentiment." Merriam (1926) in a study of four leaders identifies six attributes of a leader, and three of them involve (in varying degrees) the ability to sense public opinion. For instance, one essential skill of a political leader is an "unusual sensitiveness to the currents of political thought and feelings"

6. I want to thank Stanley Kelley for helping to unpack Weber's argument and boiling it down to these three essential ingredients. For those interested in further analysis of Weber's essay, see Kelley (1995).

7. Actually, students hinted at the need for leaders to know the public's thinking when they wrote that leaders should communicate with voters and listen to their needs.

(Merriam 1926, 7). Wilson (1952, 42) pens a similar theme, commenting that leaders "must read the common thought." Just a few paragraphs later, Wilson (1952, 43) restates this basic theme, noting that "the ear of a leader must ring with the voices of the people."[8]

The reason I suspect that this skill went unmentioned by previous scholars is that commentators tend to think about leadership in general, not the leadership of public opinion. While there is much overlap between the two, the demands of leading a democratic nation are much different from guiding an army into battle or steering a company toward greater profits. This difference did not, however, escape political scientists at the turn of the century. And, of course, it is a skill that fits well with the general subject of this book.

What to do now? When trying to organize this somewhat chaotic list, one will find lots of redundancy between these many items. For instance, Bass notes such things as intelligence, knowledge, and insight—all of which have something in common. Weber spoke of passion while Michels wrote of the force of will. I could try to boil all of these lists into a limited number of dimensions. While a worthy exercise, it is not essential to do so since the rise of polls has not altered the likelihood that politicians will embody all of these characteristics. Instead, the introduction of polls has altered the value of a few of them to practicing politicians, making it less likely that today's officeholder will possess those particular characteristics.

Specifically, three traits often associated with leadership will be under-developed among well-informed politicians—the ability to craft good arguments,[9] the knack of discerning public opinion from bits of odd information, and a willingness to remain committed to one's positions. Each of these characteristics is important to the traditional view of a democratic leader, as described above. Politicians prior to surveys did not possess all of these talents, nor do all of today's officeholders lack them. Nevertheless, these skills, I shall argue, are now less likely to be present in politicians.

The Declining Importance of Good Arguments

"Public sentiment is everything. With public sentiment nothing can fail; without it nothing can succeed."[10] Abraham Lincoln offered this observa-

---

8. These passages from Wilson also appeared in Chapter 1.

9. This particular skill speaks to a number of traits, such as intelligence and ability to communicate with others.

10. Quoted in Jaffa (1959, 309–310).

tion during his first debate with Stephen Douglas in 1858. While the point is a bit overstated, it is sound: public opinion (or sentiment) is indeed a powerful weapon in any politician's arsenal. The problem for Lincoln and Douglas, however, was that public sentiment at the time tended to be, as Bryce argued, "confused," "incoherent," and "amorphous."

So, how did these politicians know whether the electorate was on their side? The short answer is that they did not. They had guesses and perhaps even had faith in their guesses, but there surely was doubt. In addition, there was not likely to be much consensus about the accuracy of those guesses. Politicians of that era, therefore, were uncertain about the state of public opinion, while representatives from the contending camps often disagreed on what it was. The inability to measure public opinion accurately led to disagreements and gave both sides the opportunity to claim that the citizenry supported their cause.

Consider, for example, the debate over the entrance of the United States into the League of Nations. Woodrow Wilson claimed that the electorate supported the treaty. In Ogden, Utah, for example, the President stated that "I am certain, after crossing the continent, that there is no sort of doubt that 80 percent of the people of the United States are for the League of Nations" (Link 1966, V63, 426). Lodge, in contrast, felt that it was newspaper editors, teachers, and other elites who supported the treaty. The public "did not," according to Lodge (1925, 426), "understand the treaty at all." This perceived lack of genuine support for the treaty among "the man in the street," "shopkeepers," and the "farmer" gave Lodge (1925, 146) reason to oppose the treaty, as signed by Wilson. As the debate unfolded, politicians from both camps "repeatedly claimed that public opinion was on 'their side' " (Tulis 1987, 158). While Wilson spoke to large, supportive crowds on the West Coast, opponents of the treaty, such as Senators Johnson and Poindexter, also drew impressive turnout for their speeches (Flemming 1932, 340–1). Without reliable and impartial evidence, neither side during the struggle could rebut the other successfully on this point.

Another indication of how politicians could differ so widely regarding the condition of public opinion can be found in series of articles published in the Philadelphia *Press* during August 1886, about the important issues of the day. These stories report various politicians' estimates of what were the pressing issues. A future President—Benjamin Harrison—thought, for instance, that "gerrymandering" was the question of primary importance. Senator Allison thought that "railroad regulation was the most burning topic." Another senator talked about prohibition. A New York politician turned his sights on financial policy. Other political leaders stressed the debate over tariffs. Patrick Collins stated strongly that "there are no issues."[11] These divergent views highlight not only the many signals that politicians could receive about the state of public opinion, but also how their own political agendas surely affected their "interpretation" of those signals.

By comparison, consider the attention that politicians gave to the issue of crime during 1994. As mentioned in a previous chapter, nearly all the fifty governors addressed this issue in their State of the State Addresses. While California's Pete Wilson and others talked tough about crime, Bill Clinton was working very hard at getting his crime bill through Congress. Politicians of all stripes agreed that crime was an important issue. That widespread agreement was hardly accidental. Poll after poll showed that crime was a central concern to voters and that interest got the attention of support-seeking politicians.

Because prior to polls disagreements erupted frequently over what the electorate wanted, politicians had to be able to marshal the best possible case for their positions to be successful. Lincoln did not have the luxury of a Gallup Poll that might have said that 56 percent of the citizens in the North supported the Emancipation Proclamation. Instead, he had to argue before other, often doubting, politicians about why this controversial policy was essential to the war effort. Without a sound argument by Lincoln, it would have been unclear why the country should move in that particular direction. If Lincoln had tried to evoke the will of the people, a rival politician could just as easily have made the opposite claim.

Successful politicians, operating under such conditions of uncertainty, need therefore to be able to convince other politicians and citizens about the merits of their positions, which places a premium on that skill. With officeholders (and their advisers) frequently disagreeing about what the public wanted, politicians had to turn to other criteria when deciding what policies to support. Perhaps for these reasons, Woodrow Wilson (1952, 59) argued that the "dynamics of leadership lie in persuasion."

The ability to offer a convincing set of reasons for a particular policy is less essential, however, in today's political environment. With public opinion polls, there is more certainty associated with the public's preferences. This reliability extends into a general consensus among politicians that polls do reflect the public mood, curtailing the frequency of disagreements that occurred in the pre-poll era. For example, Beal and Hinckley (1984,

---

11. All this material was reported in Nevins (1933, 288–89).

75) explicitly state that information from polls helps "to resolve staff policy disputes." Instead of interpreting letters or newspapers, polls provide more "objective" information that leaves less room for debate. As a result, politicians, rather than saying "we should adopt this policy for the following reasons . . . ," now can state that "two-thirds of the American public support this action . . . . " With the power of public opinion behind one's cause, as Lincoln indicated, the task of convincing other decisionmakers becomes less difficult. Even in the early years of polls, FDR used them to buttress his case before Congress (Kernell 1993). FDR irked the opposition by doing so, because disagreeing with the President gave the impression that they were ignoring the wishes of the electorate—and such anti-democratic moves put them in a bad light with voters. In the Nixon White House, Katz (1993, 24) reports that "public opinion polls were not just a barometer of popular attitudes, but were used by the administration to persuade others in the government to support the President's program." In particular, Katz (1993) argues that Nixon used the evidence from polls to blunt Congressional attempts to undermine his policies in South Vietnam. More recently, a headline from a *Wall Street Journal* article about Clinton's intention to reform the health care system read: "Poll Shows Stunning Backing for an Overhaul, Giving the President a Big Boost" (Stout 1993, 1). Fishkin (1991, 49) observed that "with the Bush presidency, we have reached the point where a secretary of state, when questioned about the merits of his foreign policy, cites favorable poll results." Former Senator McClure labeled these types "wet-finger politicians"—the members of Congress who "spend more time sampling the political winds than reading policy papers" (Oreskes 1990, 16).

Perhaps Peggy Noonan's (1990, 249) observation is most telling: "Polls are the obsession of every modern White House and every political professional, Republican or Democratic . . . . In every political meeting I have ever been to, if there was a pollster there his own words carried the most weight because he is the only one with hard data, with actual numbers on actual paper." Given that the results from public opinion polls are treated as sound and reliable estimates of the electorate's views, politicians can now, if the poll results permit it, legitimately claim that the public backs them on particular issues or decisions. Politicians who fail to pay close attention to those results risk being attacked as undemocratic.

Our national leaders, in short, have less need than their predecessors for crafting convincing arguments in support of their positions. Tulis (1987, 188) makes a similar point, noting that surveys help "reduce political debate to assertions of policy stands, focusing attention upon what sides citizens take, and how many of them take them, rather than on the complexities of what they stand for."[12] If so, the kinds of politicians elected today may reflect that change since shifts in the surrounding environment lead to adaptations by the species. In the current political environment, survival no longer depends so heavily on developing sound arguments; we can then expect a withering of that skill among our political figures.

A few data exist to support this hypothesis. Tulis's (1987) content analysis of presidential speeches since the nineteenth century lends credence to this interpretation. According to these data, 94 percent of Inaugural Addresses and State of the Union Addresses by presidents prior to polls developed some sort of argument. Tulis, while he examines Lincoln, also includes such forgettable names as James Buchanan, Millard Fillmore, and Rutherford B. Hayes. In similar presidential speeches since and including Truman, only 27 percent of the speeches presented an argument.[13] If one turns to the electoral arena, further confirmation of Tulis's data can be found. John Young (1991) has shown that only about a quarter of Bush's and Dukakis's public statements during the 1988 campaign tried to educate or persuade the public on matters of policy.

Recent American presidents, like Reagan or Johnson, seem not to have the image of being skilled in presenting convincing public arguments. These politicians stand in contrast to our impressions of Lincoln and Wilson, who were thought to be very skilled in the art of persuasion. It is important to be mindful, however, that few historians hold many of the nineteenth-century presidents in high regard. But even so, Tulis's evidence suggests that presidents of that era offered arguments in their major addresses to the nation. Perhaps that is why politicians like Mario Cuomo stood out during his tenure as Governor of New York, because he remained one of the few true practitioners of the rhetorical arts.[14]

12. Jamieson (1988) also talks about the declining eloquence of political leaders, but her analysis does not address the role of polls. Instead, she focuses on changes in such things as liberal arts education—yet another independent variable in what is sure to be a multivariate explanation.

13. These data come from Tulis's (1987, 143) Table 5.5.

The speeches of presidents "prior to polls" include only those who served during the nineteenth century, since these documents were the only ones available (Tulis 1987). The "post polls" speeches include those from the Truman era through the third year of Carter's term. See Tulis (1987) for a more detailed account of these data.

14. Perhaps the best example of Cuomo making a powerful argument in public is an address on abortion that he gave to the students of Notre Dame. He laid out with great care how a Catholic politician could support a woman's right to choose.

Less Commitment to Positions on Issues

Besides changes in the need for politicians to marshal convincing arguments, other shifts in the characteristics of our elected officials may have
taken place. As noted in Chapter 2, politicians prior to the advent of polls
had to rely on such things as attendance at rallies, the content of personal
letters, the views of trusted associates, and their own instincts when gathering information about the electorate's views. Such sources will tend,
however, to point in the same direction as the sentiments of the politician.
Friends are friends, in part, because they share similar perspectives on politics. At the same time, activists who attend political rallies generally will
be supporters, further reinforcing the politicians' views on issues. These
reinforcing effects are compounded by the uncertainties associated with
public opinion, since elected officials may interpret the existing information as consistent with their prior beliefs.[15] Converse and Pierce (1986,
655) make just this point, contending that poorly informed politicians
tend "to fill in estimates of district sentiments with personal convictions."

William Jennings Bryan, for example, had good reason to believe that
the issue of free silver would carry him to the White House. The crowds
at his speeches were large and supportive, letters were pouring in urging
him to pursue the free coinage of silver, and many journalists thought he
would win (Jones 1964; Anderson 1981; Colletta 1968). This belief in the
power of free silver continued even after his loss to McKinley in 1896. As
Bryan (1896, 626) himself argued shortly after the election, "bimetallism
emerges from the contest stronger than it was four months ago." That perception would lead Bryan to carry much the same banner four years later.
Bryan's support of free silver was genuine; but the strength of that support
can also be tied to the kind of information that he received. The letters
Bryan received were largely from the faithful, urging him to continue to
press forward on this issue (Colletta 1968). The crowds attending his political rallies were made up largely of silverites, giving Bryan even further reason to believe that he was striking a responsive chord with this public.

Consequently, Bryan's (and many other politicians') estimates of public
opinion were *dependent* on his own personal views, which, in turn, led to
a reinforcement of those views. By hearing the views of lots of like-minded
people, Bryan became susceptible to a type of groupthink. This dynamic
may have led politicians in the "pre-poll" era to be more committed to the
issues and concerns that they raised. It is not that politicians always started

---

15. One could think of this entire process as an example of "Group Think" (Janis 1983).

as committed supporters of a particular policy. Rather, the process of reinforcement helped to encourage such commitment.

Politicians in the pre-poll era, of course, changed views on issues. I do not want to suggest otherwise. Shifts may have been due to a genuine change of heart or to a detection of movement in public opinion. But my point is only that given the sources of information, the perceptions of public opinion were highly related to the personal judgments of the politicians, reducing the prospects of *perceiving* any changes in the public's views.

The rise of the sample survey severs this connection between the judgments of politicians and their sources of information. A random sample of the electorate provides an *independent* reading of public opinion.[16] Even though politicians trust their own judgments and those of like-minded friends, they want to have reliable, external checks on their assessments, and polls provide that function (Kelley 1956, 53). That check was simply less available prior to polls.

The external, independent reading supplied by polls may, however, conflict with the politician's own views more often than in the past. Consider Ronald Reagan. During much of the 1970s, Reagan supported making Social Security voluntary (Drew 1981). Yet during the 1980s, Reagan always claimed to be a supporter of Social Security. Why? Perhaps because he knew from polling data that to oppose this sacred cow would cost him politically. If Reagan had not had access to such data, he might have paid attention to the views of close advisers and to the large, supportive crowds that surely would have turned out to hear him express his opposition to Social Security. Such experiences might have reinforced Reagan's opposition to this program and might have led him to adopt different tactics as he entered the 1980 campaign.

A way to think about this argument is to view politicians' public statements on policy as a function of three independent variables: their own

16. The ability of polls to provide an independent reading of opinion has additional implications. For example, prior to surveys, national politicians surely had to rely, in part, on the judgment of local party officials for their reading of local opinion (see Smith 1939, 394–5). But polls make those judgments less important. If so, politicians have less of a stake in maintaining strong, local organizations, since their knack for "keeping an ear to the ground" is less valuable. And as we know, local party organizations have greatly weakened over the last fifty years. At the same time, the *national* party organization could be expected to gain in strength, since it could usefully house a survey research center. And again, we have witnessed the national party grow in organizational muscle over the last quarter of a century. (see Herrnson 1988).

I do not, however, want to dwell on this implication. The story about the changing fortunes of party organizations is a complicated one and not directly relevant to the main thrust of this book. But this theory does yield a new hypothesis.

personal views, their assessment of public opinion, and their judgment of what relevant activists want. Prior to polls, these three variables were intertwined, often tapping similar things. I have noted the contamination between one's own views and one's assessment of public opinion. In addition, Ginsberg (1986) has argued quite forcefully that those interested in politics (i.e., activists, newspaper editors, business leaders) were largely responsible for generating "public opinion" before the advent of mass surveys. Thus, on average, these indicators tended to send the same message to politicians. But polls change how the equation works, so to speak. Now judgments about public opinion are much less entangled with personal views and with the views of activists.

As a result, the estimates of opinion are now more likely than in the past to point in different directions from other sources. If so, conflicts and tensions will arise more often now between a politician's personal views and what positions will maximize public support. To maintain popularity, politicians will have to alter more frequently their statements on policy to conform with estimates of public sentiment. But those individuals who stick to their initial preferences and refuse to change will, on average, have a tougher time gaining public support. Their opponents will seize on such "mistakes," arguing that the current officeholders are "out of touch" with the public's wishes and that the opposition speaks for the true interests of the people. Therefore, politicians who are unable to shed commitments to particular issues will be less likely to have a long and successful career in politics than those who are able to bend with the shifting political winds.

Today's politicians, as a result, should be less committed to their publicly stated views. They have learned over the course of their careers to jettison certain positions when doing so serves their political fortunes. Politicians of the pre-poll era were not purer in motive. It is simply that reinforcing (and biased) information made it easier to form commitments to issues. If so, this is simply one further reason to suspect that politicians elected today differ systematically from their counterparts of seventy-five years ago.

The Decline of "Gut" Instincts

For those fans of the *Godfather* trilogy, there is a scene in the second movie that captures the notion of "gut" instincts. Michael Corleone, who had seized control of the family, is in Cuba in the late 1950s negotiating with corrupt government officials from Batista's regime about possible arrangements for casino gambling. On his way to those meetings, his limousine is stopped in the street because of a disruption by rebels. During this disruption, a rebel grabs one of the police officers and detonates a grenade buried in his outfit, killing himself and the officer. Corleone bends forward from his perch in the back of the car, clearly noticing this ultimate act of sacrifice. In subsequent meetings, government officials claim that the rebels are not a serious threat and that in no way will they interfere with the pending deal. The Godfather disagrees, recalling the story of the rebel blowing himself up to take out one police officer. Based on this one brief but revealing episode, Corleone views the rebels as a serious threat because of their commitment to the cause.

Of course, as we know, Corleone's instincts were "correct." The rebels do take over Cuba, and Castro has held power for more than thirty-five years. The point of this brief story is simply that small pieces of information can provide politicians (or mobsters) with a handle on the political tides. Such talent was especially important prior to polls. Often politicians had to judge opinion from the content of a handful of letters from constituents or perhaps from the tone of newspaper editorials. Such indicators, as discussed in Chapter 2, were (and are) far removed from tapping the opinions of a representative cross-section of Americans. As a result, an important skill for successful politicians was the ability to interpret correctly the trends of public opinion. Robert LaFollette once noted that "Theodore Roosevelt is the ablest living interpreter of what I would call the superficial public sentiment of a given time, and he is spontaneous in his reactions to it." This comment was made "caustically," according to Hofstadter (1974, 297), surely because LaFollette, a frequent rival, had often been outflanked by Roosevelt's ability to sense the public's views.

It is difficult to identify these instincts precisely. The reason may be that these talents can be thought of as more of an art than a science. Merriam (1926, 48), for instance, argued that Woodrow Wilson "interpreted public opinion in somewhat the same fashion as a poet or an artist would shape a view or a sentiment." Heckscher (1991, 276) agreed that Wilson relied "on political instinct and an almost mystical identification with the people." He was forced to do so, according to Heckscher, because he lacked "modern polling techniques." Childs (1940, 50), borrowing from some ideas of Bryce, stated that "the task of identifying public opinion is essentially an art; that only those gifted with the 'flair' which 'long practice and a sympathetic touch bestow' can hope to succeed in practice."

However defined, it is reasonable to believe that such talents, or "gut" instincts, are less essential today with the rise of public opinion polls.

Given that politicians live and die at the polling booth, actors who survive on the political stage long enough to become good leaders probably can sense the direction of the blowing wind. A politician's inability to make sound judgments will lead to a shorter career and fewer opportunities to leave a mark on society. But now a politician can read a public opinion poll and absorb the frequency of certain responses to get a feeling for the prevailing winds of public opinion. There is less need to interpret the public mood from an assortment of odd indicators. The data, so to speak, are much more manageable and "scientific" than in the past. There is no longer as much art to the process or as much uncertainty. The art now involves interpreting the impact of differently worded questions on the measurement of public opinion, which in itself has become a "scientific" subfield (Schuman and Presser 1981; Tanur 1992). Interpretation can still be valuable, but, by comparison, the need for such acute political instincts is far less crucial.

Generational Change

The changes in the skills of politicians reported above are likely to be more applicable today than in the early years of polls. As noted in Chapter 3, politicians like Truman were skeptical about the value of polls. Members of Congress at the time shared this skepticism (Allard 1941). Herbst (1993, 91) summarizes this situation in the early days of polls, observing that "policymakers, on the whole, were reluctant to trust this new means of assessing public opinion because they believed they already possessed effective repertoires for measuring public sentiment." Interviewing a sample of former members of Congress about how much they used polls in the 1930s and 1940s, Herbst's data suggested that perhaps just a third made some use of surveys. In contrast, Margaret Conway (1984) finds now near universal use of polls among members of Congress.

The initial lack of reliance on polls make sense. These politicians had been raised in an era prior to surveys and had witnessed some of the problems with the early polling efforts. Thus, there should have been a tendency to distrust the value of polling data. Such distrust makes even more sense among those politicians who won office—they had captured office without the benefit of polls. Why change something that works?

However, given that polls have been around for over fifty years and have become increasingly accurate, the recent generations of politicians should reflect more fully the changes described above. These actors have cut their political teeth with polls as part of the process. There is no longer any mystery to polling, and politicians probably fear that if they do not make use of surveys, the opposition might. In fact, as early as the 1950s, generational differences were emerging. In a study conducted in 1953 by Carl Hawver (1954, 125), a generational gap existed among members of Congress in their use of polls. For Representatives who were under forty years old, 38 percent either intended to use or were using polls. That proportion fell to 16 percent for members of Congress between the ages of forty and forty-nine. In the oldest cohort (fifty and above), only 9 percent indicated any interest in polls. Some thirty years later, politicians of all ages and at all levels of government were making extensive use of polls (Conway 1984; Martin 1984).

How Bad are these Changes?

One might interpret these changes in the skills of politicians as a troubling development for democratic government. There is indeed cause for concern, but not all the shifts pose problems. First, the declining need for politicians to develop their own instincts about public opinion need not be a big deal. Politicians, whether poorly or well-informed, still have the desire to discover the electorate's views. The change is that as opposed to relying on their non-poll indicators and their own judgment, they use a different mechanism. This mechanism is more reliable and accurate than their own personal assessments, which allow politicians to base decisions on better information. That change is potentially a good thing. Some observers may wish that politicians possessed some set of uncanny instincts about the public. It may also be comforting to think that politicians can "connect" to the people in an informal and less institutionalized manner. And while those romantic ideas have appeal, they can also lead to more errors in reading public opinion, which, in turn, encourage the pursuit of questionable policy.

Observers may also express serious concerns about the claim that modern politicians, on average, tend to be less committed to their views on issues. There is a widespread belief that we want officials who are willing to stand up to the public and take a tough stand. So when Bill Clinton changed his mind about his policy for gays in the military, critics attacked him for waffling. It is reasonable to prefer politicians who have certain core beliefs that drive their conduct of government. We may not agree with those views, but at least we respect them.

While this is a noble ideal, it does run counter to some of the demands required of a *democratic* leader. Unlike leaders in business or in the military, elected officials have a responsibility to act in ways consistent with what the public wants. So, when politicians change their views on an issue because of a change in public opinion, such "waffling" can be viewed as evidence of responsiveness to the electorate's wishes. This debate, of course, bears on the long-standing controversy over whether politicians should act as trustees or delegates. I shall save the direct discussion of this matter until the concluding chapter. I simply want to note that if politicians are willing to shift positions on issues in response to changes in the public's desires, such a development can also be interpreted in a favorable light.

The final change in the skills of politicians is, however, troubling, especially within the context of the broader argument I develop. If politicians, by using the results from polls as a kind of crutch, have less skill in crafting sound arguments, then their ability to engage in Wilsonian leadership is in doubt. As one may recall, Wilsonian leadership requires politicians to rally the public toward their stated views on issues. One way to get the electorate "on board" is to explain why a particular policy makes sense. That task often requires a good argument. If politicians present a sound set of reasons for doing something, then the public (and relevant elites) are more likely to agree with it. Of course, the opposing side too will try to make their case against the particular course of action. If they too are skilled in the rhetorical arts, the public is more likely to hear good reasons not to pursue this policy. The end result is a deliberative process that will be shaped by the relative merits of the various positions.

This situation becomes especially important to those who see democracy as a process that uplifts and enriches the lives of citizens. Yet if politicians in the era of polls are less likely to engage in such dialogue and instead offer a series of assertions, the public and country are less well off. So this last change in the average characteristics of politicians is disconcerting and something that will draw further comment in the concluding chapter.

Conclusion

It is easy to misinterpret the arguments developed in this chapter. One might get the impression that the politicians of yesterday tended to be individuals of great principle, keen intellect, and sound judgment, while officeholders today are merely political chameleons who are willing to change their color at a moment's notice. Such impressions miss the point. The logic of this theory suggests that changes in available information alter the typical skills and traits that promote long and successful political careers. The personal goals of politicians have *not* changed. Instead, the increase in information has altered how these goals play on today's political stage, which makes the talents normally associated with "leadership" less valued now, thereby giving birth to a new kind of politician.

There is another way to think about these changes that captures in broad strokes what may be occurring. William Riker (1990) talked about two types of politicians: the heresthetician and rhetorician.[17] The former tries to gain political advantage by changing the dimensions of political conflict. So, for instance, if a politician faces defeat on an issue, the heresthetician will try to inject new issues into the debate to gain political advantage.[18] Thus, as the 1992 election began, Bush raised the issue of family values in an effort to deflect attention from a failing economy and to refocus concern on matters that would work for the President and against Clinton. Rhetoricians, in contrast, seek to persuade other relevant political actors about the merits of their position. So rather than introducing a new dimension, for instance, the politician here tries to convince voters to shift their views on the issue. In spatial terms, the rhetorician tries to bring the median citizen closer to their own position (i.e., leadership); the heresthetician searches for those issues where their views align with the median citizen.

Given the ideas presented earlier, it seems reasonable to argue that politicians in the pre-poll era were more likely than politicians today to be skilled rhetoricians. That is, politicians in the 1800s were more committed to particular issues, because of reinforcement, and had more practice at developing good arguments in support of their positions. Such talents are consistent with Riker's notion of a rhetorician. In today's era, however, politicians should be better at practicing the art of heresthetics. With a better handle on the public's preferences, politicians today should be able to manipulate agendas with greater skill and confidence. Rather than trying to persuade

---

17. The study of rhetoric, of course, has a long and hallowed history, with Aristotle's *On Rhetoric* being the most famous contribution. The notion of a rhetorician used here, however, follows Riker's lead by distinguishing between two types of politicians. Hence, the vast and interesting literature that deals with rhetoric is not directly relevant to this discussion.

18. See Riker (1986, 1990) for some interesting examples of this kind of behavior.

voters to adopt their positions, politicians can better identify an alternative "winning" issue and can try to inject that into the debate. At the same time, politicians have a better idea about which issues are likely to be costly and can thus try to avoid discussion on such topics (recall Chapter 4).

Keep in mind that I am not arguing that all politicians today are herestheticians, while their predecessors were rhetoricians. Obviously, both types of politicians have existed during each era (and many politicians possess both sets of skills). My point instead is that the *relative* frequency of these *types* of politicians may have changed. That is, the political environment today promotes the skills of herestheticians rather than rhetoricians; prior to polls, the need to develop good arguments, for instance, promoted the skills of rhetoricians.

Whether this change undermines the conduct of politics is open to dispute. But regardless of the merit of such a change, it does suggest a need to reconsider the criteria we use when identifying leaders. On average, leadership is associated more with the rhetorician than the heresthetician. In fact, the definition of leadership that I have offered explicitly involves persuasion. At times, this persuasion requires politicians to convince already committed citizens to change their minds, and at other times, to convince people to form new opinions—a much easier task. The normal notion of leadership does not usually concern manipulation of agendas. Of course, such action could constitute "leadership." That is, by pointing the electorate in a new direction, politicians practice leadership. Whether those new avenues are the best ones for the electorate is a question I shall leave for the last chapter.

In the end, some may still question whether we really should adjust our standards of leadership as they apply to democratic politicians. Just because the skills of politicians may have changed, must we adjust our long held notions of a leader? One could simply respond that we should hold our officials to high standards and it is incumbent upon officeholders to meet them. Perhaps. The problem is that these standards do not reflect the tension embedded in the idea of a *democratic* leader very well. As noted above, what some may call "waffling" could also be called responsiveness. And it is important that our standards reflect this underlying tension, and a move toward Riker's heresthetician might help.

Regardless of where one might fall in such a discussion, it is important to realize that modern politicians may systematically fall below our conventional standards of a "leader," leading to additional (unwarranted?) attacks on politicians. Part of political life entails criticism from opponents, journalists, and observers—it goes with the territory. But if the level and frequency of attack increase because the skills of politicians shift while our standards do not, then concerns arise. Perhaps so much criticism will be heaped on our elected officials that government will become less effective and the public's trust in governmental institutions will weaken. Clearly, the gridlock in Washington during the 1980s and early 1990s and the general distrust of elected officials are not just functions of the forces described here. Nonetheless, it is possible that outdated expectations may be part of the story. In final analysis it is simply important that we think about these standards. Such introspection in and of itself is a worthy exercise and may allow for a better understanding of the demands a democratic society places upon its elected officials.

I now want to turn attention to one final set of implications that flow from this theory: the workings of political change. So far I have ignored, for the most part, the behavior of the opposition. But by including them in the story, this theory yields a new account of partisan change, in general, and realignment, in particular.

MORE ECHOES, FEWER CHOICES:
POLITICAL CHANGE AND OPINION POLLS

IN THUMBING THE PAGES OF HISTORY,
one can find issues of such force and importance that they literally redefined politics. These issues not only alter many of the landmarks that help orient the political compasses of citizens and politicians, but they also recast how these actors actually think about politics. Slavery is probably the best example of that kind of issue in American history. For much of the nineteenth century, slavery was critical in defining the political debate. Politicians and their parties rose and fell around the heated struggle that surrounded the so-called "Peculiar Institution." Near the end of that century, with the Civil War now a more distant memory, controversy erupted over the free coinage of silver. While that issue was not as searing as slavery, it still gave rise to one of the most enduring political figures of the time, William Jennings Bryan, and established the Republicans as the dominant party for the next three decades. The Great Depression and the ensuing economic hardship unhinged that arrangement, prompting, among other things, a debate over the proper role of government in our economic lives. This struggle gave Franklin Roosevelt the opportunity to transform the Democrats into the majority party.

If such issues are the engine that both drive and redefine politics, my theory about politicians has important ramifications for how that process works. At the core, the theory contends that information supplied by polls has altered how officeholders respond to issues. The claim also must hold for the opposition. If the joint behavior of well-informed officeholders and office-seekers is different from that of their less well-informed forebearers, we can expect changes in how issues shape and mold the political process. The new responses of well-informed politicians, when considered in conjunction with the public's likely reaction to those actions, require that we rethink our theories of partisan change.

The theory, simply put, predicts that politicians will no longer differ on issues of great importance to the public; instead, politicians will disagree (from time to time) on less pressing issues. Yet a core component of partisan change (e.g., realignments) has been polarization between parties (or politicians) on some highly important issue. Without polarization, *critical* realignments[1] may now be a thing of the past. Instead, the electorate will turn increasingly to other criteria when choosing which politicians to support, such as the contenders' personal characteristics, general performance in office, and politicians' views on less pressing issues. The end result will be a more volatile political system, with no party (or politician) likely to dominate the political system for any length of time.

This theory, as a result, provides a new way to understand the often contradictory interpretations of political change that have been made over the last few decades. Some scholars contend that realignments never did occur, offering a different theoretical perspective to explain both the events of the last few decades and of the previous century (Carmines and Stimson 1989; see also Schafer 1991). Others have argued that change, which has been accumulating since the 1930s, did finally yeild a realignment in the 1980s (Lawrence 1993; Miller 1991; Miller and Shanks 1991). Still others see a dealignment afoot, contending that parties have weakened and will continue to do so (Burnham 1970; Wattenberg 1990). The argument developed here suggests that most of these scholars are right, to a certain degree. There has been no critical realignment over the last thirty years, as Carmines and Stimson claim. But it is not because Sundquist (1983) and others were wrong—realignments did in fact unfold in the past. Rather, well-informed, rational politicians now avoid the mistakes of Stephen Douglas and Herbert Hoover, which prevents sharp breaks in the political system. Without a galvanizing issue to (re)structure politics, many citizens do not develop the kinds of partisan loyalties that admirers of Franklin Roosevelt or William Jennings Bryan

---

1. For the record, a "critical realignment" is a sharp and enduring shift in the electoral balance between the two major parties (see Key 1955).

possessed. The lack of a strong partisan anchor for the electorate is, of course, consistent with the evidence of a dealignment, as reported by Wattenberg and others.

To make these arguments, this chapter will first show how this theory about politicians applies to the study of realignment. With that task completed, I shall deduce what the theory predicts for the joint behavior of politicians competing for the public's support. The accuracy of this prediction, in turn, will be assessed by examining two past realignments and recent potential realignments. Last I shall discuss what this theory says for how political change now occurs under the ascedance of polls.

A Change of Scenery

To consider the implications that arise from the joint behavior of politicians, we need to move the argument away from the explicit context of governing. As it stands now, the officeholder attempts to maximize popularity in an effort to secure action on public policy in the short run, and to gain reelection in the long run. That goal of maximizing public support still drives the actions of officeholders and the opposition. But rather than the electorate approving or disapproving of officeholders, citizens now choose to support one of two rival sets of politicians.[2] By "support," I am not talking just about votes. Instead, competing sets of politicians struggle for dominance within what might be loosely called a "party system."[3] That is, an arrangement where politicians compete for support centered around some fundamental issue or dispute that structures that competition, such as slavery prior to the Civil War.

Given this new context, the choice facing citizens now involves their "standing decision" to support one of two sets of politicians—a concept similar to the oft-discussed idea of partisanship. As Fiorina (1981) pointed out, citizens' choice of parties involves a calculation of competing politicians' views on salient issues—the so-called "running tally."

This shift of contexts is a natural one for the theory developed here. First, politicians, when forging new party systems, are engaging in an important form of leadership—the moving of an electorate toward a new way of thinking. In fact, Sundquist (1983, 144) places "the variable of lead-

---

2. I could refer to parties instead of politicians. Such a move is reasonable and consistent with the thrust of this argument. But because this book focuses on politicians, I have stuck with the term.

3. See Sartori (1976) for a discussion of the differing ways to define a party system.

ership" at the center of his accounts of past realignments. One cannot study the New Deal realignment without developing a deep appreciation of Franklin Roosevelt's talent as a political leader. He drew the battlelines and then proceeded to defend those positions with great acumen.

Second, the study of realignment provides a surprisingly good fit for the spatial approach adopted here. The competition for the enduring commitment of the public, which is so central to realignment, can be captured effectively by a unidimensional continuum. A quick scan of the literature demonstrates the implicit and often explicit references to spatial logic. Burnham (1970, 7), for starters, argued that in a realignment "issue distances between the parties are markedly increased." Sundquist (1983, 14) viewed a realignment as "those redistributions of party support, of whatever scale or pace, that reflect a change in the structure of party conflict and hence the establishment of a new line of partisan cleavage on a different axis within the electorate." Clubb, Flanigan and Zingale (1980, 31), on the other hand, argue that a realignment involves the "formation of a new distribution of partisan loyalties in the electorate." Finally, Carmines and Stimson (1989) contend that highly salient issues help forge partisan change in the electorate. Each of these four descriptions has obvious spatial overtones.[4]

With the connections between realignment and the theory developed, I now turn to what this theory suggests about partisan change. To start this discussion, I raise a conceptual issue that has gone unaddressed in previous discussions of realignment.

Differentiation v. Polarization

That parties or politicians differ on issues is central to the political process. The classic unidimensional model provides a way to illustrate the importance of differentiation. In *An Economic Theory of Democracy*, Downs uncovered a "rationality crisis" for citizens. In the "bare bones" theory, competing politicians (or parties) adopted the median position in the distribution of opinion. That act was rational for vote-seeking politicians, given such assumptions as no uncertainty about public opinion. But in so

---

4. One important difference does emerge, however, between most theories of realignment and the unidimensional assumption. Sundquist (1983) and Schattschneider (1975) view a realignment as a two-dimensional space. A new, important issue cuts across the existing distribution of opinion, generating partisan change. Aldrich (1983a) in fact incorporates just such an idea in his multidimensional spatial model of realignment. Even though these approaches have much appeal, I shall stick with the unidimensional assumption for the reasons noted in Chapter 1.

doing, citizens lacked a choice, since there was no difference on the issue between the two sets of politicians. Hence, a rationality crisis arose for voters. Of course, modifying the basic assumptions eliminates the dilemma: rational politicians can in fact move away from the median position, and thereby offer citizens a choice.

Nonetheless, the simple model highlights the significance of differentiation for citizens' choices. Politicians must disagree on at least one issue for citizens to be able to act rationally in their selection of which set of politicians to support. While some differentiation allows voters to cast *ballots* rationally, it may not be enough for them to develop a standing commitment to a particular set of politicians (or party). Previous work on partisan realignment stresses the importance of *polarization* on issues (Burnham 1970; Sundquist 1983; Carmines and Stimson 1989). Politicians (i.e., parties) must stake out starkly different positions on an important issue to set in motion partisan change. The presumption is that such differences give citizens reason to recast their partisan loyalties. Without polarization on such issues, citizens lack the incentive to alter existing attachments or to form new ones.

But how does one distinguish between polarization and differentiation? At first, the differences seem obvious: polarization involves dramatic or stark differentiation. But that statement does little to address the problem. What constitutes "stark differentiation"? Herein lies the rub. We may be able to agree that some gaps between politicians' views on issues constitute polarization, and others do not. But an inevitable gray area arises. Figure 6.1 attempts to capture this matter by providing three examples of politicians offering different positions on an issue. It is reasonable to label the case of A and A' as differentiation—not polarization. On the other hand, the distance between C and C' surely constitutes polarization. B and B' represents the tough call. Is the space between B and B' wide enough to be called polarized, or is the gap closer to just differentiation? At what point would the gap be wide enough to constitute polarization? Conversely, if the distance between B and B' shrunk, at what point would it become differentiation? The answers are unclear, underscoring the conceptual uncertainty of these terms.

I do not need to settle these issues. Instead, the critical points are, first, that not all differentiation is polarization. There has been a tendency among scholars to assume that if politicians differ on an issue, then that gap constitutes polarization. It may. But such a conclusion may also be hasty. Second, it is polarization that is necessary for critical realignments

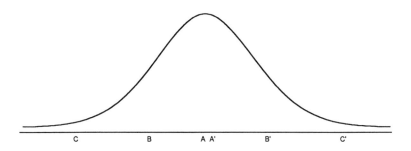

FIGURE 6.1 Polarization v. Differentiation

to unfold. Differentiation is not sufficient to generate sharp breaks in the political system. If one accepts these two claims, we can begin to consider how polls, by altering the joint response of politicians to issues, have affected the way political change unfolds.

Competition, Highly Salient Issues, and Information

The stuff of realignments comprises barn-burning issues like slavery, free silver, and the economic collapse that resulted in the Great Depression. These issues, of course, easily fit the bill of what I have termed "highly salient." Because such issues serve as sparks for political change, I shall limit my initial focus to how politicians behave in regard only to those kinds of issues that helped to shape politics for decades prior to, during, and after their resolution.

When an issue is salient to the electorate, the theory offers some straightforward predictions for the joint behavior of competing politicians. To start, if politicians lack good information about the electorate's views on issues, disagreements can arise among politicians about the best position to adopt. Since politicians are, by definition, uncertain about the distribution of opinion, they must make educated guesses about its true shape. These judgments will often be different, especially since poorly informed politicians rarely relied on the same sources of information when making their calculations (recall Chapter 2). As a result, we can expect poorly informed politicians to disagree from time to time on what positions to adopt on highly salient issues. Figure 6.2 illustrates this scenario. These disagreements mean that politicians will periodically polarize on these issues (i.e., C and C' in Figure 6.1).

The situation changes, however, when politicians possess complete information. Both camps, under this new assumption, can adopt the "true" median position in the distribution of opinion for that highly salient issue. The two sides will attempt to stake a claim to the so-called center. As a result, in a world filled with well-informed politicians, we should see very little disagreement on issues of great importance to the public. Recall that in our theory, the opposition has an incentive to differentiate itself slightly from the officeholder. So to use the examples presented in Figure 6.1, the A and A' scenario would be a good representation of the predicted outcome.

The prediction of A and A' holds even *without* the assumption that polls provide complete information. Randall Calvert (1985) has demonstrated (theoretically) that parties (or politicians) will adopt the median position under conditions of both certainty and uncertainty. But the key to Calvert's claim is that both sets of politicians have the *same* view of public opinion, even if it is the same flawed view. Thus, when politicians have similar assessments of public opinion, polarization on highly salient issues should not occur. Polls, if conducted correctly, should paint much the same picture of the electorate's views for competing politicians. Of course, different questions and question-wording can produce different findings,

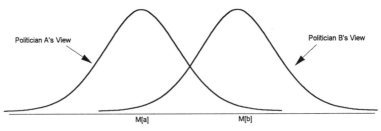

M[a]: Politician A's perception of Median Voter

M[b]: Politician B's perception of Median Voter

FIGURE 6.2 Polarization on Issues

but the numerous polls, both public and private, should provide a check on politicians forming widely divergent impressions of public opinion. Consequently, for this argument about declining polarization to hold, one does not even have to make the strong assumption that polls provide complete information.

The key to my argument, then, is that prior to polls politicians often developed alternative views of the median position of public opinion. But by sampling the public randomly, different perceptions should disappear. It is this crucial shift that predicts an end to polarization on *highly salient issues*.

Some may question this theoretical result. For instance, could polarized positions be a rational response for politicians when the shape of public opinion is bipolar? If the views of the electorate are not normally distributed, but rather take on a polarized distribution, the result might lead politicians to stake out vastly different positions on that issue (see figure 6.3). Thus, politicians can take polarized positions, because of a sharp split in the electorate (Downs 1957, 118–19). Such a strategy is not rational, however, for politicians within the assumptions of my theory. Both sets of politicians would still be better off competing at the center, because that would maximize their support. Even though nearly all citizens would be dissatisfied with those positions, the rational voter would still choose between the lesser of two evils. More important, if one politician (A) adopts a position in the center of one of the poles, a rational competitor (B) should move toward that position and become the majority party (see figure 6.4).[5] Thus, given the desire to maximize support, rational politicians should try to take similar positions on highly salient issues—regardless of the shape of public opinion.[6]

If one moves beyond the traditional Downsian assumption that politicians act as a team, an additional source of polarization may arise. Polarization, for example, might come from the nominating system.

5. Barry (1970, 114) makes a similar point, arguing that a party that moves to the left to attract some extremist voters risks losing the election. If a party adopted that strategy, its opponent should match that position and thus secure a clear majority of the votes.

6. One might argue that if politicians take the center in a bipolar distribution, they could alienate enough voters to encourage the entrance of third parties into the fray. With competition from the outside, the parties might be forced to take opposing positions in an effort to quell the attacks from insurgent groups. But in the U.S., at least, third parties have a difficult time competing because of the election laws, which makes this possibility less likely (Rosenstone, Behr, and Lazarus 1984). Nonetheless, for the purposes of this argument, I shall assume a closed two-party system.

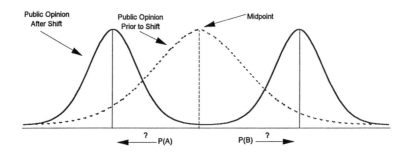

FIGURE 6.3 Downsian Strategies of Competing Politicians in a Bipolar
Distribution of Public Opinion

Polsby (1983) contends that the current arrangement encourages splits
within the parties. With factionalism, one extreme group could capture
the party and polarize the political debate. If one assumes, however (as I
do), that factions seek to gain public support, these groups should still
adopt positions that maximize their chance for victory in the general election. And these positions, given the availability of polls, should not be
polarizing. So regardless of the nominating system, polarization can
emerge only if one moves beyond the classic assumption that politicians
seek to maximize public support in the short run.

For those who remain unconvinced that polls have altered how politicians react to highly salient issues, there is one final consideration. With
surveys, mistakes can be corrected much more quickly than in the past.
The GOP, for example, distanced itself from Goldwater immediately after
the debacle of 1964. The data from polls (in conjunction with the election
results) showed that there was no silent conservative majority hiding
somewhere in middle America. Similarly, the Republicans, following
Clinton's victory, spent time identifying Bush's errors, especially as candidates began to draw battlelines for the 1996 nomination. In contrast, the
Democrats stuck with Bryan after 1896, nominating him in 1900 and 1908.
Nor did the Republicans react very swiftly to changes in the early 1930s
(Weed 1994), leaving a legacy that even the "me-too" campaigns of the
1940s could not overcome. This ability to correct mistakes more quickly

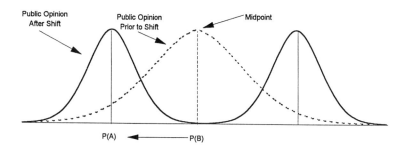

FIGURE 6.4 The Rational Response of a Competing Politician in a Bipolar Distribution of Public Opinion

than in the past is an important impediment to the realignment process. David Butler and Donald Stokes (1976) argued that partisan differences must persist for a while if real partisan change is to unfold. Hence, politicians, armed with polls, will avoid offering the electorate *enduring* polarized positions on highly salient issues, even if mistakes are made. Voters who pay only sporadic attention to politics needs those sharp differences to persist for a while, or they may well miss the boat.

The basic point—that as politicians become more informed, the differences on highly salient issues shrink—draws both theoretical and empirical support from recent work by Morton (1993) and Kollman, Miller and Page (1992). Morton has run a series of experiments, varying the amount of information that politicians possess. When these decisionmakers have incomplete information, their platforms diverge. But "as candidates acquire information on voters' preferences, convergence of platforms increases significantly" (Morton 1993, 389). Kollman and associates (1992), using simulations, also found that convergence of candidates increases as information about the views of voters increases—even if the parties (or candidates) are ideological.

Ginsberg (1976) provides further evidence that supports my hypothesis that polarization has declined since the advent of polls. According to Ginsberg's content analysis of the Democratic and Republican platforms, from 1940 to 1968 there was a .017 average difference between the parties' views on issues.[7] So parties have differed on some issues since the introduction of polls. But between 1844 and 1936, which constitutes the pre-poll era, the average difference between the parties' platforms was .073, which is more than *four* times greater than that between 1940 and 1968. In addition, the frequency of "polarized" elections has dropped dramatically since the advent of polling. Of the eight elections from 1940 to 1968, the Goldwater-Johnson contest exhibited the greatest difference between the parties' platforms: .041. No other election during this period approached that difference. But from 1844 to 1936, more than 50 percent of the elections showed a *greater* difference between the parties' platforms than that witnessed in the 1964 campaign. In fact, for those "polarized" contests from 1844 to 1936, the average difference was .175, which is more than a fourfold jump over the differences found in 1964. Thus, while the Johnson-Goldwater election is often seen as unusual in the "choice" that it offered the electorate, Ginsberg's data suggest that such differences were common before the introduction of polls.[8]

The End of Critical Realignments?

The claim made above has sizable implications for the study of partisan realignments. Most scholars agree that a crucial ingredient in any realignment is that the parties must stake out clearly different positions on issues of high salience to the public (see, for instance, Burnham 1970; Sundquist 1983; Carmines and Stimson 1981, 1984, 1989). Without polarized parties, citizens will lack the incentive to alter existing partisan attachments or to form new ones. Now, however, knowing the public's views on highly salient issues, rational parties should *not* adopt vastly different positions on those matters. Consequently, the public opinion poll may have fundamentally

---

7. I chose 1940 as the cut-off point since Gallup began its polling of the national electorate in 1937 and FDR started to use information from polls more heavily as war started to break out in Europe. Even if one adopts later elections as starting points, it does not alter the basic finding.

One might also quarrel with the use of platforms to study the positions politicians take on issues, since they are documents more closely tied to the parties than to individual officeseekers. Although true, I do not make a big distinction between politicians and parties, since I treat both as unitary actors. In addition, the nominee (or politician) usually has a very big role in the platform anyway, blurring the utility of this distinction (Maisel 1994).

8. Ginsberg's data do not include the last six presidential elections. It is unlikely, however, that these contests would change the basic finding. Even if one assumes that every election from 1972 to 1992 had differences between the parties similar to those Ginsberg reported in 1964, which is highly unlikely given the Ford-Carter, Dukakis-Bush, and Clinton-Bush races, parties still differed about *three* times more on issues before polls.

altered the process of partisan change, casting a monkey wrench into our theories of realignment. No longer should we expect sharp, durable changes normally associated with periods of "critical" realignments.

The question now becomes, of course, whether polls have altered the behavior of politicians so as to make polarization on highly salient issues irrational and hence very rare. Answering this question is not easy, since there is no way to be sure whether politicians would act differently with or without access to polls. Nonetheless, I shall marshal some evidence to support this claim. First, by examining two past realignments, I can show whether party leaders did in fact try to read public opinion and whether their decisions about which policies to pursue were based on those assessments. So, did Williams Jennings Bryan believe that the issue of free silver would carry him and the Democratic party to the White House in 1896? Or did his ideological commitment to bimetallism lead to his call to arms?

It is, of course, politicians' concern about policy, as opposed to their interest in votes, that poses a serious rival explanation for why polarization on a salient issue might arise.

My second source of evidence involves evaluating the current political situation to determine whether potential critical realignments may have been diffused by politicians offering similar views on divisive issues.

The Realignment of the 1890s   Most historians and political scientists agree that the 1890s was a period of partisan realignment (Clubb, Flanigan and Zingale 1980; Kleppner 1970). Obviously many ingredients were necessary for this partisan transformation to occur, but among them was the polarization of the Democrats and Republicans on the issue of free silver (Sundquist 1983). In 1896, the Republicans, led by Mark Hanna and William McKinley, opposed the coinage of silver at a 16-to-1 ratio, advocating instead the gold standard and "sound money" (Glad 1964). The Democrats adopted a very clear and opposing stance. As the 1896 platform states, "we demand the free and unlimited coinage of both silver and gold" (Johnson and Porter 1973, p. 98). In staking out this position, the Democrats deserted the conservative faction led by President Cleveland and instead nominated Williams Jennings Bryan.

The young politician from Nebraska strongly supported his party's plank endorsing free silver. The Cross of Gold speech at the convention perhaps best represents his position, but Bryan also traveled across the country (both before and after the convention) campaigning on the issue of free silver. One might interpret Bryan's fervent support of bimetallism as the motivating force behind his crusade. Perhaps. But, according to Hofstader (1973, 245), Bryan in 1892 claimed not to know anything about free silver and supported it only because the "people of Nebraska are for free silver." Such a statement suggests his commitment to free silver was at least partly tied to judgments about public opinion. But even more important, the debate over whether Bryan was motivated by policy or by a desire for public support is moot. Whether he was driven by his devotion to bimetallism or not, Bryan had good reason to believe that his position on free silver would in fact lead him to victory—given the measures of public opinion available at the time.

As noted in Chapter 5, many of Bryan's campaign speeches drew enormous crowds (Jones 1964; Hollingsworth 1963). Anderson (1981) reports that Bryan "spoke to crowds of 50,000 in Columbus, 10,000 in Springfield, and 40,000 in Toledo, all in McKinley's own Ohio." Anderson (1981) then notes that "so large were his crowds elsewhere that predictions of his victory were commonplace." Bryan also received an unusually large number of favorable letters from voters—further evidence of the public's support of free silver (Colletta 1968). These kinds of measures gave Bryan reason to believe he was hitting a responsive chord with the public. Many observers at the time thought the issue had broad appeal. As one historian writes, "the emergence of the silver issue in the West and South [was] the dominant issue in the minds of what *appeared* to be a majority of people in those sections" (Jones 1964, 179, my emphasis). Sundquist (1983, 152), too, reports that many Democratic politicians thought that the money issue would give them "a clear and reliable national majority, for 'the people' had the strength of numbers against 'the interest.' " The problem is that these judgments were based on unsystematic data, thus giving Bryan a plausible but mistaken belief that the issue of free silver would provide him a majority of the electorate's support on election day.

There were additional reasons to believe that the issue of silver would maximize public support. President Cleveland, a Democrat, had presided over a major recession in 1893, and unless the Democrats distanced themselves from him, defeat appeared certain (Jones 1964; Glad 1964). In a nonpartisan book published just before the start of the 1896 general election, the "unbiased" view was "that a fight on free silver was the best issue" for the Democrats.[9] Given the economic problems facing Cleveland's administration, changing the focus of the campaign was important if the

9. See *The Parties and the Men* (1896, 340), copyright by Robert O. Law. This book had no official author. Instead, it promoted itself as an unbiased look at the 1896 election, providing accounts of the Populist, Republican, and Democratic conventions of that year. As best as I can tell, it was designed to serve as a guide to the campaign.

Democrats were to have any reasonable chance of winning. Riker (1982, 1986) has shown that politicians in the minority have an incentive to inject new issues (or dimensions) into any political debate.

Bryan also thought that the issue of free silver would allow him to conduct a campaign pitting the common man against the wealthy; such rhetoric might garner even more support. The Democratic nominee, as a result, carried his message directly to the electorate, believing that if he could talk directly to citizens, he could secure even more votes than if he conducted the typical front-porch campaign (Hollingsworth 1963, 84). In short, one can easily interpret the behavior of Bryan and his followers as support-maximizers, given the situation facing them and the available information on public opinion.

While Bryan had good reason to believe that he had found a winning issue, uncertainty existed about how the public would react to this stance on coinage of silver. Jones (1964) expresses this uncertainty facing the party: "The decisive factor in the election of 1896 would be the action taken by the industrial worker. Neither of the Democratic factions (conservative and free-silver) was in a position to understand or accurately to predict how this group of voters would act. To a very large extent, they based both their nightmares and their rosy dreams in mistaken predictions of what he would do (pp. 242–43)." If polls had been available, much of the guesswork surrounding these two factions would have been avoided.

Interestingly, even after the defeat in the 1896 election, Bryan remained convinced that the free-silver issue would help him win in 1900. McKinley won a number of narrow pluralities in some crucial states, which gave Bryan reason to believe that the public would still support the coinage of silver at the 16-to-1 ratio (Jones 1964; Anderson 1981). There was also great speculation that industrialists had threatened workers with pink slips if they supported the populist from Nebraska. Bryan (1896, 625) himself spoke just after the election about "the coercion practiced by corporate employers." Such threats may have undercut Bryan's support. Finally, McKinley greatly outspent Bryan in the campaign. This additional money may have helped McKinley, especially in those tightly contested states (Glad 1964). Thus, the election results need not be interpreted as a repudiation of free silver, making it reasonable for the Democrats to call once again for free silver in the election of 1900.

The Realignment of the 1930s   The realignment of the 1930s also can be seen, in part, as a product of opposing politicians making different assessments of public opinion. In 1932 few politicians seemed to think that there was any fundamental shift in public opinion. The concern, instead, was with solving the Great Depression; both Democrats and Republicans offered vague proposals to meet this economic calamity. Warren (1967, 258), for instance, argues that "even after the platforms were announced, the only clear division appeared on the Prohibition issue and even that difference practically disappeared before November." FDR and Hoover made little mention of having the government manage the economy. In fact, much discussion centered on federal spending, with Roosevelt frequently attacking Hoover for a "huge deficit" that "has brought us to the verge of bankruptcy." The Democrats, FDR pledged, would initiate a "25 percent reduction in expenses" as a way to stop the "Republican extravagance."[10]

Given the rhetoric of the 1932 campaign, the GOP had little reason to believe that their positions on government intervention in the economy would soon be out of line with most voters. The Democrats were not offering radical proposals in 1932; rather, they simply were trying to take advantage of the problems that faced the incumbent Republican administration. The GOP defeat in 1932 was attributable, therefore, to a very sour economy. There had been economic downturns in the past, and the GOP had remained the majority party. Why would this time be any different?

While in 1932 the Democrats and Republicans were offering similar views, the situation had changed by the next election. In 1936, polarization between the two camps surfaced over what role the federal government should play in the economic lives of the public. The Republicans continued to support having state and local governments provide economic relief to the less fortunate. In 1932, for instance, the Republican platform viewed "the relief problem as one of State and Local responsibility" (Johnson and Porter 1973, 341). In 1936 the GOP remained consistent, criticizing the New Deal as usurping "the rights reserved to the states and to the people" and calling for the return of relief programs to local authorities (Johnson and Porter 1973, 365–66). This same document also attacked the New Deal's effort to create government jobs as a temporary and costly solution to unemployment. All in all, Republicans in 1936 remained committed to relying "on the character and virtue, self reliance, industry and thrift of the people," *not* "on the wisdom and power of the government" (Johnson and Porter 1973, 370).

---

10. These quotations come from a campaign flyer distributed during FDR's 1932 presidential campaign. This flyer is available upon request.

Roosevelt and the Democrats, by comparison, showed marked changes in their positions by 1936. While the 1932 Democratic platform was vague on its solutions to the Depression, the 1936 document reflected a commitment to an activist federal government. The 1936 platform contended that the federal government should protect "the family and home," establish "opportunity for all the people," and aid "those overtaken by disaster" (Johnson and Porter 1973, 360). The Democrats had clearly adjusted their position after the 1932 election. Since the Republican politicians remained committed to minimizing the federal government's role, polarization emerged.

Even though strong disagreements arose, it was still unclear how much support the Democrats could expect to receive because of this change in their position. The public appeared to be giving mixed signals about whether they supported the government's new role in the economy. In 1934, the Democrats scored major victories in the midterm elections, suggesting that their programs were popular with voters. Yet by 1935, there was reason to believe that an anti-New Deal sentiment was growing in the country. First, the Republicans captured the New York State Assembly, which many political observers interpreted as a defeat for the New Deal. As FDR's campaign manager, James Farley, recounted: "The Democrats fared rather badly in a few of the state elections that year, and naturally those minor victories were hailed by the opposition as a trustworthy sign of shifting political winds" (Farley 1938, 291).[11] The second hopeful sign for the Republicans was the emergence of the so-called Liberty League (Farley 1938, 291). This organization of wealthy business people was dedicated to defeating Roosevelt in the 1936 election (see Freidel 1990, 203). There was also growing concern, in some quarters, that the New Deal was wasting too much money. Perhaps the public's support for an activist federal government was limited. Walter Lippmann, who had been an ardent supporter of the New Deal in 1933, became a harsh critic by 1935 (Weed 1994, 84). Even the hard-core New Deal Democrats were unsure how popular their programs were, as shown by their continued support of a balanced budget (Freidel 1990).

Few political analysts thought that the Democrats would have an easy time in the 1936 election. Clyde Weed (1994, 78), in the most thorough study to date of the Republican's response to the New Deal, reported that

---

11. Weed (1994, 92) reports that the chairman of the Republican Senatorial Campaign Committee, immediately after the off-year vote claimed: "The voice of the people in yesterday's election was a powerful rebuke to the New Deal."

a former member of Congress in 1935 thought that the "Democratic party may split up" over the New Deal. A few months later a well-known journalist, Gerald Swope, wrote that "FDR is slipping fast." According to Weed (1994), these kinds of perceptions were widespread. Roosevelt himself felt the 1936 election would be close, contending that "we are facing a very formidable opposition on the part of a very powerful group among the extremely wealthy and centralized industries" (Schlesinger 1960, 572).[12]

These few pieces of evidence show that the available estimates of public opinion did not point in a clear direction. This ambiguity made it difficult for the Republicans to decide which course to take. As Schlesinger (1960, 524) observed, "The Republican Party had been in inner turmoil since its staggering losses in the midterm elections of 1934. This disaster had re-opened the perennial family dispute whether the party should stand by its ancient principles or whether it should liberalize itself to keep up with changing times." If better information had been available, it might have been easier to resolve this "family" dispute.

But without clear evidence of what would be the best course of action, the Republicans took a middle road, nominating the moderate Kansas Governor, Alf Landon, for president. The two extremes of the party, Hoover on the right and Idaho Senator William E. Borah on the left, received little support at the convention. Landon represented a compromise position, since he sought to attack the New Deal for its excesses, not for its repeal or extension. Landon commented that "as I see it our basic issue should be the waste and extravagant expenditures of this administration." Landon, however, was willing to "fight along whatever line (that) seems to have the best hope of winning" (Landon quoted in Schlesinger 1960, 537).

The problem, of course, was that he was unsure of which issues to stress. As the campaign began, evidence suggested that attacks on the New Deal might attract enough votes to win the election. A statistician for the Du Pont Company supplied the figures showing the public's growing distaste for the New Deal. The results from a *Literary Digest* poll (not the famous one) confirmed this claim, showing that "majority of the people were opposed to the New Deal" (McCoy 1966, 264). Third, most newspapers opposed Roosevelt's re-election, indicating to many observers that support

---

12. FDR also feared that Huey Long might take away enough votes in 1936 to allow the Republican to win in a three-way contest (Barone 1988). This concern, which ended when Long was murdered in Baton Rouge, may have further fueled the Democrats' uncertainty about the upcoming 1936 election.

for the New Deal might indeed be soft (Freidel 1990, 203). Finally, Landon, like Bryan forty years earlier, was welcomed by large and receptive crowds following his nomination, suggesting that the public might be receptive to attacks on the New Deal (McCoy 1966, 282–3).

This kind of evidence may have given Landon reason to believe that anti-New Deal rhetoric would garner public support. Landon's attacks on the New Deal, which grew stronger as the campaign progressed, served to polarize the two nominees (and their parties) even further. In September, for instance, Landon stated that the Roosevelt administration believed that "the government must play a greater and greater part in managing the details of our daily lives . . . The Republican party, on the other hand, utterly rejects this philosophy" (Landon quoted in McCoy 1966, 302). By October, Landon began to attack Roosevelt as a threat to the "American form of government." Near the close of the campaign, Landon made his view quite clear, stating: "I am willing to trust the people. I am willing to stand up and say openly that I am against economic planning by the government. I am against the principles of the Agricultural Adjustment Act" (McCoy 1966, 335).

Even in the middle of the campaign Landon's anti-New Deal position was reasonable, given what he and the GOP knew of public opinion. Many observers, for instance, still thought Landon was capable of defeating Roosevelt (Schlesinger 1960; Weed 1994). The state of Maine, which conducted its presidential balloting in September, had gone for Landon by a larger margin than it had for Hoover in 1932. Perhaps the most famous estimate of public opinion was the *Literary Digest*'s poll, showing Landon the winner over Roosevelt. Such evidence fueled the hopes of the GOP (Schlesinger 1960; McCoy 1966). Even the Gallup organization conducted a state-by-state analysis in 1936 that suggested a possible Republican majority in the Electoral College (Weed 1994, 105). Perhaps it was not until election night, when FDR carried every state but Maine and Vermont, that the Republicans became convinced that the public had shifted their views and left them in the minority. Of course, even then they did not have access to detailed surveys of public opinion, but most Republican leaders felt a change in position was necessary. Beginning in 1940, the Republicans began to run the "me-too" campaigns, which supported the basic ideas of the New Deal. But by then the Republicans had been established as the minority party.

It seems clear that both the Democrats in the 1890s and the Republicans in the 1930s had reason to believe that their positions on what turned out to be the "realigning" issues were not out of step with the public's views. In both cases, the parties did appear to rely on estimates of public opinion when making strategic decisions. The problem is that informal sources of public opinion are often misleading. In short, polarization can be attributed, at least in part, to the availability of flawed data, leading rational politicians to stake out different positions on the realigning issue.

"Thwarted" Realignments?   Has the advent of polls led rational politicians to adopt similar positions on salient issues, thereby thwarting potential realignments? I cannot answer that question definitively, but I can build an empirical footing for my claim. First, has there been a critical realignment since the introduction of polls? If the answer is no, then we have established at least a necessary condition for this thesis. Second, how have politicians responded to highly salient issues over the last thirty years? Have the contending forces in fact adopted similar positions, or have they polarized? How do these reactions compare with those of politicians 100 years ago?

To begin, there is little evidence to suggest that a *critical* realignment has taken place since the New Deal.[13] Classical realignment theory predicted that a realignment should have occurred between the late 1960s and early 1970s. That prediction has gone awry. In fact, despite being long in the tooth, parts of the New Deal Party System are still in force (Sundquist 1983; Carmines and Stimson 1984, Carmines, Renton and Stimson 1984; Kelley 1988). The electorate, for example, continues to evaluate the parties and candidates along what Kelley (1988) has termed "New Deal" issues (see also Geer 1992a and Krasno 1995). In addition, the parties continue to debate about the proper role of government in our economic lives. But, at the same time, clear change has unfolded. Most prominently, there have been shifts in the coalitional makeup of the parties (see Petrocik 1981; Stanley, Bianco, and Niemi 1986). But few interpret those changes as evidence of a *critical* realignment.[14]

At the time of this writing, political scientists are still trying to digest the meaning of the 1994 midterm elections. Some observers have inter-

13. Some observers have argued that the change over the last sixty years has yielded what Key (1959) once called a secular realignment (see, for instance, Lawrence 1991). Namely, that piecemeal change has led to the end of the New Deal party system.

14. Actually, Sundquist (1983) contends that coalitional shifts should unfold during the course of a party system. Over time groups will align themselves with the party that best represents their interests. But that alignment can often be delayed at the start of the party system because of the durability of old loyalties and simple inertia. Hence, some changes in the coalitions may be a delayed effect of the original realignment that occurred years earlier.

preted the Republican gains in both the House of Representatives and the Senate as a clear sign of realignment. It is far too early, however, to make any final pronouncements, especially since the off-year elections of 1995 were favorable to the Democrats. The most systematic analysis to date of the 1994 elections comes from Alan Abramowitz (1995). He contends that the changes in Congress reflect a genuine shift, but one that more suggests a competitive balance between the parties than an enduring GOP majority. That interpretation squares with data from the Gallup Poll gathered in 1995 that shows both parties have comparable favorability ratings among the national electorate.

Regardless of one's interpretation of the 1994 elections, the key remaining question is whether well-informed politicians have avoided taking polarized positions on highly salient issues. To answer that question, I collected data from the Gallup organization and the party platforms since 1960. In each presidential election year, I identified the issue that was most important to the public, as measured by Gallup,[15] and then analyzed the relevant section of the party platforms that spoke to that issue. Table 6.1 reports the most salient issue to the public.

In all nine cases, it would be difficult to distinguish the parties' views on these important issues.[16] In scanning the list, the controversy over integration in 1964 seems a prime candidate for polarization by the parties.[17] Yet stark differences fail to arise in the parties' rhetoric. The Democrats, for example, trumpeted the 1964 Civil Rights Act, calling for the end of "discrimination in the use of public accommodations, in employment, and in the administering of Federally assisted programs" (Johnson and Porter 1973, 671). The Republicans, on the other hand, called for the "full

15. Gallup asks their sample: "What do you think is the most important problem facing this country today?" They tend to ask this question two or three times each year. I used the results in those surveys to identify the most important issue to the public. See *The Gallup Poll* volumes edited by George Gallup for the actual data used.

16. As part of some other research, I have examined the political advertisements aired on television by the major candidates in presidential elections from 1960 to 1992. These data too indicate that very few differences exist between the candidates on these issues. In fact, about 80 percent of all appeals on issues made by presidential candidates were nondirectional in nature (Geer 1993), making it hard for citizens to perceive differences between the contenders. But given that television spots are usually only 30 seconds long, I thought this test a bit unfair. Hence, I turned to the party platforms.

17. Issues such as inflation, war, and unemployment are classic "valence" issues (Stokes 1963, 1993), which exhibited no polarization among the parties. Both parties, instead, pledge their commitment to ease inflation or stimulate employment, blurring any possible differences between them.

Table 6.1 *Most Important Problem*

1960	Relations with the USSR	1980	Inflation
1964	Integration	1984	Threat of War
1968	Crime	1988	Deficit
1972	Vietnam	1992	Unemployment
1976	Inflation		

SOURCE: *The Gallup Poll*

implementation of the Civil Rights Act of 1964, and all other civil rights statutes, to assure equal rights and opportunities guaranteed by the Constitution to every citizen" (Johnson and Porter 1973, 683). Another prime candidate for polarization would be Vietnam in 1972. But again stark differences failed to materialize. The Democrats pledged to end the war by "an immediate and complete withdrawal of all U.S. forces in Indo-China" (Johnson and Porter 1973, 812). The GOP blunted differences by calling for a "*settlement* of the Vietnam war which will permit the people of Southeast Asia to live in peace under political arrangements of their own choosing" (Johnson and Porter 1973, 850, my emphasis).

Sundquist (1983) supports these general interpretations. He examined the three most divisive issues of the 1960s and 1970s (race relations, Vietnam, and the "social issue") and concludes that the parties "straddled" each of them. Page and Brody (1972, 984) also found that "there was . . . little difference between Nixon's and Humphrey's stated views on Vietnam policy." This controversial war certainly could have brought about polarization, especially if politicians had paid attention to the many protests that dotted the country's landscape. But boisterous crowds no longer deceive politicians about the distribution of opinion, as they once deceived Williams Jennings Bryan and Alf Landon.

How do these cases compare with those of the pre-poll era? Did the parties/politicians hedge on the salient issues as indicated above, or did they offer clear differences on such matters? We, of course, know that the parties did go in different directions on issues such as slavery, free silver, and the New Deal, but what about other highly salient issues?

By scanning political history from the time between the conclusion of the Civil War and the advent of polls,[18] a number of issues clearly appeared

18. I focus on the post Civil War era because neither major party presented platforms until the 1844 election, and at the outset these documents were exceptionally short—especially the Whigs.'

to be controversial and probably salient to the public.[19] The tariff is an obvious choice in the period between the Civil War and the New Deal; that issue helped to define the political debate for decades. Reconstruction, which arose immediately following our bloodiest conflict, is another good candidate. The parties had heated debates over this policy. Prohibition was also an issue that sparked lots of attention—enough to spawn a constitutional amendment. Of final interest was the dispute over the League of Nations.

In each case, the issues demonstrated a *more*[20] polarized debate than that which was exhibited in the previously discussed cases. In 1868, the Democrats called for an "immediate restoration of all the states to their rights in the Union." (Johnson and Porter 1973, 37). The GOP, in contrast, supported the policy of Reconstruction to avoid allowing the people of the "States lately in rebellion" to face "anarchy or military rule" (Johnson and Porter 1973, 39). One need not be sophisticated to detect a marked difference between the parties on how best to let the Confederate states rejoin the Union.

The longstanding debate over the tariff also reflected a clear difference between the parties. Consider that in 1904 the "Democratic party has been, and will continue to be, the consistent opponent of that class of tariff legislation by which certain interests have been permitted, through Congressional favor, to draw a heavy tribute from the American people" (Johnson and Porter 1973, 131). The Republicans, by comparison, supported a "consistent protective tariff" (Johnson and Porter 1973, 137). These differences persisted for decades and were not confined to the 1904 campaign. In 1924, for example, the Democrats attacked tariffs as unfair and favored the repeal of the Fordney-McCumber Tariff Act. The GOP supported the tariffs as "protection to our productive industries" (Johnson and Porter 1973, 260).

With regard to the League of Nations, differences once again arose between the parties in the 1920 presidential campaign. The Democrats offered their support of the League as the very first substantive issue it addressed in the platform. The Republicans opposed the League, as signed by Wilson in Paris. For prohibition, the Democrats in 1932 advocated "the repeal of the Eighteenth Amendment" (Johnson and Porter 1973, 332). The GOP sought to maintain the integrity of the amendment, largely because

---

19. I, of course, cannot be sure of what issues were salient to the public—just as the politicians of the time could not be certain. But the issues I chose seemed to enjoy a widespread perception of importance.

20. Given the earlier discussion about the concept of polarization, it is much safer to speak of less or more polarization, as opposed to saying that there is or is not polarization.

they felt it important to enforce the laws of the land. The GOP did hedge a bit here, because they were willing to allow the individual states "to deal with the problem as their citizens may determine." (Johnson and Porter 1973, 348–49). These particular differences are not as stark as in the other cases above. Whether they constitute polarization is open to debate; but the more important point is that all these four examples paint a picture consistent with the central thesis of this chapter.

Two Possible Objections

Many observers would object to the earlier conclusion about integration and civil rights, arguing that racial concerns have in fact been a "polarizing" issue (Edsall and Edsall 1991). There is little doubt that race has been a central and divisive component of politics in this nation. One need only think of the civil rights movement and how the Democratic response unhinged the once "solid South." The politics of race continue today—whether in the form of Clarence Thomas or Willie Horton. But divisiveness is not the same as polarization. The public may well split on an issue, but politicians may still be hedging by offering positions that are more moderate.

Carmines and Stimson (1984, 1989) make the best case for race as a polarizing issue, uncovering evidence of sharp differentiation in the electorate concerning desegregation. While the electorate may have diverged on this and other racial issues since the 1960s,[21] the case is far less clear for politicians. When coding the platforms of both parties, Carmines and Stimson (1989, 56) do show that both parties paid more attention to the subject in the 1960s than in the 1950s. But increased attention says little about the publicly stated views on the topic by politicians (or by parties). I have already reported the respective parties' stated views on integration in 1964. When examining the specifics of the platforms with regard to civil rights, the differences continue to be muted. In 1968, for instance, *both* parties proposed ending discrimination and eradicating the causes of poverty and racism (Johnson and Porter 1973). Twelve years later, both parties continued to pledge to end the effects of discrimination (Johnson 1982). It is not surprising that politicians on both sides of the aisle support civil rights. Few politicians are going to be explicitly discriminatory. The topic is ripe for what Stokes (1963, 1993) terms "valence" politics. That is,

---

21. Alan Abramowitz (1994) has questioned the import of race for the electorate, finding little evidence that racial issues shape the partisan attitudes of white Americans. See also Harold Stanley (1987) for an argument that white southern voters are not as racially motivated as many assume.

where elected officials avoid stating clear positions on issues and instead try to link themselves with a good outcome like civil rights. Some disagreement surfaces among politicians on how to achieve this goal, but few (other than David Duke) question the goal.

Another possible objection to my conclusion is that I have focused too much on polarization as the catalyst for realignment. Perhaps such issues as race and Vietnam were not salient enough to the public to lead to a reshaping of the party system. This argument, in part, is based on the belief that the issue surrounding the New Deal—the federal government's role in the economy—is, and is likely to remain, central to most citizens' choices of party. While few issues match the power of the Great Depression, realigning issues need not possess such force. The issue of free silver in the 1890s, for instance, was an important problem, but only part of the electorate appeared concerned about the matter—primarily the agrarian interests in the West and the financial interests in the East (Glad 1960, chapter 3). Yet the issue of free silver is credited with realigning the party system. While one cannot be sure, it seems reasonable to believe that such issues as the Vietnam War, race relations, or the so-called "social issue" were at least as salient to the public as the concern over monetary policy in the 1890s. In 1968, for instance, data from the National Election Studies (NES) indicated that about half of the electorate thought Vietnam was the most important problem facing the nation.

Even if these recent issues were important only to some of the public, it is worth recalling that realignments need not entail massive change in the partisanship of the electorate. Only a portion of the public needs to change, either through conversion or mobilization, for a new party system to emerge (Andersen 1979). Thus, there is reason to believe that some of the issues since the Great Depression could have led to a realignment of the party system—especially in light of the decline in the electorate's commitment to parties over the last two decades.

Low-Salience Issues and Partisan Change

While I have argued that the process of partisan change has been altered by polls, I have yet to suggest what the new mechanisms are. Even if critical realignments have gone the way of dinosaurs, political change obviously has not. How does it now unfold? One way, I shall argue, involves how politicians respond to issues that are salient to only a handful of citizens.

In a previous chapter, I showed that well-informed politicians rationally can adopt differing (polarized?) positions on issues that are not central to the public. These positions can represent an effort to engage in leadership, to pay off party activists (or relevant interest groups), or to pursue personal policy objectives. Whatever the goal, we can expect well-informed politicians to offer differing positions on issues that are not salient to the public. So when politicians differ on such issues as the death penalty or gays in the military, those differences give a *small* portion of the electorate, such as members of the NRA, reason to shift or to adjust political loyalties. Because each group of politicians will have a different set of these kinds of issues, the change will be slow. The debate over gays in the military may give the Republicans a small boost in some quarters, while aiding the Democrats in others. At the same time, the GOP's stand on lessening environmental regulations will further chip away at some loyalties, while strengthening loyalties in others.

To illustrate how this modified process of political change can work, I shall show how a few hypothetical issues might alter the public's long-term support of politicians. I will start this demonstration with six assumptions.

1. 100 citizens reside in the polity.
2. There are two sets of competing politicians.
3. There is a single highly salient issue that defines the citizens' commitment to either set of politicians.
4. 55 of them have a standing commitment to politicians from Group A.
5. 45 of them have a standing commitment to politicians from Group B.
6. This standing commitment is a function of which politicians offer the position closer to the citizens'.[22]

Let me first backtrack a bit by considering the amount of change "realigning" issues generate when politicians are well and poorly informed. This detour will help to underscore the shift in partisan change.

Assume that a new, extremely salient issue has entered the political arena, and that it is important to 80 percent of the citizenry (i.e., 80 individuals). Of those people, 45 support the new issue to some degree and the other 35 oppose it. Group A, not knowing that distribution of support, announces its opposition to the new issue. It turns out that their sources of information came mostly from the 35 people who opposed the issue,

---

22. There are other assumptions underlying this hypothetical scenario. For a more complete listing see Chapter 1.

which biased their perceptions of public opinion. Group B, on the other hand, comes out in favor of it. This mistake by Group A gives the opposition 45 supporters and only 35 for themselves. There are still, of course, 20 citizens from the previous cleavage. If we assume that these people stick with the old loyalties in the same proportion as in that previous distribution, [23] the end result is a new majority set of politicians:

	Before New Issue	After New Issue
Group A	55	46
Group B	45	54

This case, although a highly simplified one, illustrates the basic contours of partisan change. Now let us consider the same issue (i.e., salient to 80 with 45 favoring it and 35 opposing it), but with politicians having access to good information about public opinion supplied by polls. Group A and Group B, with the same view of public opinion, adopt positions very close to the ideal point.[24] The public perceives little difference between the politicians on this issue, giving them little reason to alter their existing loyalties. The end result is that Group A stays in the majority, perhaps losing or gaining one or two supporters along the way.[25] And as any other potentially realigning issue enters the political arena, politicians act in such a way as to undercut its potential for shifting the political balance of power.

While well-informed politicians diffuse realigning issues, some non-salient issues can generate political change. Figure 6.5 represents two alternative distributions for issues that are salient to only a small portion of the polity. For Issue 1, politicians have little reason to polarize. While the dispute matters only to a handful of the electorate, the respective politicians still stand to gain support by adopting the middle position. Moreover, if B chooses to adopt an extreme position, A would get even more support, since A and B would no longer be dividing that small group.

23. To make this calculation, I multiplied the 20 remaining people by .55 (the old level of support for Group A). That yields 11 people, which I added to the new supporters of Group A, yielding 46 total followers. The same procedure (20*.45) nets Group B an additional 9 supporters—54 in all.

24. Recall that in my original theory there is some differentiation among the two sets of politicians. Officeholders get to adopt the ideal position, forcing the opposition to adopt a slightly different stance to ensure that the public does not give those in power all the credit for this issue. See Chapter 1 for the complete argument.

25. Even though the similar positions adopted by the two sets of politicians will deter most people from forging new loyalties, citizens at the very center of the distribution may detect genuine differences between the parties. If so, then a few people may change their partisan loyalties. There would not be a lot of these people and the net effect of this change would be small.

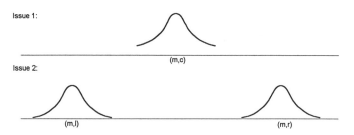

The distribution of preferences for ONLY that subset of the electorate that finds the issue salient.

FIGURE 6.5 Two Types of Low Salience Issues

The situation is different, however, for Issue 2. The median position is unlikely to make citizens from either side of the spectrum happy. If politicians stake out such a view, supporters at either extreme would have little reason to align themselves with those politicians. Recall that citizens do *not* have to make a choice on the basis of that issue; they can support either set of politicians based on existing views on previous issues.

If politicians from A adopted the position in the middle of the left-hand part of the distribution (m,l), those people in that region would lend their their support to A. Group B could do the same for the right-hand side (m,r). Because these individuals are at the extreme of the spectrum, it is also possible that "support" might include such things as money and workers for campaigns. These additional goodies are not part of the original theory. But as shown in Chapter 4, politicians can pursue such secondary goals when their overall popularity with the public is not threatened.

One might note, however, that Brian Barry (1970) argues that adopting the modal position in a distribution of opinion is not rational for politicians. His argument applies, however, when an issue is salient to all voters, and when the citizens must choose on the basis of that issue. Here, the issue is salient to only those few at the extreme. For those who do not find it salient, other issues will shape their support of politicians. Hence, most citizens, as in the original Downsian model, do not face a choice between the lesser of two evils.

Political change thus unfolds as certain issues of low salience chip away at the loyalties of a few citizens. But in the aggregate, these processes should lead to only minor shifts in the partisan balance of the parties. To illustrate this process, let us return to the simulation presented above and consider an issue that is salient to only 10 percent of the electorate—half of those people are on the "right" and half on the "left." If politicians from Group A and B play to the respective poles, then they may be able to add as many as five new supporters to their ranks (recall the electorate has only 100 people in it).[26] But each side would have the same number of new supporters, which means this hypothetical issue will have no aggregate effects on the respective standing of the parties. Interestingly, we could see coalitional shifts within this aggregate stability. That is, groups like African-Americans or textile workers may align themselves with one of the groups, creating change in *who* supports the two groups while the net division of support shows little change.

Now, of course, some of these low-salience issues may have more people on the "left," while others will favor the "right." But across a large number of such issues, the aggregate change still should be small. Given this claim, we should see only minor shifts in the partisan leanings of the electorate during the era of polls. The NES has collected data on party identification in the mass public since 1952, which allows us to test this hypothesis. These time series data show only small ebbs and flows in the electorate's support of the parties (see Stanley and Niemi 1994, 158). For instance, 51 percent of the electorate either identified themselves as Democrats or leaned toward the Democratic party in 1960. By the time of Jimmy Carter's election, the proportion stood at 52 percent. In 1992, the share of Democrats in the electorate was at 49 percent. On the Republican side of the ledger, the proportions for those same years were 37, 33, and 39. These data are consistent with the predictions of this argument.

Abortion: A Case in Point   Abortion provides an interesting case that illustrates how well-informed politicians can react to nonsalient issues. The two major parties have disagreed on this issue since the 1970s.[27] Even though abortion has been of great concern to certain interest groups, it

---

26. Now some of these people may already have been supporters. That overlap is not an important issue here, unless one camp has more or less overlap than the other. But for this argument I shall assume that the issue cuts the same for both groups.

27. The parties did not make explicit references to abortion in the platforms until 1976—two years after *Roe v. Wade*. The parties at that point started to stake out their respective ground. The Democrats in their 1976 platform opposed a constitutional amendment that would ban abortion. The Republicans, in contrast, endorsed that proposed amendment. There was, however, some hedging by both party platforms on this issue. By 1980, the battle lines were much clearer.

was not very salient to the mass public during the 1970s and early 1980s.[28] As a result, the GOP could adopt an anti-abortion stand that attracted a small number of loyal supporters who contributed money and time to the Republican party. At the same time, the Democrats could adopt a strong pro-choice position in an effort to appeal to various women's groups who might also offer support to the party. Abortion, in short, was an ideal "Issue 2"—a concern that has strong adherents on both sides of the spectrum.

The situation changed a bit, however, in the latter part of the 1980s. The salience of the issue began to grow. Prior to that time, the issue was not very important to the public—probably because the Supreme Court in *Roe v. Wade* protected a woman's right to an abortion. However, Supreme Court cases in the mid-1980s and early 1990s began to chip away at this precedent, leading some observers to predict its reversal. This possibility apparently led to an increase in the salience of this issue to the public.[29] As this issue grew in importance, the GOP's position threatened to be costly at the ballot box. These kinds of concerns led party elites to debate openly about whether they should moderate their view on this increasingly controversial issue. In 1990, for example, the New York Republican Party officially drafted a platform that supported "reproductive rights for women."[30]

During the 1992 campaign, Vice-President Quayle claimed that abortion was an issue that required more contemplation, and he was unwilling to take a hard-line stand on the matter. This statement stood in contrast to his longstanding opposition to abortion. Quayle's adjustment came on the heels of Barry Goldwater's proclamation that the GOP had better abandon its pro-life position if it wanted to compete successfully in presidential elections. More recently, the chairman of the Republican party, Haley Barbour, stated that "if we make abortion a test of being a Republican, we need our heads examined."[31]

28. In searching the Gallup Poll Indexes between 1970 and 1985, abortion rarely was mentioned as a most important problem by the public.

29. In October 1989, Gallup conducted a poll about the public's views on abortion, comparing the findings to those of a similar poll 10 years earlier. Among those who favor the overturn of *Roe v. Wade*, the proportion who view a candidate's position on abortion as the "most important" issue increased from 12% in 1979 to 27% in 1989. For those who oppose the overturn of *Roe v. Wade*, 50% view abortion as "not too important" when choosing candidates in 1979. That percentage shrunk to 28 ten years later. These data indicate an increase in the relevance of this issue to voters when selecting candidates.

30. See *New York Times* National edition, May 5, 1990, p. A1

31. Quoted in Thomas Edsall (1993, 15). Actually, the remark by the new chairman, Haley Barbour, indicates a shift in the emphasis on the abortion issue, not a switch in positions.

Many Republicans, in short, scrambled toward the median—just as predicted by this theory. The Democrats, too, modified their rhetoric, because they could no longer support what the Republicans labeled "abortion on demand." The public may well support a woman's right to choose, but there is only limited support for abortion under any circumstance.[32]

In short, as the issue became more salient (i.e. more people entered the distribution of opinion), rational politicians could no longer afford the luxury of a nonmedian position. This situation may have changed , however, with the election of Bill Clinton. His appointees to the Supreme Court have been more supportive of a pro-choice position than those selected by Reagan and Bush. Those additions to the Court make it harder to overturn *Roe v. Wade*, lessening the salience of this issue to the bulk of people who want to ensure a woman's right to an abortion. However, there remains a sizable group of activists, largely situated on the right, who remain ardently opposed to abortion. This group's activism continues to give the GOP incentive to support the pro-life camp.

A Few Implications

The claim that critical realignments are a thing of the past has a number of implications for the study of partisan change. One involves the formation of new party systems. If polls make it unlikely that parties will take polar positions on realigning issues, partisan change will be halting and more piecemeal. It will also be hard to identify the starting and ending points of a party system. That variable, so to speak, shifts from being dichotomous to continuous. Certainly, many scholars have argued that ongoing and fluid change has been characteristic of the party system since the New Deal (see, for instance, Carmines and Stimson 1981; Sundquist 1983; Carmines, McIver, Stimson 1987; Greenberg 1995). Consequently, political scientists may want to stop looking for realignments in the classic mode. It is unlikely that any one election or even set of elections can be pointed to as realigning. The discipline, therefore, may want to focus much greater attention on the "gradual transformations of the party sys-

Politicians realize that "flip-flops" are costly, and given the many issues facing the polity, an adjustment in agendas is often the rational move (see Geer 1992). But if the issue of abortion heats to a boiling point, ducking the issue will no longer work. At this point, it would be very interesting to see whether the GOP behaves as predicted by this theory.

32. A Gallup Poll in January 1991 indicated that only 31 percent of the public favored abortion "under any circumstance," 53 percent "under certain circumstances," and 14 percent "under no circumstances."

tem" than on the "abrupt" change normally associated with critical realignments (Carmines and Stimson 1984, 152).

Another implication of this argument involves the electorate's attachments to parties. With rational parties offering similar views on highly salient issues, voters should have less incentive to develop a strong commitment to one party. If both parties offer similar views on such issues, it may be harder than in the past to develop a strong attachment to one party. One should therefore expect the strength of partisanship to decline. Numerous studies have documented the electorate's waning support for parties (Nie, Verba and Petrocik 1976; Wattenberg 1990; Beck 1984). A commonly cited reason for this erosion of partisan support is that the rise of candidate-centered campaigns and the growth of the mass media have made parties less relevant to voters' political choices. While these arguments have obvious merit, the theory presented here provides an additional explanation. The rational behavior of well-informed parties has minimized the differences between the parties and has led to a weakening of the electorate's commitment to them.

Without clear differences on salient issues, much of the public will not be able to base choices between the parties on such concerns. When parties do offer vastly different positions on less pressing issues, the more activist segment of the public may select parties on that basis. But if parties offer much the same view on important issues, most citizens will have to consider other criteria when selecting parties. For example, the differing personal characteristics of the candidates provide an obvious way to choose among them. If so, we should see more emphasis on candidate's traits by the public; indeed, survey data support this claim.[33] But the usual explanation is found in the rise of primaries and the advent of television. No one has suggested that the increasing importance of candidates' personal traits might be tied to changes in the kinds of positions that politicians adopt on issues. I do not want to suggest that my explanation is superior to these others. I have no basis for such a claim. Instead, this theory offers another independent variable for that equation.

Besides traits, the public also will be more likely now than in the past to form partisan ties on the basis of the relative performance of the parties in office. Such information would not be costly, making it an attractive way for voters to select parties. If the governing party does a good job while

---

33. Since the 1950s, the mass public has increasingly made more references to the personal traits of the presidential candidates (see Geer 1992).

in power, the electorate will likely increase their support of that party. If, on the other hand, the governing party oversees a sluggish economy, the electorate should increase its support of the opposition. Citizens appear to be behaving in this manner. Fiorina (1981), for instance, has marshalled impressive evidence demonstrating that an individual's partisanship reacts to retrospective evaluations of the parties. MacKuen, Erikson, and Stimson (1989) also find that the partisan division in the electorate responds to changes in the economy. Of course, not all voters would act in this manner. But with an aging party system and weak partisan loyalties, more and more citizens may adjust their support of the parties in the face of short-term forces.

If these arguments have merit, we can expect, in turn, greater volatility in the electorate's support of parties and politicians, since they will not be offering vastly different views of the world. Different views on important issues provide a kind of anchor for the public; without such an anchor, the public is more likely to be moved by shifting political tides. Stokes (1993) finds evidence of greater volatility in politics, contending that this pattern can be tied to the increasing use of valence issues by politicians. Valence issues are not the stuff of enduring commitments and can lead to a fickle electorate. Consider the rise and fall of Jimmy Carter or George Bush. Bush, in particular, held a Gallup Poll rating of 90 percent, only to fall victim to Bill Clinton less than eighteen months later. Stokes (1993, 19) ties the rise of valence politics and volatility to the changes in the "means of the communication between leaders and the led." By that he meant the rise of television. But the decline of "position politics" is also predicted by behavior of well-informed politicians who avoid adopting unpopular positions on issues by repackaging them into valence form.

While the bulk of the electorate lacks any partisan moorings, activists and interest groups may develop strong loyalties. Well-informed politicians can strategically use issues to buy the support of activists and interest groups. The information supplied by polls allows politicians to pick and choose those kinds of issues that will not be costly at the ballot box, but will help add financial contributors and workers to any pending campaign. Poorly informed politicians would be less willing to engage in such behavior because of the risks associated with it. If polls have altered those calculations, then we can expect single-issue groups to flourish in this new environment, which in fact seems to be the case. Pundits and scholars have complained about the rise of single-issue interest groups that have carved niches for themselves in the political landscape. Among the reasons for this development may well be the ability of today's politicians to cater to their needs.

Finally, the argument suggests that our party system should get increasingly competitive. We can expect sharp short-term shifts in the support of politicians, as a weakly committed electorate swings toward a leader who oversees a prosperous economy and a tranquil international scene (or swings against someone who governs during bad times). But with both sides possessing good information and putting that information to good use, we should witness a party system that moves toward a close partisan balance. Certainly, there has been a decline in the areas of the country that use to be dominated by one party, with the South being the most known example of this trend. And the 1994 midterm elections, as mentioned earlier, may well usher is an era of genuine competition for partisan control of the House of Representatives (Abramowitz 1995). Such trends are consistent with the notion of an increasingly competitive party system.

Conclusion

This chapter has sought to flesh out the possible implications that the rise of polls had regarding how political change works. The implications presented are far-reaching. Not only are critical realignments a thing of the past, but the political system should also become more volatile and subject to short-term forces. No longer does the public have that strong mainstay that helped them weather the various political storms that periodically engulf us. Some may worry about this rise in volatility, given the predisposition of many to favor stability over instability. But, on the other hand, such an electorate may give politicians additional incentive to pay attention to the public's wishes, which may encourage even more responsiveness. Of course, that then gets us into the debate over whether elected officials should be followers or leaders of public opinion. I will save that general debate for the next and final chapter.

LEADERSHIP, DEMOCRACY, AND INFORMATION:
FINAL THOUGHTS

THIS BOOK BEGAN WITH A STORY
about George Washington touring the countryside on horseback in pursuit
of public opinion. I then contrasted that image of a cantering president with
that of Bill Clinton surrounded by computer printouts describing, with
great statistical precision, the latest indicators of the electorate's attitudes.
That juxtaposition highlights the central claim of this book; namely, that the
advent of survey research has transformed politicians from being poorly
informed to well-informed about public opinion. By developing a theory
about officeholders that casts information in a lead role, I have been able to
offer a new way to think about political leadership; shown how the advent
of polls has altered the prospects for that leadership; argued that politicians
now will develop skills different from those of their forebears; and contended
that the process of political change has been altered by survey research.

These all ideas have rested upon a very simple theory about how politicians behave. It may give some readers pause. Politics is rarely as simple as
I have assumed. For instance, Bill Clinton, when developing an economic
package in 1993 that could navigate the treacherous waters of Congress,
did not just let data from public opinion polls determine his decisions.
The President was surely influenced by the views of Washington insiders,
members of Congress, loyal friends, and his spouse. Nonetheless, polls
played a central part in the process.[1] Stanley Greenberg conducted numer-

_____

1. It should be noted that the views of advisers will also be influenced by data from polls, providing an indirect effect for polls.

ous surveys during this period, giving Clinton a handle on how he might proceed. Clinton did not consume every frequency count in Greenberg's printouts, but the data often had an effect on the President's thinking— such as helping to scuttle the BTU tax (Woodward 1994). Other "variables" may, however, have been more important in shaping Clinton's decisions, such as the role of the "deficit hawks" in the administration's decision-making process (Woodward 1994).

That interpretation may well be true. But the argument presented here is *historical* and *comparative*. Hence, we need to compare how Bill Clinton made his decisions with how, for instance, FDR enacted the now fabled New Deal legislation. It is that kind of comparison that highlights the potential importance of the information presented by polls. FDR did not have evidence about what proportion of the public favored the National Recovery Act or how many people opposed governmental support of agriculture. Clinton, on the other hand, knew what fraction of the public would be willing to pay higher taxes for deficit reduction, what percentage favored a cap in entitlements, and whether the public wanted a jobs program or more cuts in spending (Woodward 1994).

The critical question, therefore, is not whether polls are the most important variable in the decision-making process—surely an unanswerable question—but, instead, how have polls changed the general character of the decisions made by politicians? It is this question that lies at the core of this book.

The very nature of this question encourages one to look at the forest as opposed to the trees. The objective of this kind of endeavor, as James DeNardo (1985, 5) reminds us, is "to show how things fit together, to reveal connections and relationships that otherwise are difficult to discern. . . . The process of boiling things down to essentials is the heart of the matter, and this process demands not literalism but abstraction." This book offers only a road map to the relationship between information and politicians. Future studies can fill in the many details left out here.

In the pages that remain, I embark on an all too short journey that addresses what this argument has to say about the study of leadership, democratic theory, and the future relationship between politicians and public opinion.

Toward a Revised Conception of Leadership

Leadership is one of the most overused and misused terms in our political discourse.[2] We use it to lavish praise on our heroes. And we never

2. There is little question that leadership draws a tremendous amount of attention. On August 1, 1994, I located 5,938 published articles that dealt with the topic of leadership. Of those,

apply it to our enemies, tarring them instead with labels like demagogue or dictator. We have some general sense that democratic leaders are those people who accomplish good things. But exactly what a "good thing" is may well be unclear and, of course, what is good to one person may not be good to another. So when FDR was striking blows at the business elites of this country during the 1930s, many viewed his attacks as evidence of great leadership, while opponents blasted those same attacks as "a demagogic appeal to the masses of the working people of this country."[3] Leadership, according to conventional wisdom, is the kind of phenomenon that is hard to describe ahead of time. But you will know it when you see it.

That kind of approach to the study of political leadership makes scholarly advance slow going. Not only is the label "leader" or "leadership" often politically motivated, but also few agree on what actually constitutes leadership. The end result is confusion. This book has sought, by charting a theoretically rigorous course, to lessen this confusion.

If we step back for a moment, I have addressed two major types of democratic leadership—both of which have a well-established tradition in the literature. The first, Periclean leadership, consists of politicians taking their case to a skeptical, if not hostile, public, and attempting to convince that doubtful electorate of the error of their ways. This form of leadership is not only the hardest to accomplish, since politicians must convince people to alter existing preferences, but it is also the most risky for elected officials. If these efforts fail to get the public to shift their views, the next election may not be kind to these officials. Because of the risks and difficulty of the task, Periclean leadership is usually viewed as the ultimate test of a politician's skill.

Wilsonian leadership, the second type, consists of politicians rallying an unengaged public toward their position on a particular issue. This form of leadership makes fewer demands upon the persuasive skills of politicians, since officeholders are writing on what is largely a blank slate. While perhaps easier to accomplish, this type of leadership still requires that office-

---

1,617 concerned explicitly *political* leadership. These articles were "located" using Arizona State University's library system (CARL), which indexes journal and periodical articles published since 1988. By June 1, 1995, the number stood at 7,330 and 2,033, respectively. In just 10 months there was a 25 percent increase in the number of articles on this topic. That increase is a tribute to interest and importance of this subject.

3. Alfred Smith leveled this attack at Roosevelt in a response to FDR's now famous "Forgotten man" speech in April, 1932 (see Freidel 1990, 70).

holders identify problems and persuade the public to join their cause.

This theory casts doubt on the utility of that typology for understanding leadership of public opinion. First, and foremost, my argument has been that Periclean leadership is something that rational politicians practice only by mistake. So the belief that democratic leadership involves those instances where politicians tame public opinion is misguided. These incidents of "leadership" can be interpreted as followership gone awry. And even more important, the rise of polls has provided politicians with sufficient information about public opinion to avoid such mistakes now and in the future. So even these misguided attempts at followership (previously thought of as leadership) are anachronisms.[4] The end result is that the Periclean leader is really an empty cell in the leadership matrix.

This is an important claim, especially in light of the widespread belief that our nation is suffering from a lack of good (Periclean) leaders. Garry Wills (1994, 12), for instance, asks "how often have we heard that we lack great leaders now, the clearly virtuous kind, men like George Washington and Abraham Lincoln?" We need only to turn on the television to hear commentators complain that Bill Clinton is not "showing enough leadership on this issue" or that Congress "failed to lead on that bill." The general assumption is that we could become great again with a great leader to guide us. All the nation's problems would be solved if we could just find someone who either cuts down apple trees or splits rails. James MacGregor Burns has long grumbled about a shortage of leadership. And he is not alone. Alan Brinkley (1994) chimed in with a recent article titled: "What's wrong with American Political Leadership?" Bruce Miroff (1993, 359) views the 1990s as a "particularly bleak time for American political leadership." John Gardner (1990) simply asks "Why do we not have better leadership?" It is a widely held belief that there are too few politicians who have the courage to challenge the public and reorient their thinking on an important policy.[5]

---

4. Just as a reminder, I do not claim that polls preclude politicians from making errors when judging the state of public opinion. But even when mistakes are made, the constant monitoring of public opinion by polls allows them to be corrected quickly. In addition, trial balloons of various sorts can be floated in an effort to reduce even further the residual uncertainty. As a result, errors are likely to be short-term in nature and hence, only transitory, providing few opportunities for an extended attempt at (mistaken) leadership. It is reasonable to assume that any successful effort to change entrenched public opinion would need a good deal of time to take place.

5. In a recent issue of *National Civic Review*, James Kunde (1994, 17) wrote about the nationwide call "for more effective leadership." This call, which reflects the widespread concern about the lack of leadership, has yielded a dramatic increase in programs in universities, local communities, and corporations that seek to promote leadership.

The usual explanations for the relative absence of Periclean leadership mostly focus on either institutional or personal forces. James MacGregor Burns (1984, 101) contends that the absence of effective leadership is tied to the "system," which is "rooted more in institutional and intellectual forces than personal ones." Alan Ehrenhalt (1991) is more pointed than Burns, arguing that changes in the electoral system, such as the rise of the direct primary, have allowed more ambitious and self-centered politicians to gain office than in the past. Gardner (1990), on the other hand, sees the root of the problem in a lack of training. Lots of people have the potential to be good leaders, but we are not cultivating those talents.

Wills (1994) takes a different tack in answering this question. Leadership in a democracy along the lines of Thucydides' description of Pericles is rare and may not occur at all. The public is supposed to have some say in the process, and simply to give ourselves over to the judgments of another contradicts the notion of democratic rule. As Wills (1994, 12) writes, in "a democracy, supposedly, the leader does not pronounce God's will *to* the people but carries out what is decided *by* the people." Thus, for Wills a leader is also a follower, and the expectation that we need a gifted politician to guide us is misplaced.

Wills's empirical and normative claim draws theoretical support from my argument. Periclean leadership will indeed be rare. But this book's argument puts a much different spin on the matter than does Wills. The lack of Periclean leadership is not because democratic leaders are supposed to be followers; that has always been the case. Instead, politicians now have enough good information about the electorate's preferences to be effective followers of public opinion. Periclean leadership (by mistake) was possible at one time, but polls enable politicians to know what the people want, which permits them to act on those preferences. Thus, scholars who wonder why there are no "George Washingtons" anymore have not considered carefully enough the context facing politicians today. We should *not expect* rational, well-informed politicians to engage in such behavior. And even when they did in the past, it was not a deliberate attempt to steer the public on a new course. Thus, there is little reason to bemoan a lack of Periclean leadership, as defined by most scholars.

There is one final point about the rise of polls worth mentioning in this discussion about great leaders and Periclean leadership. Opinion surveys provide political observers with better information to judge whether politicians are standing up to the gusts of public opinion or being blown around by them. Thus, where journalists and pundits could not be sure why Andrew Jackson opposed Nicholas Biddle and the national bank, we now can judge the president's actions in light of public opinion data. So when Clinton announced his intention in June 1995 to balance the Federal budget in ten years, and with the evidence from polls that showed the widespread public support to eliminate the deficit, that decision was widely interpreted as followership, not leadership. But without polling data, political commentators would have lacked that critical piece of information when assessing Clinton's motives. Perhaps his decision to compromise with the Republicans might have been viewed less critically, since his actions did increase the chances that the cuts in Medicaid and Medicare would not be as deep as sought by the House Republicans. Such an outcome could well be viewed in a favorable light.

Thus, the information from polls not only makes followership on important issues more likely, but also makes it easier for observers to identify such moves. With the uncertainty lifted around many presidential actions, some of the luster surrounding those actions is sure to rub off as well. It seems reasonable to assume that Lincoln's Emancipation Proclamation would have been treated differently by both contemporary and historical observers if Gallup's grandfather had released a poll in June, 1862, showing that 72 percent of Northerners favored setting the slaves free.

Redefining Leadership in Information-Rich Societies   According to this analysis, the discussion of leadership in the era of polls should center on Wilsonian leadership. How should our conception of leadership change to fit this new context? What should we now expect of our politicians? Certainly concepts and standards are dynamic, responding to shifts in the environment in which they are used. We have already seen that the concept of public opinion went through a metamorphosis with the advent of polls. It is now time to update our view of leadership.

Leadership involves a two-step process. First, politicians identify a set of nonsalient issues to tackle. (Recall that rational, well-informed politicians address all salient issues as followers.) Second, they marshal the troops around their stated position on the issue. This two-step process requires that we approach leadership differently. To begin, democratic leadership of public opinion should *not* be thought of as getting people to change their views on issues. Some citizens in this process will surely shift their views, but, more important, leadership becomes highly intertwined with politicians shaping and defining the public's agendas. Since politicians face a large number of nonsalient issues at any one time, the *choice* of which issues they address takes center stage. That choice has been an implicit part of previous definitions of leadership, but now it becomes an explicit part of it.

Chapter 1 offered a definition of leadership that spoke to both the Periclean and Wilsonian strands:

Democratic leadership occurs either when politicians move an existing distribution of opinion toward their stated position OR when they create a distribution of opinion favoring their stated position.

The definition still applies, but the first part is not as plausible in the era of polls. That point has already been made. What has not been included in this discussion involves the role of the agenda. We heard in a previous chapter talk about "hard" and "easy" Wilsonian leadership. The hard Wilsonian leadership involved tackling those issues that were important to the polity but would not be sure winners for the politician. The easy form, as one might expect, involved those issues that were sure winners but may not be all that crucial to the country.

With those concerns in mind, I now am able to present a fuller definition of democratic leadership that better captures these matters:

Democratic leadership occurs when politicians create a distribution of opinion favoring their stated positions on a set of issues that are important to the well-being of the polity.

It is, of course, open to debate which issues are critical to the "well-being of the polity." But the point is that leadership involves more than just generating public support for a position on an issue. It concerns tackling those issues that are likely to improve the condition of those citizens in the polity.

We also need to reconsider what constitutes a good leader in democratic regimes. If leadership now involves molding opinion around issues that "are important to the well-being of the polity" as opposed to changing opinion, we need to adjust the criteria used to identify good leaders. There is an idealized notion that the ultimate leader is someone who is genuinely public-spirited without even a hint of self-interest. This pursuit of the common good is facilitated by a keen intellect and uncanny judgment. The pure leader is someone who comes before the people and shows them the error of their ways. By the force of argument and the use of a silver tongue, such a leader is able to convince the public to chart a new course that will move the nation forward. This kind of person fits very much the Periclean notion of leadership.

Such skills are still valuable. But in modern, information-rich democracies, they are less essential. And, in fact, efforts to shift the direction of public opinion could just as easily be labeled "demagogic" and "antidemocratic." Instead, good leaders are those politicians who build a political agenda that not only gains the public's support, but also addresses important political problems. An effective leader in the modern age, therefore, must be able to look down the road to see what issues *will* be important. By picking and choosing the right issues, the politician can indeed become a leader, but not the kind of leader we often find placed on pedestals by previous work.

An Assessment   There is a tendency among political observers, pundits, and scholars to expect politicians to be Periclean leaders. But this perspective is problematic. At the core, it misunderstands how politicians operate in democracies. Those who hold elected offices owe their positions to the public. The ballots cast during the last election gave them the opportunity to be in government; if these individuals want to continue in their positions past the time allotted in their current terms, they will have to face the electorate for approval again. Consequently, much of being a politician in a democracy, as Garry Wills reminds us, involves *following* the wishes of those who sent you to govern.

We should not expect democratically elected politicians to be "leaders." Or more accurately, we should not expect them to be the kinds of leaders who defy public opinion. Such actions are likely to result in unemployment. Before polls, politicians could in fact stumble into leadership because they did not know what the public wanted. But with the rise of surveys, we need to adjust our expectations. In so doing, we might develop a better appreciation for the talents, skills, and constraints under which politicians operate. That might lead to less criticism, which often immobilizes our elected officials.[6]

Having said all this, we still can expect rational politicians to engage in a kind of leadership that rallies the public to a cause. For those issues that are not important to the public at the moment but nonetheless are press-

---

6. This idealized view of leaders is not without merit. It can be used to judge other types of political actors, such as activists. Although the Martin Luther Kings and Susan B. Anthonys are not officially part of this theory, they can be expected to possess such talent. Their loyalty to a cause gives them the incentive to pursue it single-mindedly. Since they do not need a majority of the public to support them on election day and instead seek a small cadre of dedicated followers to spread the word, such skills are invaluable. So when I question the Periclean leader, I am doing so only as that standard applies to democratically elected politicians.

ing concerns that face the polity, politicians can exhibit leadership. They can identify those issues and attempt to convince the public that the issues should be addressed. This kind of leadership squares with Key's idea of latent public opinion—issues that lurk on the horizon. Democratic politicians have an incentive to tackle these kinds of problems. Not only will they receive credit for solving them, but they will also gain both support and votes. If a politician fails to address the problems that are likely to arise in the future, the opposition may be able to seize on them. That outcome could lead to the defeat of the officeholder at the next election. In short, there are incentives for politicians to practice certain kinds of leadership—but not the type that is often idealized by those who perceive a lack of national leadership.

Within this adjusted view of leadership, there is a problem. Well-informed politicians may duck the hard issues that lie on the horizon and instead address the easy ones. By taking this route, politicians may be undermining the nation's future. This possibility is a real one, especially when we see politicians stressing such issues as family values and patriotism. The opposition does have the incentive to attack those in power for not addressing relevant issues. So, the competitive context may help lessen this concern. But the opposition also may see merit in ducking the hard issues. There is one sure-fire consolation, however. If the issue becomes salient down the road, well-informed politicians will address it at that point. So the timing may not be ideal, but the officeholder, armed with polls, will address those issues of concern to the electorate. Thus, responsiveness does work—perhaps not with the best timing, but politicians will react.

Bringing Back Periclean Leadership?   Some observers may still want leaders to be cut from Periclean cloth, feeling that such individuals will be best able to keep the democratic ship well outfitted. Usually, the supporters of this view have little faith in the ability of the public to make good decisions (e.g., Michels 1915; Schumpeter 1950; Lippmann 1925; Tulis 1987). For them, the Periclean form of leadership is essential. The uninformed public, in this view, is prone to error, and great leaders are needed to keep the nation on the proper course. That view may well be correct. But given this theory, we would need to provide politicians a different set of institutional incentives to accomplish that goal. By placing them in an environment where they must constantly seek the public's support, they have much reason to pay close attention to the public's views. Perhaps we should make officeholders less responsive to public opinion by lengthening terms or establishing term limits. Such recommendations have been offered over the years, with the debate over term limits being in full swing at the time of this writing (see Will 1992a).

Those solutions not only have anti-democratic overtones, but also carry their own risks. While such moves might promote good public policy because they rely more on the skill and judgment of leaders, it could just as easily be labeled elitist. By insulating politicians from the wishes of the electorate, the system would place less power in the hands of the public and greater power in the hands of those who control government. Such developments are anti-democratic, at least as the term is defined by most political theorists (e.g., Dahl 1989; Held 1987). The counter to this claim is that the winds of public opinion, as detected by polls, are not reflective of the public interest or of what some scholars have termed public sentiment (Ginsberg 1986; Tulis 1987; Nisbet 1975). It is not unreasonable to claim that polls often give a snapshot of the electorate that is not a true indicator of what the public would want after carefully deliberating an issue. But if one accepts this argument, we are back in the nineteenth-century trap—how do we know what public sentiment is? Where can we find it? Should we trust elites to tell us? By evoking the idea that public opinion is not measurable by polls, we open ourselves to the unending interpretations of what the public really wants without asking them directly.[7]

Polls do partially reflect short-term forces, but at least we have confidence that they are measuring something that is real. And as noted earlier, when one aggregates the views of all citizens, the indicators seem reasonable. Key (1966) once reminded us that "voters are not fools." Now, Popkin (1991) and Page and Shapiro (1992) provide further evidence of this point. While surely public opinion could be more informed and efforts should indeed be made on this front, at least the views of the electorate are part of the equation.

There are additional risks associated with any institutional changes like term limits. For starters, the types of candidates who seek and win public office will be systematically different. As I argued in Chapter 5, environmental changes lead to shifts in the skills of politicians. And we can expect that those who seek offices with term limits (or longer terms) will be different from those who seek offices without those rules. How it would play

---

7. Fishkin (1991) has offered a very inventive solution to this problem that draws on the logic of polling. He contends that if we draw a small, random sample of people to discuss important issues, like the nomination of presidential candidates, we can encourage the kind of deliberation that will yield informed opinion. The "deliberative opinion poll" has generated a great deal of interest and debate. While it represents an important solution, I shall not deal with it here.

out is not entirely clear, but Fiorina's (1994) analysis indicated that term limits would alter the pool of candidates seeking office in legislatures. With the prospects of a short career, potential candidates are more likely to have the financial resources and the leisure time to dabble in politics for a few years. Such a shift might not only lead to legislatures that may be less representative of the population, but it might also give Republicans an edge over Democrats, since the former are more likely to have candidates with free time.

One could respond that term limits will encourage the type of candidate who is more public-spirited and more committed to the public good, as opposed to one whose aim is to be re-elected (Will 1992a). That may well be true. But that view reflects once again the common confusion between leaders and elected politicians. And, however one feels about my claims, it is essential that we dispel this confusion.

Implications for Representative Theory

In its mythical form, classical democratic theory describes a polity in which all citizens participate directly in government. The hope is that these participants have equal power and influence in shaping policy. As a result, there are no leaders (or politicians) making decisions on behalf of the populace. That mythical description has proved elusive as an operating model for government. Even in ancient Athens, the birthplace of democracy, a few select leaders arose, directing and influencing the conduct of government (Ober 1989). The best-known example, of course, is Pericles' efforts to rally the Athenian people to engage Sparta in a naval war.

As governments began to cover larger geographic areas and greater numbers of people, that theory became even less tenable and fell into disfavor (Dahl 1989). But in the eighteenth century, Montesquieu and Rousseau[8] wrote about how the concept of representation could make democracy possible. By selecting a small number of people to represent the interests of a large number of citizens, it was possible to eliminate "the ancient limits on the size of democratic states and transform democracy from a doctrine suitable only for small and rapidly vanishing city-states to one applicable to the large nation-states of the modern age" (Dahl 1989, 29). Perhaps just as important, the arguments behind representation

---

8. Dahl (1989) notes that Rousseau in the *Social Contract* rejected the concept of representation. But that view is "inconsistent with both his earlier and later writings" (Dahl 1989, 29).

ended the masquerade that all citizens had equal governmental influence by giving a select few the responsibility of running the government. This idea spread quickly in intellectual circles, allowing democratic theory to make a comeback.

With the emergence of representative democracies, the relationship between the officeholder and the public became the foundation on which modern democratic theory rested. Politicians were now the conduit through which the views of the public would flow and be expressed in actual public policy. But how was representation supposed to work? How should public officials represent the interests of the public? What is the best way for this institution to work? These and other questions arose. Surely the best-known controversy centers around the longstanding question: "Should (must) a representative do what his constituents want, and be bound by mandates or instructions from them; or should (must) he be free to act as seems best to him in pursuit of their welfare?" (Pitkin 1967, 145). Much debate has surrounded the Burkean distinction of trustees versus delegates.

Scholars have approached this question from theoretical, normative, and empirical angles. Despite the many efforts, no agreed upon answer has emerged. As Hanna Pitkin (1967), who wrote the most comprehensive and definitive book on the subject, comments, "what is most striking about the mandate-independence controversy is how long it has continued without coming any nearer to a solution."

When plumbing the depths of this dispute, the importance of information possessed by the elected officials becomes crystal clear. And once exposed, it provides new insights into this centuries-old debate.

Classic trustee representatives need not worry about what the public wants, since they are supposed to use their own expertise in making choices about policy. Of course, if they seek re-election, trustees would like to know public opinion.[9] With such information, they could highlight those issues that the public supports and downplay those that would draw the electorate's ire. In addition, for those issues where the politician is not sure what to do, the direction of public opinion could break the tie. A complete disregard for the electorate's wishes may, in short, lead to ouster from office at the next election. So vote-seeking trustees will benefit from accurate information about the views of the people they represent. But it is not absolutely essential to their task in the short-run.

---

9. Burke himself in the famous speech to the electors at Bristol stated that constituents' "wishes ought to have great weight" with their representative.

For delegates, however, knowledge of constituents' preferences is a must—without it they cannot perform their representative role. How can a politician do as instructed without good instructions? Delegates, in sum, cannot be delegates without accurate information about public opinion.

It is for these reasons perhaps that Hanna Pitkin (1967, 188) claims that the "accurate transmission of popular feelings . . . is a prerequisite to representation." Yet as Pitkin (1967, 220) later notes, a politician "seldom has access to accurate information about what views and interests they [constituents] do have." Without good information, the theoretical walls around the delegate conception of representation begin to crumble. In fact, the debate over delegate versus trustee representation can be settled on practical grounds. Delegate representation prior to polls was not possible in the large, populous electorates of the modern era. Once electorates grew, politicians simply lacked any institution through which they could receive clear and accurate instructions from their constituents. While debate from both theoretical and normative perspectives was still reasonable, the matter was a dead issue for the actual operation of government.[10]

Now, of course, it was still possible that poorly informed politicians could act as delegates for some issues. There might be a very strong current of opinion that embedded itself in a series of protests or a string of editorials in local newspapers. Politicians in the nineteenth century did have ways to detect public sentiment. But as we have seen, these mechanisms were often flawed and, more important, they were open to interpretation. So while a politician could cloak himself in the attire of a delegate, no one could be certain of it, and the opposition would surely question those judgments. Without an agreed upon and reliable way for politicians to find out what the public wanted, delegate representation was very hard to accomplish.[11]

The rise of the public opinion poll, however, has lessened, perhaps even eliminated, the practical difficulties facing delegate representation. Politicians can now uncover what their electorates want them to do. And since nearly all political actors accept polls as legitimate indicators of public opinion, survey research has reinvigorated this longstanding debate. Polls can indeed be considered an institution that not only links politicians

---

10. As is so often the case, Key (1961, 482) clearly understood this problem: he argued that the "practice of constituency instructions to representatives has long since ceased, in part because of broadening of the suffrage and the direct election of representatives left no organ competent, either legally or practically, to issue instructions."

11. Of course, politicians could *try* to be delegates. But, as before, outcomes, not intentions, are the focus of this book.

and citizens, but also allows the public to issue instructions to representatives. It is possible for elected officials to gather information very quickly on what the public wants on nearly any issue. It would be costly to run polls so often and within particular districts, but it is possible. In fact, some members of Congress have sought to develop a polling organization that will accomplish exactly that (Clymer 1994). Of course, for national leaders, such operations have been in force for more than three decades (Jacobs 1993).

Political representation, then, falls into three different eras.

1. Era of Restricted Suffrage, 1640–1800.[12] Politicians could determine the state of public opinion, because of restricted suffrage within geographically small districts.
2. Era of Expanded Suffrage, 1800–1940. With growth in population and the extension of suffrage to more and more people, politicians could no longer accurately discern the views of constituents.
3. Era of Polls, 1940–present. Despite very large constituencies, the public opinion poll allowed politicians to gain good information about the views of citizens.[13]

The view that polls could in fact play this critical role in representative theory rests on a particular conception of public opinion—one not shared by all. One may attack polls as measuring something less than the public's "real" views or claim that the public is so woefully informed that their instructions should be ignored. But by doing so, we would, once again, be forced to abandon the delegate conception of representation as a practical guide to government. Perhaps that is a good thing, but we risk undermining any aspirations to building a true democracy. As Key (1961, 7) once observed, "unless the mass views have some place in the shaping of policy, all the talk about democracy is nonsense." We will, of course, quibble over what constitutes "some place." But even holding that debate aside, the mass views can have only "some place" in determining the conduct of government when public officials know what the public wants. Polls provide at least a chance to learn about what the electorate wants. Of

---

12. I use 1640 as the starting point because that date marks the beginning of the Levellers movement in England. The Levellers advocated a number of reforms, including wider suffrage. One could easily adopt a different date, since the 1600s witnessed a series of struggles over suffrage in England (Hirst 1975). Any date prior to 1600 would be questionable, however, since elections were rarely contested (Hirst 1975, 12).

13. Kelley's (1983) work on mandates inspired this notion of three stages. Kelley argues that survey research provides the opportunity for political observers to identify and measure the kind of mandate an election bestows on the winner. Prior to polls, the requirements behind a mandate could only be met when the electorates were small—as in the time of Burke.

course, as other technological advances arise, politicians may abandon polls. These new advances may be even better at tapping the electorate's views. But until that breakthrough emerges, polls provide the best alternative for those who want to see the public directly affecting the policies of government.

Leadership v. Democracy

Democracy and leadership are two concepts that form, at best, a rocky marriage. As Dahl (1985, 152) observes, "the question of leadership has always been difficult for advocates of democracy, and not least for its theorists." Since leaders exercise more influence in government than average citizens, the criterion of equality among all members of the polity, which is a linchpin of much democratic theory, is violated (Dahl 1989; Green 1993). So, any discussion of the importance of leadership to democracies is often awkward. But, at the same time, history shows that no regime has ever existed without some set of leaders running the show.

One way to ease tensions in this marriage is to alter the criteria for a democracy. Schumpeter (1950, 269) provides the most famous example of this strategy, arguing that "the democratic method is that institutional arrangement for arriving at political decisions in which individuals acquire the power to decide by means of a competitive struggle for the people's vote." A democracy, therefore, becomes "a mechanism which allows the registration of broad desires of ordinary people, while leaving actual public policy to the few who are sufficiently experienced and qualified to make it" (Held 1987, 166). There is only a loose relationship between the elected and the electors. As Schumpeter (1950, 284–85) comments, "democracy does not mean and cannot mean that the people actually rule in any obvious sense of the terms 'people' and 'rule.' " Instead, voters select the set of leaders who will be viewed as the legitimate decisionmakers in government.

Some defend this view of democracy as not only realistic but also essential to the preservation of liberty. These proponents have little faith in the capacities of the public to make good choices. Democracy is just a set of institutions that allows the electorate to select leaders periodically. This process ensures some modest level of responsiveness and encourages turnover in government if the leadership becomes corrupt or blind to the needs of the voters.[14]

---

14. Riker (1982) presents a different look at the relationship between leadership and democracy. By evoking social choice theory, Riker contends that when there are more than two posi-

The other way to ease this tension is to move toward more participatory forms of democracy (Pateman 1970; Barber 1984; Macpherson 1977). Under these kinds of arrangements, efforts are made to give citizens a more direct say in government. By accomplishing this goal, more power is given to the public and less to the upper echelons of leaders. No one argues that all leadership roles can be eliminated by these schemes. But as Held (1987, 258–59) comments, participatory democracy "fosters human development, enhances a sense of political efficacy, reduces a sense of estrangement from power centres, nurtures a concern for collective problems, and contributes to the formation of an active and knowledgeable citizenry capable of taking a more active interest in governmental affairs."[15] This model moves democracy beyond being just an institutional arrangement for choosing leaders to a process that improves the lot of all citizens in the polity.

These two opposing schools of thought provide a handle on the continuum that exists over the proper relationship between democracy and leadership.[16] Obviously, one school of thought favors more democracy. Members of this camp want to see a system that creates more equality and participation and places more faith in its public than in its leaders. The other school favors more leadership. They see excessive public influence as a dangerous thing and prefer instead to place faith in leaders who face periodic checks on their power.

The information made available by polls provides a different way to ease this tension. With good data about public opinion, politicians can now identify both those issues that are important to the public as well as the electorate's views on them. For highly salient issues, it is now possible to give the public a say in the direction of public policy. Polls, therefore, provide a way for politicians to detect the "public will" in some cases.[17] At

---

tions on an issue there is no way to aggregate preferences that ensures the fair reflection of the public's views. Thus, the "public will" is elusive. Riker, hence, rejects the idea that public officials act on behalf of the view of the public. Instead, he favors a Schumpeterian democracy where voters use the ballot to control officials, who in turn control government.

15. Steven Finkel (1985) provides important empirical support for this claim.

16. Let me emphasize that my treatment of these schools of thought does little justice to the depth and quality of arguments offered by the numerous scholars in this field. My objective is only to sketch a very rough picture of these two views so as to draw implications this theory has for this longstanding issue.

17. Social Choice theorists, such as Arrow and Riker, would take issue with this claim. Even for salient issues, there is no way to aggregate preferences in a way to ensure that the "public will" has been detected. However, if politicians perceive that a "public will" exists, then, for the purposes of this theory, it remains important to pursue this line of reasoning.

the same time, polls also show the large mass of issues that the public does not find very important and about which they possess highly unstable views. For those issues, politicians now know that there is not any "public will." In these cases, it is not possible for politicians to act in a purely democratic manner. Instead, they must make judgments about which issues might become important or which issues might yield them additional public support. In short, politicians must practice leadership.

Polls allow politicians to conduct a kind of democratic triage. For the highly salient issues, the rational politician acts in a manner consistent with the public's will. For those issues that are highly unlikely to capture the public's attention, politicians can follow the classic trustee strategy. Then for those issues that might become important, politicians can tackle the subset that will yield them the most public support.

This triage will not work perfectly. Important issues will be ducked, and silly ones will be stressed. It will also be difficult to know precisely what the public wants, because of the problem of aggregating preferences. But if one compares this situation to that facing politicians prior to polls, there is a genuine opportunity to balance the competing views. Democracy kicks in for those issues salient to the public, while leadership enters the picture for less pressing matters. The tension does not end. But good information eases it.

For those observers who want democracy to educate and develop the skills of the electorate, this scenario can be viewed positively. In trying to capture the public's attention regarding the nonsalient issues, politicians will be educating the citizenry. Officeholders will place issues on the public's agenda in an effort to increase their support. If these efforts are unsuccessful, rational politicians either will abandon the issue (and turn to other concerns) or adjust their views on the issue to correspond to the views of an engaged public. On the other hand, scholars who worry about excessive reliance on an uninformed public can draw some comfort from this outcome. The public, according to this theory, dictates policy only when they have well-developed, clear preferences on an issue. In such cases, the judgment of the public is likely to be better than it might be for new, untested issues that emerge on the political scene.

From Opinion Polls to Focus Groups

As Al Gore's "information highway" begins to connect all corners of the country (and the world), it is easy to imagine that technology will dramatically increase the prospects of gathering more and better information about public opinion than currently exists. We can only speculate at this point about what kinds of information politicians will have at their disposal in the coming years. Constant referendums could be taking place via telephones, computers, or even television. A member of the House of Representatives may literally be able to sample thousands of households about how to vote on a particular bill just before entering the chamber to cast that ballot. The possibilities are nearly endless. Just as James Bryce (1895, 29) never anticipated that some method could be invented that would tap the views of citizens on a weekly basis, we too cannot imagine the types of changes that surely will unfold in the coming decades. We can be confident, however, that these shifts in information will alter how politicians behave and will change the relationship between the leaders and the led.

In recent years, there has been one addition to how politicians gather information that is worthy of comment here in the closing pages of this book: the focus group.[18] Although the focus group has been around for a long time, it has been gaining popularity among politicians of late (Polsby and Wildvasky 1991; Delli Carpini and Williams 1994). The most famous use of a focus group in electoral politics led to the production of the Willie Horton advertisement in 1988. The information gleaned from focus groups indicated that Michael Dukakis was vulnerable on the issue of crime, leading to the airing of a series of political advertisements on TV of which the Willie Horton spot was the most famous (Moore 1992). The rise of the focus group provides an interesting contrast to the public opinion poll. As opposed to drawing a large, representative sample, the focus group usually relies on a small number of like-minded people—usually around ten individuals. There is no pretense that these individuals are representative of the public as a whole (Delli Carpini and Williams 1994). In fact, Stanley Greenberg contends that "the more homogeneity, the more revealing" (Kolbert 1992, 21). A particular group, like Reagan Democrats or undecided voters, will be asked a series of open-ended questions. There is no standardized format, as with polls. Instead, the "quirky interactions of a dozen or so adults" shape the kinds of information researchers glean from these encounters (Kolbert 1992, 20).

Despite the unscientific feel of these devices, they are becoming staples in the diets of politicians. George Bush used focus groups during his presidency in an effort to sound out reactions to possible themes and policies

18. For a thorough and thoughtful discussion of focus groups, see Delli Carpini and Williams (1994).

(Kolbert 1992). President Clinton has made extensive use of these devices (Woodward 1994). For instance, Greenberg (1993) conducted six focus groups (and a series of polls) to understand the attitudes and likely behavior of Perot voters. Because this mechanism uses a small number of citizens, it provides a cheap way to get some useful information about public opinion.

In particular, focus groups permit probing that gives insights into the underlying reasons behind the public's support for particular policies, filling some of the holes in the data supplied by surveys. As Scott Walker (1992, 41) argues:

> The strengths of a focus group are different from those of a poll. A focus group will not tell you whether a position is mostly favored or mostly opposed by the electorate. A focus group will tell you how voters approach issues, how much thinking they have done about issues, how deeply they care about different issues, what wording resonates best when taking a stand on an issue, and how willing the voters are to accept and believe more information on a topic.

Delli Carpini and Williams (1994, 64) continue:

> Focus groups can illuminate aspects of public opinion that are less accessible through traditional methods. In particular, focus groups are valuable in revealing the *process* of opinion formation, in providing glimpses of usually *latent* aspects of this process, and in demonstrating the *social* nature of public opinion.

Obviously, focus groups provide useful information about public opinion. But, as a result, this increasingly popular device has repercussions for the argument developed here. Because focus groups provide a handle on the underlying dynamics of public opinion, they can give an indication of what Douglas Arnold (1990) calls "potential preferences." Because of the in-depth approach of focus groups, politicians can use these devices to see what public opinion might look like down the road. They can see what topics excite and irritate citizens. For instance, Bush's people found out that members of their focus group did not have any favorable response to his State of the Union message until he said that "government is too big and spends too much" (Kolbert 1992, 20). Focus groups also help to provide politicians with ideas about how to package issues. The Reagan administration wanted to give the Strategic Defense Initiative (SDI) a catchy name that would play better with the public. Focus groups were part of that effort.[19] Focus groups offer important insights about public opinion that are not available through polls.[20] For those issues that are important to the public, polls provide a good handle on both their direction and salience, but for less pressing issues, things are a little more dicey. While polls tell politicians which issues are not currently important to the public and what the electorate's tentative views are, surveys do not always provide a reliable measure of underlying preferences. Focus groups can supply such insight that, in turn, gives indications of what opinion may look like in the future. Of the large number of non-salient issues on the horizon, which are most likely to capture the public's attention? What position is the electorate likely to adopt on each issue? Politicians worry about the future shape of public opinion. JFK, for instance, fretted over what to do with Vietnam. He knew that pulling out would kill him politically, since losing that territory to the Communists would give the Republicans a field day. At the same time, a full-scale commitment might be unsuccessful and would certainly result in lots of casualties—another unacceptable outcome to the American people. Kennedy chose a middle course, hoping to postpone such unpopular choices at least until he won re-election.[21] Arnold (1990, 68) summarizes this concern effectively when observing that politicians

> ignore inattentive publics at their peril. Latent or unfocused opinions can quickly be transformed into intense and very real opinions with enormous political repercussions. Inattentiveness and lack of information today should not be confused with indifference tomorrow. The cautious legislator, therefore, must attempt to estimate three things: the probability that an opinion might be aroused, the shape of that opinion, and its potential for electoral consequences.

While polls do provide some information about the three items that Arnold mentions, focus groups can supply additional clues about potential preferences, by probing deeper into the public mind.

---

19. Hedrick Smith (1988, 703) also reports that the Reagan team wanted to use the name "missile shield." But "star wars" could not be shaken from the public consciousness.

20. Despite the popularity of focus groups, they are unlikely to replace polls as the major mechanism for detecting public opinion. Polls measure the views of the entire electorate in systematic ways, making them much more reliable indicators of opinion than focus groups. This claim is especially true for highly salient issues. It is also true that through various question wordings, polls can also provide hints at potential preferences.

21. See Reeves (1993) for an account of Kennedy's presidency. The above discussion is drawn from that volume.

Focus groups do not provide a foolproof measure of potential preferences. The unrepresentative sample, combined with the "quirky" dynamics of the groups, prevents that. However, this device does provide a more systematic way of judging preferences than interpreting the actions of a crowd or the content of the mail. With a more controlled setting, politicians can test different ideas with different groups to detect patterns. These devices are obviously tapping into something, given the increased use of them. And if presidents and other politicians continue to employ focus groups, they will become institutionalized as part of the political process, thereby increasing their legitimacy and potential impact on politicians.

The ability of focus groups to offer an increased sense of potential preferences will allow politicians to choose issues more strategically. For those issues that seem to be lurking on the near horizon, officeholders will want to fire preemptive shots in an effort to get credit for the issue and to be able to define it in the most favorable terms. Politicians may also be better able to choose a set of issues that are more likely to draw a public response—or what I earlier termed "easy" Wilsonian leadership. Of course, lots of issues will still grab the stage for which politicians will be unprepared. Too many unexpected events will unfold and too many unanticipated reactions will take place to make this process anything close to a science. But when such issues suddenly erupt, politicians will have polls and focus groups to provide quick readings about how best to proceed. At the very least, politicians, armed with both focus group and poll data, will be better able to tiptoe between the various landmines that mark the political battlefield.

Final Thoughts

The advent of the public opinion poll helps fuel the longstanding debate over whether we should seek more democracy or more leadership. The importance of polls (and of focus groups to a far lesser extent) is that they do provide genuine opportunities for the public to increase their influence on the political process. George Gallup made exactly this point in the 1940s. This initial optimism has been tempered, however. There are real dangers associated with surveys, ranging from politicians becoming slaves to the whims of the public to the fear that polls allow politicians to manipulate the public.

Whether one sees polls as a threat or as a boon to democracy depends, in large part, on the kind of faith one has in the skills of the public. For those who think that the public makes informed decisions, one can hail polls as an opportunity to give citizens a greater say in the government. But for the doubters, the advent of polls makes politicians slaves to a fickle public that is frequently incapable of making informed decisions. What constitutes an "informed decision" is very open to debate. If one wants nearly all the public to know such things as which party controls Congress and what the various alternatives are on a controversial piece of legislation, then the public will come up short. If, on the other hand, we alter the criteria of what constitutes an informed choice, the public can look informed (see Kelley 1983; Popkin 1991; Page and Shapiro 1992).

But whichever side one favors, this theory suggests that the fate of democratic regimes rests more today than in the past on the ability of citizens to make good judgments. Sixty years ago politicians were often uncertain about what the public wanted. It was possible for them to interpret what the public wanted, which gave elected officials room to maneuver. But the rise of the public opinion poll places additional responsibility on the shoulders of the public. Where before a poorly informed electorate was not all that consequential, since it could not communicate their views to politicians very well, it now becomes more important. So the attention by political theorists and social scientists to creating a more engaged and informed democratic citizenry is absolutely essential in today's politics (e.g., Barber 1984; Fishkin 1991). Politicians now are able to follow instructions on important issues; it is therefore critical that those instructions are sound.

Struggles over how to promote good government either through more reliance on the public or through more reliance on elites will not end (and certainly will not be solved in these pages). These struggles have been going on for centuries and will continue through the centuries that follow. The struggle itself is a good thing. Samuel Huntington (1981) reminds us that the tension between the ideal and the actual often provides the engine for change. Our institutions always come up short when compared with the theories on which they rest. These gaps lead to calls for improvements and revisions. But by the time any reforms have been enacted, the criteria change again. So even if we managed to establish a much more participatory democracy, theorists will have quill in hand to revise the standards of such regimes. The pursuit of good government is constant and unending. If it were otherwise, we would risk decay and collapse.

We can expect further changes in political life, as information becomes increasingly available. Polls are just an intermediate step in an enduring battle over information. The danger is not that more information is bad.

Nor do I want to suggest that as more information becomes available, we may be opening Pandora's box. To the contrary, information is a great asset. Moreover, any efforts to suppress information are surely even more dangerous. But genuine concern arises in the differing use of this information across different segments of the polity. As polls, focus groups, and other devices become part of every politician's bag of tricks, will citizens also take advantage of the political information that is available to them? The amount of information that people can tap about politics (or any other topic) is awesome, ranging from their local newspapers to cable television to the internet. But even though such information can be secured by "clicking a mouse," my fear is that most people will not take the time and the effort. Politicians have a vested interest in acquiring good political information and will take all steps to do so. Average people do not have that kind of incentive. They are more interested in paying the bills, going bowling, and rooting for the New York Mets. Consequently, the balance of information between what the public knows and what public officials know may get increasingly out of whack. That development could lead to additional advantages for politicians.

Representative government requires an exchange of information between the people and politicians. As J. R. Pole (1983, 89) notes, "it would be virtually impossible to construct a theory of democracy which did not include" a *two-way* flow of information. Polls alter that flow, potentially generating a dangerous gap in the exchange of information that could become very troubling. When that point might arise is unclear. Perhaps we have already reached it. I do not know. But increasingly we will be entering uncharted waters at rapid speeds. And we do need to ensure that we find ways for *all* relevant decisionmakers to make use of good information as they make respective choices. In this way, we can ensure that democratic societies gain the benefits from the availability of that information. It is that task that demands our attention as we embark on the twenty-first century.

Abramowitz, Alan I. 1994. "Issue Evolution Reconsidered: Racial Attitudes and Partisanship in the U.S. Electorate." *American Journal of Political Science* 38:1–24.

Abramowitz, Alan I. 1995. "The End of a Democratic Era: 1994 and the Future of Congressional Elections." *Political Research Quarterly* forthcoming.

Abramowitz, Alan I., Ronald B. Rapaport, and John McGlennon, eds. 1986. *The Life of the Parties*. Lexington: University Press of Kentucky.

Albig, William. 1956 [1939]. *Modern Public Opinion*. New York: McGraw Hill.

Aldrich, John H. 1983a. "A Spatial Model with Party Activists: Implications for Electoral Dynamics." *Public Choice* 41:63–99.

Aldrich, John H. 1983b. "A Downsian Model with Party Activism." *American Political Science Review* 77:974–90.

Allard, Winston. 1941. "Congressional Attitudes Toward Public Opinion Polls." *Journalism Quarterly* 18:47–50.

Altheide, David L. and Robert P. Snow. 1979. *Media Logic*. Beverly Hills: Sage.

Altschuler, Bruce E. 1990. *LBJ and the Polls*. Gainesville: University of Florida Press.

Andersen, Kristi. 1979. *The Creation of a Democratic Majority*. Chicago: University of Chicago Press.

Anderson, David D. 1981. *Williams Jennings Bryan*. Boston: Twayne Publishers.

Arizona Republic. 1991. "Bush Will Seek Health Care Plan by '92 Election." November 11, A1.

Arizona Republic. 1993, January 17, A19.

Arnold, R. Douglas. 1990. *The Logic of Congressional Action*. New Haven: Yale University Press.

Baker, Russell. 1991. "Pollsters: The Oracle of Today." *Arizona Republic,* November 11, A15.

Barber, Benjamin. 1984. *Strong Democracy.* Berkeley: University of California Press.

Barber, James David. 1977. *The Presidential Character.* 2nd ed. Englewood Cliffs: Prentice Hall.

Barone, Michael. 1988. "Power of the President's Pollsters." *Public Opinion* 3:2–4, 57.

Barry, Brian. 1970. *Sociologists, Economists, and Democracy.* Chicago: University of Chicago Press.

Basler, Roy P., ed. 1953. *The Collected Works of Abraham Lincoln.* New Brunswick: Rutgers University Press.

Bass, Bernard, ed. and rev. 1981. *Stogdill's Handbook on Leadership.* New York: Free Press.

Beal, Richard S. and Ronald H. Hinckley. 1984. "Presidential Decision Making and Opinion Polls." *The Annals of The American Academy of Political and Social Science* 472:72–94.

Beck, Paul Allen. 1984. "The Dealignment Era in America." In Russell J. Dalton, Scott C. Flanigan, and Paul Allen Beck, ed., *Electoral Change in Advanced Industrial Democracies.* Princeton: Princeton University Press.

Beniger, James. 1986. *The Control Revolution: Technological and Economic Origins of the Information Society.* Cambridge. Harvard University Press.

Berke, Richard. 1993. "Clinton Advisor Says Polls had a Role in Health Care Reform." *New York Times.* December 9, A17.

Bernays, Edward. 1923. *Crystallizing Public Opinion.* New York: Boni and Liveright Publishers.

Bernays, Edward. 1928. *Propaganda.* New York: H. Liveright.

Blondel, Jean. 1987. *Political Leadership.* London: Sage Publications.

Blum, John Morton. 1977. *The Republican Roosevelt.* Cambridge: Harvard University Press.

Blumer, Herbert. 1948. "Public Opinion and Public Opinion Polling." *American Sociological Review* 13:542–554.

Bogart, Leo. 1972. *Silent Politics: Polls and the Awareness of Public Opinion.* New York: Wiley Interscience.

Brace, Paul and Barbara Hinckley. 1992. *Follow the Leader.* New York: Basic Books.

Brace, Paul and Barbara Hinckley. 1993. "Presidential Activities from Truman through Reagan: Timing and Impact." *Journal of Politics* 55:382–98.

Brehm, John. 1993. *The Phantom Respondents.* Ann Arbor: University of Michigan Press.

Brinkley, Alan. 1994. "What's Wrong with American Political Leadership?" *Wilson Quarterly* (Spring):447–54.

Brody, Richard. 1991. *Assessing the President*. Stanford: Stanford University Press.

Brown, Richard D. 1989. *Knowledge is Power*. New York: Oxford University Press.

Bryan, William Jennings. 1896. *The First Battle*. Chicago: W.B. Conkley Company.

Bryce, James. 1895 [1888]. *The American Commonwealth*. New York: MacMillan.

Bryce, James. 1921. *Modern Democracies*. New York: MacMillan.

Budge, Ian, David Robertson, and Derek Hearl. 1987. *Ideology, Strategy and Party Change: Spatial Analyses of Post–War Election Programs in 19 Democracies*. New York: Cambridge University Press.

Budiansky, Stephen, Art Levine, Ted Guest, Alvin P. Sanoff, and Robert J. Shapiro. 1988. "The Numbers Racket: How Polls and Statistics Lie." *U.S. News and World Report*: July 11, 44–47.

Burke, Edmund. 1987 [1789]. *Reflections on the Revolution in France*. J.G.A. Pocock, ed. Indianapolis: Hackett Publishing Company.

Burke, John P. and Fred I. Greenstein, eds. 1989. *How Presidents Test Reality*. New York: Russell Sage Foundation.

Burnham, Walter Dean. 1970. *Critical Elections and the Mainsprings of American Politics*. New York: Norton.

Burns, James MacGregor. 1963. *The Deadlock of Democracy*. Englewood Cliffs: Prentice–Hall.

Burns, James MacGregor. 1970. *Roosevelt: The Soldier of Freedom*. New York: Harcourt, Brace, and Jovanovich.

Burns, James MacGregor. 1978. *Leadership*. New York: Harper and Row.

Burns, James MacGregor. 1984. *The Power to Lead*. New York: Simon and Schuster.

Butler, David and Austin Ranney, eds. 1992. *Electioneering: A Comparative Study of Continuity and Change*. New York: Oxford University Press.

Butler, David and Donald E. Stokes. 1976. *Political Change In Britain*. New York: St. Martin's Press.

Caddell, Patrick. 1979. "Trapped in a Downward Spiral." *Public Opinion*: October/November, 2–8.

Calvert, Randall L. 1985. "Robustness of the Multidimensional Voting Model: Candidate Motivations, Uncertainty and Convergence." *American Journal of Political Science* 29:69–95.

Cantril, Hadley. 1967. *The Human Dimension*. New Brunswick: Rutgers University Press.

Carmines, Edward G. and James A. Stimson 1981. "Issue Evolution, Population Replacement and Normal Partisan Change." *American Political Science Review* 75:107–18.

Carmines, Edward G. and James A. Stimson 1984. "The Dynamics of Issue Evolution: The United States." In Russell J. Dalton, Scott C. Flanigan, and Paul Allen Beck, eds., *Electoral Change in Advanced Industrial Democracies*. Princeton: Princeton University Press.

Carmines, Edward G. and James A. Stimson 1989. *Issue Evolution*. Princeton, NJ: Princeton University Press.

Carmines, Edward G., John McIver, and James A. Stimson. 1987. "Unrealized Partisanship: A Theory of Dealignment." *Journal of Politics* 49:376–400.

Carmines, Edward G., Steven H. Renton, and James A. Stimson. 1984. "Events and Alignments: The Party Image Link." In Richard G. Neimi and Herbert F. Weisberg, eds., *Controversies in Voting Behavior*. Washington, D.C.: Congressional Quarterly Press.

Chappell, Henry W. and William R. Keech. 1986. "Policy Motivation and Party Differences in a Dynamic Spatial Model of Party Competition." *American Political Science Review* 80:881–900.

Childs, Harwood. 1940. *An Introduction to Public Opinion*. New York: Wiley.

Childs, Harwood. 1965. *Public Opinion: Nature, Formation, and Role*. Princeton: Van Nostrand.

Chong, Dennis. 1992. *Collective Action and the Civil Rights Movement*. Chicago: University of Chicago Press.

Christian Science Monitor. 1991, August 5, A1.

Clubb, Jerome M., William H. Flannigan, and Nancy H. Zingale. 1980. *Partisan Realignment*. Beverly Hills: Sage Publications.

Clymer, Adam. 1991a. "A Bush Campaign Chief Who Knows the Voters." *The New York Times*. December 8, A18.

Clymer, Adam. 1991b. "Politicians Take Up The Domestic Issues; Polls Suggest Why." *The New York Times*. September 15, E5.

Clymer, Adam. 1994. "Proposing to Eliminate a Polling Gap in Congress." *The New York Times*. May 15, A31.

Colletta, Paola E. 1968. "The Bryan Campaign of 1896." In *William Jennings Bryan*, ed. Paul Glad. New York: Hill and Wang.

Converse, Jean. 1987. *Survey Research in the United States*. Berkeley: University of California Press.

Converse, Philip E. 1974. "Comment: The Status of Nonattitudes." *American Political Science Review* 68:650–60.

Converse, Philip E. 1987. "Changing Conceptions of Public Opinion in the Political Process." *Public Opinion Quarterly* 51:12–24.

Converse, Philip E. and Roy Pierce. 1986. *Representation in France*. Cambridge: Belknap Press of Harvard University.

Conway, M. Margaret. 1984. "The Use of Polls in Congressional, State, and Local Elections." *The Annals of The American Academy of Political and Social Science* 472:97–105.

Cooper, John Milton. 1983. *The Warrior and the Priest*. Cambridge: Belknap Press of Harvard University.

Corbett, Michael. 1991. *American Public Opinion*. New York: Longman.

Cornwall, Elmer E. 1965. *Presidential Leadership of Public Opinion.* Bloomington: Indiana University Press.

Crespi, Irving. 1988. *Public Opinion, Polls, and Democracy.* San Francisco: Westview Publishing.

Croley, Steven P. 1994. "Imperfect Information and the Electoral Connection." *Political Research Quarterly* 47:509–24.

Cuomo, Mario M. 1990. *Lincoln on Democracy.* New York: Harper.

Dahl, Robert A. and Deane E. Nuebauer, eds. 1968. *Readings in Modern Political Analysis.* Englewood Cliffs: Prentice Hall.

Dahl, Robert. 1956. *A Preface to Democratic Theory.* Chicago: University of Chicago Press.

Dahl, Robert. 1985. *A Preface to Economic Democracy.* Berkeley: University of California Press.

Dahl, Robert. 1989. *Democracy and its Critics.* New Haven: Yale University Press.

Dahl, Robert. 1990. "Myth of the Presidential Mandate." *Political Science Quarterly* 105:355–73.

Davis, Otto A. and Melvin J. Hinich. 1967. "Some Results Related to a Mathematical Model of Policy Formation in a Democratic Society." In J. L. Bernd, ed., *Mathematical Applications in Political Science III.* Charlottesville: University of Virginia Press.

Delli Carpini, Michael X. and Bruce Williams. 1994. "The Method is the Message." *Research in Micropolitics* 4:57–85.

DeNardo, James. 1985. Unpublished manuscript. Princeton University.

Dentzer, Susan. 1992. "Health-care Gridlock." *U.S. News and World Report* 112:4, January 20, 22–24.

Dizard, Wilson P. 1985. *The Coming Information Age.* New York: Longman.

Donald, David. 1947. *Lincoln Reconsidered.* New York: Random House.

Donovan, Robert J. 1964. *The Future of the Republican Party.* New York: New American Library.

Downs, Anthony. 1957. *An Economic Theory of Democracy.* New York: Harper and Row.

Drew, Elizabeth. 1981. *Portrait of an Election.* New York: Simon and Schuster.

Dunleavy, Patrick. 1991. *Democracy, Bureaucracy and Public Choice.* Englewood Cliffs: Prentice Hall.

Dwyer, Paula, and Susan B. Garland. 1991. "A Roar of Discontent: Voters Want Health Care Reform–Now!" *Business Week*: November 25, 28–30.

Edsall, Thomas B. and Marie Edsall. 1991. *Chain Reaction.* New York: Norton.

Edsall, Thomas. 1993. "For Republicans, a New Chairman and an Easy Target." *Washington Post.* February 8–14, A15, national weekly edition.

Edwards, George C. III. 1980. *Presidential Influence in Congress.* San Francisco: W.H. Freeman.

Edwards, George C. III. 1983. *The Public Presidency*. New York: St. Martin's Press.

Edwards, George C. III. 1989. *At The Margins*. New Haven: Yale University Press.

Edwards, George C. III. 1990. *Presidential Approval*. Baltimore: Johns Hopkins University Press.

Ehrenhalt, Alan. 1991. *The United States of Ambition*. New York: Random House.

Eisinger, Robert M. 1994a. "Pollster and Public Relations Advisor: Hadley Cantril and the Birth of Presidential Polling." Paper presented at the Annual Meeting of the American Association of Public Opinion Research, Denver.

Eisinger, Robert M. 1994b. "Presidential Polling in the 1950s and Beyond." Paper presented at the Annual Meeting of the American Political Science Association, Chicago.

Ellis, Richard J. and Aaron Wildavsky. 1989. *Dilemmas of Presidential Leadership from Washington to Lincoln*. New Brunswick: Transaction Publishers.

Enelow, James M. and Melvin J. Hinich. 1990. *Advances in the Spatial Theory of Voting*. New York: Cambridge University Press.

Entman, Robert M. 1989. *Democracy without Citizens: Media and the Decay of American Politics*. New York: Oxford University Press.

Erikson, Robert S., Gerald C. Wright, and John P. McIver. 1993. *Statehouse Democracy*. New York: Cambridge University Press.

Erikson, Robert S., Norman R. Luttbeg, and Kent L. Tedin. 1991. *American Public Opinion*, 4th ed. New York: MacMillan.

Esaiasson, Peter. 1991. ''120 Years of Swedish Election Campaigns.'' *Scandinavian Political Studies* 14:261–78.

Exline, Frank. 1922. *Politics*. New York: Dutton.

Farkus, Steve, Robert Y. Shapiro, and Benjamin I. Page. 1990. "The Dynamics of Public Opinion and Policy." Paper delivered at the Annual meeting of the American Association for Public Opinion Research, Lancaster, PA.

Farley, James A. 1938. *Behind the Ballots*. New York: Harcourt.

Ferejohn, John and James Kuklinski, eds. 1990. *Information and Democratic Process*. Urbana: University of Illinois Press.

Finkel, Steven E. 1985. "Reciprocal Effects of Participation and Political Efficacy: A Panel Analysis." *American Journal of Political Science* 29:891–913.

Finkel, Steven E. 1993. "Re-examining the 'Minimal Effects' Model in Recent Presidential Campaigns." *Journal of Politics* 55:1–21.

Fiorina, Morris and Kenneth Shepsle. 1989. "Formal Theories of Leadership: Agents, Agenda–Setters, and Entrepreneurs." In Bryan Jones, ed., *Leadership and Politics*. Lawrence: University of Kansas.

Fiorina, Morris. 1981. *Retrospective Voting*. New Haven: Yale University Press.

Fiorina, Morris. 1992. *Divided Government*. New York: MacMillan.

Fiorina, Morris. 1994. "Divided Government in the American States: A Byproduct of Legislative Professionalism?" *American Political Science Review* 88:304–16.

Fishkin, James. 1991. *Democracy and Deliberation*. New Haven: Yale University Press.

Flemming, Danna Frank. 1932. *The United States and the League of Nations*. New York: Putnam.

Foner, Eric. 1988. *Reconstruction: America's Unfinished Revolution, 1863–77*. New York: Harper.

Franklin, John Hopp. 1963. *The Emancipation Proclamation*. Garden City: Doubleday.

Freidel, Frank B. 1990 *Franklin D Roosevelt: A Rendezvous with Destiny*. Boston: Little Brown, and Company.

Fysh, Peter, 1992. "Opinion Research, Liberalism and the French Right." *International Journal of Public Opinion* 4:109–26.

Gallup Poll Monthly. August, 1991, p. 4.

Gallup, George and Saul Rae. 1940. *Pulse of Democracy*. New York: Simon and Schuster.

Gardner, John W. 1990. *On Leadership*. New York: Free Press.

Garland, Susan. 1992. "Health Care: Finally, a Pulse at the White House." *Business Week*: January 20, 43.

Geer, John G. 1991. "Do open-ended Questions Measure 'Salient' Issues?" *Public Opinion Quarterly* 55:460–70.

Geer, John G. 1992a. "New Deal Issues and the American Electorate, 1952–88." *Political Behavior* 14:45–65.

Geer, John G. 1992b. "The Search for Differences." Paper presented at the Annual Meeting of the American Political Science Association, Atlanta.

Geer, John G. 1993. "Campaigns, Competition, and Political Advertising: A Look at Some Evidence." Paper presented at the Annual Meeting of the American Political Science Association, Washington, D.C.

George, Alexander L. and Juliet L. George. 1964 [1954]. *Woodrow Wilson and Colonel House*. New York: Dover Publications.

Gienapp, William E. 1987. *The Origins of the Republican Party, 1852–1956*. New York: Oxford University Press.

Giglio, James N. 1991. *The Presidency of John F. Kennedy*. Lawrence: University Press of Kansas.

Gilder, Richard W. 1909. *Lincoln the Leader and Lincoln's Genius for Expression*. New York: Houghton Mifflin Company.

Ginsberg, Benjamin. 1976. "Elections and Public Policy." *American Political Science Review* 70:41–49.

Ginsberg, Benjamin. 1982. *The Consequences of Consent*. Menlo Park: Addison Wesley.

Ginsberg, Benjamin. 1986. *Captive Public*. New York: Basic Books.

Glad, Paul W. 1960. *The Trumpet Soundeth*. Lincoln: University of Nebraska Press.

Glad, Paul W. 1964. *McKinley, Bryan, and the People*. Philadelphia: Lippincott.

Graber, Doris. 1988. *Processing the News: How People Tame the Information Tide*. 2nd ed. White Plains: Longman.

Green, Philip, ed. 1993. *Democracy: Key Concepts in Critical Theory*. Atlantic Highlands: Humanities Press.

Greenberg, Stanley B. 1993. "The Alienated." *The New Democrat*. 5:4–10.

Greenberg, Stanley B. 1995. *Middle Class Dreams*. New York: Times.

Greenstein, Fred I. 1982. *The Hidden-Hand Presidency*. New York: Basic.

Greer, Thomas. 1958. *What Roosevelt Thought*. East Lansing: Michigan State University Press.

Gunn, J. A. W. 1989. "Public Opinion." In Terence Ball, James Farr, and Russell Hansen, eds., *Political Innovation and Conceptual Change*. Cambridge: Cambridge University.

Hargrove, Erwin C. 1966. *Presidential Leadership*. New York: MacMillan.

Hargrove, Erwin C. 1989. "Two Conceptions of Institutional Leadership." In Bryan Jones, ed., *Leadership and Politics*. Lawrence: University of Kansas Press.

Hargrove, Erwin C. 1994. *Prisoners of Myth*. Princeton: Princeton University Press.

Hart, Roderick. 1987. *The Sound of Leadership*. Chicago: University of Chicago Press.

Hartley, Thomas and Bruce Russett. 1992. "Public Opinion and the Common Defense: Who Governs Military Spending in the United States." *American Political Science Review* 86:905–915.

Hawver, Carl. 1954. "The Congressman and His Public Opinion Polls." *Public Opinion Quarterly* 18:123–9.

Heckscher, August. 1991. *Woodrow Wilson*. New York: Scribner's.

Hedlund, Ronald D. and H. Paul Friesma. 1972. "Representatives Perceptions of Constituency Opinion." *Journal of Politics* 34:73–52.

Held, Richard. 1987. *Models of Democracy*. Cambridge: Polity Press.

Herbst, Susan. 1993. *Numbered Voices*. Chicago: Chicago University Press.

Herring, E. Pendleton. 1965 [1940]. *The Politics of Democracy*. 2nd ed. New York: Norton.

Herrnson, Paul. *Party Campaigning in the 1980s*. Cambridge: Harvard University Press.

Hilderbrand, Robert. 1981. *Power and the People: Executive Management of Public Opinion in Foreign Affairs*. Chapel Hill: University of North Carolina Press.

Hinckley, Ronald H. 1992. *People, Polls, and Policy Making*. New York: Lexington Books.

Hinds, Michael deCourcy. 1991. "Wofford Win Shows Voter Mood Swing." *New York Times*. November 7, A11.

Hirst, Derek. 1975. *The Representative of the People?*. New York: Cambridge University Press.

Hofstadter, Richard. 1973 [1948]. *The American Political Tradition and the Men Who Made It*. New York: Vintage Books.

Holcombe, A. W. 1923. *The Foundation of the Modern Commonwealth*. New York: Harpers.

Hollingsworth, J. Rogers. 1963. *The Whirligig of Politics*. Chicago: University of Chicago Press.

Hotelling, Harold. 1929. "Stability in Competition." *Economic Journal* 39:41–57.

Huntington, Samuel P. 1981. *American Politics: The Promise of Disharmony*. Cambridge: Belknap Press.

Ifill, Gwen. 1993. "Clinton Sees Need to Focus his Goals and Sharpen Staff." *New York Times*. May 5, A1 and A14.

Iyengar, Shanto and Donald R. Kinder. 1987. *News That Matters*. Chicago: University of Chicago Press.

Jacobs, Lawrence R. 1992a. "The Recoil Effect: Public Opinion and Policymaking in the U.S. and Britain." *Comparative Politics* 24:199–217.

Jacobs, Lawrence R. 1992b. "Institutions and Culture: Health Policy and Public Opinion in U.S and Britain." *World Politics* 44:179–209.

Jacobs, Lawrence R. 1993. *The Health of Nations*. Ithaca: Cornell University Press.

Jacobs, Lawrence R. and Robert Y. Shapiro. 1992a. "Public Decisions, Private Polls: John F. Kennedy's Presidency." Paper presented at the Annual Meeting of the Midwestern Political Science Association, Chicago.

Jacobs, Lawrence R. and Robert Y. Shapiro. 1992b. "Leadership and Responsiveness: Some New Evidence on the Johnson Presidency." Paper presented at the Annual Meeting of the American Political Science Association, Chicago.

Jacobs, Lawrence R. and Robert Y. Shapiro. 1993a. "Leadership in a Liberal Democracy: Johnson's Private Polls and Public Announcements." Paper presented at the Annual Meeting of the Midwestern Political Science Association, Chicago.

Jacobs, Lawrence R. and Robert Y. Shapiro. 1993b. "Studying Substantive Democracy: Public Opinion, Institutions and Policymaking." Paper presented at the Annual Meeting of the American Political Science Association, Washington, D.C.

Jacobs, Lawrence R. and Robert Y. Shapiro. 1994a. "Disorganized Democracy: The Institutionalization of Polling and Public Opinion Analyses during Kennedy, Johnson, and Nixon Presidencies." Paper presented at the Annual Meeting of the American Political Science Association, New York.

Jacobs, Lawrence R. and Robert Y. Shapiro. 1994b. "Issues, Candidate Image, and Priming: The Use of Private Polls in Kennedy's 1960 Presidential Campaign." *American Political Science Review* 88:527–41.

Jacobs, Lawrence R. and Robert Y. Shapiro. 1995a. "The Rise of Presidential Polling: The Nixon White House in Historical Perspective." *Public Opinion Quarterly* 59:163–195.

Jacobs, Lawrence R. and Robert Y. Shapiro. 1995b. "Public Opinion in President Clinton's First Year: Leadership and Responsiveness." In Stanley A. Renshon, ed., *The Clinton Presidency*. San Francisco: Westview Press.

Jacobs, Lawrence R., Robert Y. Shapiro, Eli C. Schuman. 1993. "The Polls—Poll Trends: Medical Care in the United States—an Update." *Public Opinion Quarterly* 57:394–428.

Jacobson, Gary. 1990. *The Electoral Origins of Divided Government*. San Francisco: Westview Press.

Jaffa, Harry. 1959. *The Crisis of the House Divided*. 2nd ed. Chicago: University of Chicago Press.

Jamieson, Kathleen Hall. 1988. *Eloquence in an Electronic Age*. New York: Oxford University Press.

Janis, Irving L. 1983. *Groupthink*. 2nd ed. Boston: Houghton Mifflin.

Johnson, Donald B. 1982. *National Party Platforms of 1980*. Urbana: University of Illinois Press.

Johnson, Donald B. and Kirk Porter. 1973. *National Party Platforms, 1840–1972*. Urbana: University of Illinois Press.

Jones, Bryan D. 1989. "Causation, Constraint and Political Leadership." In Bryan Jones, ed., *Leadership and Politics*. Lawrence: University of Kansas Press.

Jones, Stanley L. 1964. *The Presidential Election of 1896*. Madison: University of Wisconsin Press.

Kagay, Michael. 1991. "The Use of Public Opinion Polls by *The New York Times*: Some Examples from the 1988 Presidential Election." In Paul J. Lavraka and Jack K. Holley, eds., *Polling and Presidential Election Coverage*. Newbury Park: Sage.

Kahneman, Daniel and Amos Tversky. 1984. "Choices, Values, and Frames." *American Psychologist* 39:341–50.

Katz, Andrew Z. 1993. "Antiwar Opinion, Democratic Legislatures, and Interventionist Policy Reversals in Three Cases." Paper presented at the Annual Meeting of the American Political Science Association, Washington, D.C.

Kellerman, Barbara, ed. 1986. *Political Leadership: A Source Book*. Pittsburgh: University of Pittsburgh Press.

Kelley, Stanley, Jr. 1956. *Professional Public Relations and Political Power*. Baltimore: Johns Hopkins University Press.

Kelley, Stanley, Jr. 1983. *Interpreting Elections*. Princeton: Princeton University Press.

Kelley, Stanley, Jr. 1988. "Democracy and the New Deal Party System." In Amy Guttman, ed., *Democracy and the Welfare State*. Princeton: Princeton University Press.

Kelley, Stanley, Jr. 1995. "Politics as Vocation: Variations on Some Themes from Max Weber." Paper presented at conference in "New Perspectives on Party Politics," Princeton, New Jersey, October 27–28.

Kelley, Stanley, Jr. n.d. "Party Politics." Unpublished manuscript, Princeton University.

Kernell, Samuel. 1993. *Going Public: New Strategies of Presidential Leadership*. Washington, D.C.: Congressional Quarterly Press.

Key, V. O. 1955. "A Theory of Critical Elections." *Journal of Politics* 17:3–18

Key, V. O. 1961. *Public Opinion and American Democracy*. New York: Alfred Knopf.

Key, V. O. 1966. *Responsible Electorate*. New York: Random House.

Kingdon, John. 1968. *Candidates for Office; Beliefs and Strategies*. 2nd ed. New York: Random House.

Kingdon, John. 1984. *Agendas, Alternatives, and Public Policy*. Boston: Little Brown Company.

Kleppner, Paul. 1970. *The Cross of Cultures: A Social Analysis of Midwestern Politics 1850–1900*. New York: Free Press.

Kolbert, Elizabeth. 1992. "Test-Marketing a President." *New York Times Magazine*, August 30, 18.

Kollman, Ken, John H. Miller, and Scott E. Page. 1992. "Adaptive Parties in Spatial Elections." *American Political Science Review* 86:929–38.

Kosterlitz, Julie. 1991. *National Journal*: November 11, 2806.

Kramer, Michael. 1991. "The Voters' Latest Ailment: Healthcare." *Time*: November 11, 51.

Krasno, Jonathan S. 1995. "Interpreting the 1994 Elections." Paper presented at "New Perspectives on Party Politics," Princeton, New Jersey, October 27–28.

Kuklick, Bruce. 1988. *The Good Ruler*. New Brunswick: Rutgers University Press.

Kunde, James E. 1994. "American Renewal: The Challenge of Leadership." *National Civic Review* 83:17–25.

Lacayo, Richard. 1994. "Lock'em Up." *Time*: February 7, 50–3.

Ladd, Everett C. and John Benson. 1992. "Technology and the Changing Landscape of Media Polls." In Thomas E. Mann and Gary R. Orren, eds., *Media Polls in American Politics*, Washington, D.C.: Brookings Institution.

The Lancet. 1991. "Bush Plays Safe on Health Care Reform." August 31, Volume 338:561.

Lane, Robert E. and David O. Sears. 1964. *Public Opinion.* Englewood Cliffs: Prentice Hall Inc.

Lanoue, David J. 1988. *From Camelot to the Teflon President.* New York: Greenwood Press.

Lasswell, Harold D. 1941. *Democracy Through Public Opinion.* New York: George Banta Publishing Company.

Lawrence, David G. 1991. "The Collapse of the Democratic Majority: Economics and Vote Choice Since 1952." *Western Political Quarterly* 44:797–820.

Lewis, I. A. 1991. "Media Polls, the *Los Angeles Times* Poll, and the 1988 Presidential Election." In Paul J. Lavraka and Jack K. Holley, eds., *Polling and Presidential Elections Coverage.* Newbury Park: Sage.

Lewis-Beck, Michael S. and Tom W. Rice. 1982. "Presidential Popularity and Presidential Vote." *Public Opinion Quarterly* 46:534–37.

Link, Arthur, ed. 1966. *The Papers of Woodrow Wilson.* Princeton: Princeton University Press.

Lippmann, Walter. 1922. *Public Opinion.* New York: The Free Press.

Lippmann, Walter. 1925. *The Phantom Public.* New York: Harcourt, Brace.

Lodge, Henry Cabot. 1925. *The Senate and the League of Nations.* New York: Scribner's.

Loomis, Burdett. 1988. *The New American Politician.* New York: Basic Books.

Lowell, Lawrence. 1913. *Public Opinion and Popular Government.* New York: Longman's Green and Company.

Luke, Timothy W. 1989. *Screens of Power: Ideology, Dominance, and Resistance in an Information Society.* Urbana: University of Illinois Press.

Machiavelli, Niccolo. 1947 [1532]. *The Prince.* Thomas G. Bergin, ed. and trans. Arlington Heights: Harlan Davidson, Inc.

MacKean, Dayton. 1940. *The Boss.* New York: Russell and Russell.

MacKuen, Michael B., Robert S. Erikson, and James A. Stimson. 1989. "Macro-Partisanship." *American Political Science Review* 83:1225–42.

Macpherson, C. B. 1977. *The Life and Times of Liberal Democracy.* Oxford: Oxford University Press.

Maisel, L. Sandy. 1994. "The Platform-Writing Process: Candidate Centered Platforms in 1992." *Political Science Quarterly* 108:671–698.

Maney, Patrick J. 1992. *The Roosevelt Presence.* New York: Twayne.

Mann, Thomas E. and Gary R. Orren, eds. 1992. *Media Polls in American Politics.* Washington, D.C.: Brookings Institution.

Martin, John L. 1984. "The Genealogy of Public Opinion Polling." *The Annals of The American Academy of Political and Social Science* 472:12–24.

Mayhew, David R. 1974. *The Electoral Connection.* New Haven: Yale University Press.

Mayhew, David R. 1991. *Divided We Govern: Party Control, Lawmaking and Investigations, 1946–1990*. New Haven: Yale University Press.

McCoy, Donald R. 1966. *Landon of Kansas*. Lincoln: University of Nebraska Press.

McCullough, David. 1992. *Truman*. New York: Simon and Schuster.

McPherson, James M. 1964. *The Struggle for Equality*. Princeton: Princeton University Press.

McPherson, James M. 1988. *Battle Cry for Freedom*. New York: Oxford University Press.

McPherson, James M. 1991. *Abraham Lincoln and the Second American Revolution*. New York: Oxford University Press.

Mencken, H. L. 1926. *Notes on Democracy*. New York: Knopf.

Mendelsohn, Harold and Irving Crespi. 1970. *Polls, Television, and the New Politics*. Scranton: Chandler Publishing.

Merriam, Charles. 1926. *Four American Party Leaders*. New York: MacMillan.

Michels, Robert. 1949 [1915]. *Political Parties: A Sociological Study of Oligarchical Tendencies of Modern Democracy*. Glencoe: Free Press.

Mill, John Stuart. 1972. *Utilitarianism, On Liberty, and Considerations on Representative Government*, H. B. Acton, ed. New York: J. M. Dent and Sons.

Miller, Warren E. 1979. "Comments on Caddell's Trapped in a Downward Spiral." *Public Opinion*: October/November.

Miller, Warren E. 1988. *Without Consent*. Lexington: Kentucky University Press.

Miller, Warren E. 1991. "Party Identification, Realignment, and Party Voting: Back to the Basics." *American Political Science Review* 85:557–68.

Miller, Warren E. and M. Kent Jennings. 1986. *Parties in Transition: A Longitudinal Study of Party Elites and Party Supporters*. New York: Sage.

Miller, Warren E. and Merrill Shanks. 1991. "Partisanship, Policy, and Performance." *British Journal of Political Science* 21:129–97.

Miroff, Bruce. 1976. *Pragmatic Illusions*. New York: Longman.

Miroff, Bruce. 1993. *Icons of Democracy*. New York: Basic Books.

Moe, Terry. 1993. "Presidential Institution and Theory." In Edwards, George C. III, John H. Kessel, and Bert A. Rockman, eds., *Researching the Presidency*. Pittsburgh: University of Pittsburgh Press.

Monroe, Alan. 1979. "Consistency between Public Preferences and National Policy Decisions." *American Politics Quarterly* 7:3–19.

Montesquieu, Charles de Secondat. 1966 [1748]. *The Spirit of the Laws*. Translated by Thomas Nugent. New York: Hafner. Book 8, chapter 16.

Moore, David W. 1992. *The Super Pollsters*. New York: Four Walls Eight Windows.

Morton, Rebecca B. 1993. "Incomplete Information and Ideological Explanations of Platform Divergence. *American Political Science Review* 87:382–92.

Mueller, Dennis. 1989. *Public Choice II*. New York: Cambridge University Press.

Mueller, John. 1970. *War, Presidents, and Public Opinion*. New York: John Wiley and Sons Inc.

Mueller, John. 1994. *Policy and Opinion in the Gulf War*. Chicago: University of Chicago Press.

Murray, Robert K. and Tim K. Blessing. 1988. *Greatness in the Whitehouse*. University Park: The Pennsylvania State University Press.

Neuman, Russell W. 1986. *The Paradox of Mass Politics*. Cambridge: Harvard University Press.

Neuman, Russell W. 1991. *The Future of the Audience*. New York: Cambridge University Press.

Neustadt, Richard. 1990. *Presidential Power and the Modern Presidents*. New York: The Free Press.

Nevins, Allan. 1933. *Grover Cleveland: A Study in Courage*. Port Washington: Kennikut Press.

Nie, Norman, Sidney Verba, and John Petrocik. 1976. *The Changing American Voter*. Cambridge: Harvard University Press.

Nisbet, Robert. 1975. "Public Opinion and Popular Opinion." *The Public Interest*: Winter, 166–92.

Nisihira Sigeki. 1983. "Political Opinion Polling in Japan." In Robert Worcester, ed., *Political Opinion Polling*. London: The Camelot Press.

Nixon, Richard M. 1982. *Leaders*. New York: Warner Books.

Nixon, Richard M. 1992. "Peace and Prosperity Depend on Our Adopting a New Internationalism." *Arizona Republic*.

Noelle-Neumann, Elisabeth. 1984. *The Spiral of Silence*. Chicago: University of Chicago Press.

Noonan, Peggy. 1990. *What I Saw at the Reagan Revolution*. New York: Random House.

Ober, Josiah. 1989. *Mass and Elite in Democratic Athens*. Princeton: Princeton University Press.

Ogle, Marbury Bladen, Jr. 1950. *Public Opinion and Political Dynamics*. Boston: Houghton Mifflin.

Ordeshook, Peter C. 1986. *Game Theory and Political Theory: An Introduction*. New York: Cambridge University Press.

Oreskes, Michael and Robin Toner. 1990. "Political Failures Are Creating a New Constituency, for Change." *New York Times Magazine*: March 18, A12.

Oreskes, Michael. 1990. "America's Politics Loses Way As Its Vision Changes World." *New York Times*. March 18, A1.

Ostrogroski, M. 1921. *Democracy in the Party System*. New York: MacMillan.

Ostrom, Charles W. and Dennis M. Simon. 1985. "Promise and Performance: A Dynamic Model of Presidential Popularity." *American Political Science Review* 79:334–58.

Page, Benjamin I. 1978. *Choices and Echoes in Presidential Elections*. Chicago: University of Chicago Press.

Page, Benjamin I. and Richard A. Brody. 1972. "Policy Voting and the Electoral Process: The Vietnam War Issue." *American Political Science Review* 66:979–95.

Page, Benjamin I. and Robert Y. Shapiro. 1983. "Effects of Public Opinion on Policy." *American Political Science Review* 77:175–190.

Page, Benjamin I. and Robert Y. Shapiro. 1984. "Presidents as Opinion Leaders: Some New Evidence." *Policy Studies Journal* 12:649–61.

Page, Benjamin I. and Robert Y. Shapiro. 1992. *The Rational Public*. Chicago: University of Chicago Press.

Paige, Glenn. 1972. *Political Leadership*. New York: The Free Press.

Paige, Glenn. 1977. *The Scientific Study of Political Leadership*. New York: The Free Press.

Palmer, P.A. 1936. "Public Opinion in Political Theory." In *Essays in History and Political Theory: In Honor of Howard McIlwain*. Cambridge: Cambridge University Press.

The Parties and the Men. 1896. Robert O. Law, Publisher.

Pateman, Carol. 1970. *Participation and Democratic Theory*. Cambridge: Cambridge University Press.

Patterson, Thomas E. 1993. *Out of Order*. New York: Knopf.

Pear, Robert. 1992. "Bush is Vague on Health Plan's Details." *New York Times*. February 7, A15.

Petrocik, John R. 1981. *Party Coalitions*. Chicago: University of Chicago Press.

Pierce, Roy and Thomas R. Rochon. 1991. "Constancy of Legislative Perceptions of Constituency Opinion: French Socialist Candidates in 1967 and 1978." *Comparative Political Studies* 23:478–97.

Pitkin, Hanna Fenichel. 1967. *The Concept of Representation*. Berkeley: University of California Press.

Pole, J. R. 1983. *The Gift of Government*. Athens: University of Georgia Press.

Polsby, Nelson and Aaron Wildavsky. 1991. *Presidential Elections*. New York: The Free Press.

Polsby, Nelson W. 1982. *What If?: Explorations in Social- Science Fiction*. Lexington: Lewis Publishing Company.

Polsby, Nelson W. 1983. *Consequences of Party Reform*. New York: Oxford University Press.

Popkin, Samuel. 1991. *The Reasoning Voter*. Chicago: University of Chicago Press.

Porado, Phillip. 1989. "Finding Faster Feedback." *Campaigns and Elections* 10(4):34.

Price, Vincent. 1992. *Public Opinion*. Newbury Park: Sage Publications.

Public Opinion, a Comprehensive Summary of the Press Throughout the World on All Important Topics. 1886–1906. Washington D.C.: The Public Opinion Company.

Putnam, Robert D. 1973. *The Beliefs of Politicians.* New Haven: Yale University Press.

Rabinowitz, George and Stuart Elaine MacDonald. 1989. "A Directional Theory of Issue Voting." *American Political Science Review* 83:93–122.

Ragsdale, Lyn. 1984. "The Politics of Presidential Speechmaking, 1949–80." *American Political Science Review* 78:971–84.

Ranney, Austin. 1983. *Channels of Power.* New York: Basic Books.

Reeves, Richard. 1993. *President Kennedy: Profile of Power.* New York: Simon and Schuster.

RePass, David E. 1971. "Issue Salience and Party Choice." *American Political Science Review* 65:389–400.

Ricci, David. 1993. *Transformation of American Politics.* New Haven: Yale University Press.

Riker, William H. 1982. *Liberalism Against Populism.* Prospect Heights: Waveland.

Riker, William H. 1986. *The Art of Political Manipulation.* New Haven: Yale University Press.

Riker, William H. 1990. "Heresthetic and Rhetoric in the Spatial Model." In James M. Enlow and Melvin S. Hinnich, eds., *Advances in the Spatial Theory of Voting.* Cambridge: Cambridge University Press.

Riker, William H. 1993. *Agenda Formation.* Ann Arbor: University of Michigan Press.

Rivers, Douglas and Nancy Rose. 1985. "Passing the President's Program: Public Opinion and Presidential Influence in Congress." *American Journal of Political Science* 29:183–96.

Robertson, David. 1976. *A Theory of Party Competition.* New York: Wiley.

Robinson, Claude. 1932. *Straw Votes: A Study of Political Predicting.* New York: Columbia University Press.

Rochon, Thomas R. 1993. Personal correspondence.

Rockman, Bert. 1984. *Leadership Question.* New York: Praegar.

Rogers, Lindsay. 1949. *The Pollsters.* New York: Knopf.

Rosenbaum, David E. 1993. "Clinton's Plan For Economy May Hinge on His Popularity." *New York Times.* April 29, A1.

Rosenstone, Steven J., Roy L. Behr, and Edward H. Lazarus. 1984. *Third Parties in America.* Princeton: Princeton University Press.

Rossiter, Clinton. 1953. *Seedtime of the Republic.* New York: Harcourt, Brace.

Rossiter, Clinton, ed. 1961. *The Federalist Papers.* New York: New American Library.

Runkel, David P., ed. 1989. *Campaign for President.* Dover: Auburn House Publishing Company.

Russett, Bruce. 1990. *Controlling the Sword: The Democratic Governance of National Security.* Cambridge: Harvard University Press.

Sandburg, Carl. 1939. Abraham Lincoln: *The War Years.* New York: Harcourt, Brace and Company.

Sartori, Giovanni. 1976. *Parties and Party Systems: A Framework for Analysis.* New York: Cambridge University Press.

Schafer, Bryon E. 1991. *The End of Realignment?* Madison: University of Wisconsin Press.

Schattschneider, E. E. 1942. *Party Government.* New York: Holt, Rinehart, and Winston.

Schattschneider, E. E. 1975. *The Semisoveriegn People.* Hinsdale: Dryden Press.

Schlesinger, Arthur. 1960. *Politics of Upheaval.* Boston: Houghton Mifflin.

Schlesinger, Arthur. 1962. "Our Presidents: A Rating by 75 Historians." *New York Times Magazine*: July.

Schuman, Howard and Stanley Presser. 1981. *Questions and Answers in Attitude Surveys.* New York: Wiley.

Schuman, Howard, Charlotte Steeh, and Lawrence Bobo. 1985. *Racial Attitudes in America.* Cambridge: Harvard University Press.

Schumpeter, Joseph A. 1950. *Capitalism, Socialism, and Democracy.* New York: Harper and Brothers.

Sinclair, Barbara. "Studying Presidential Leadership." 1993. In Edwards, George C. III, John H. Kessel, and Bert A. Rackov, eds., *Researching the Presidency.* Pittsburgh: University of Pittsburgh Press.

Sjoblom, Gunnar. 1968. *Party Strategies in a Multiparty System.* Lund, Sweden: Studentlitteratur.

Skowronek, Stephen. 1993. *The Politics Presidents Make.* Cambridge: Harvard University Press.

Smith, Charles. 1939. *Public Opinion in a Democracy.* New York: Prentice Hall, Inc.

Smith, Hedrick. 1988. *Power Game.* New York: Random House.

Smith, Richard Norton. 1993. *Patriarch: George Washington and the New American Nation.* Boston: Houghton Mifflin.

Smith, Tom W. 1990. "The First Straw? A Study of the Origin of Election Polls." *Public Opinion Quarterly* 54:21–36.

Sorenson, Ted. 1975. *Watchmen in the Night.* Englewood Cliffs: Prentice-Hall.

Specter, Michael. 1991. "In This Corner." *New York Times Magazine*, December 15, 42.

Stanley, Harold. 1987. *Voter Mobilization and the Politics of Race.* New York: Praeger.

Stanley, Harrold and Richard G. Niemi. 1994. *Vital Statistics on American Politics*, 4th edition. Washington, D.C.: Congressional Quarterly Press.

Stanley, Harrold, William Bianco, and Richard G. Niemi. 1986. "Partisanship and Group Support Over Time: A Multivariate Analysis: *American Political Science Review* 80:969–76.

Steele, Richard W. 1974. "The Pulse of the People. Franklin D. Roosevelt and the Gauging of American Public Opinion." *Journal of Contemporary History* 9:195–216.

Stern, Mark. 1992. *Calculating Visions*. New Brunswick: Rutgers University Press.

Stimson, James A. 1991. *Public Opinion in America*. Boulder: Westview Publishing.

Stimson, James A., Michael B. Mackuen, Robert S. Erikson. 1995. "Dynamic Representation." *American Political Science Review*. 89:543–65.

Stoetzel, Jean. 1983. "Political Opinion Polling in France." In Robert Worcester, ed., *Political Opinion Polling*. London: The Camelot Press.

Stokes, Donald E. 1963. "Spatial Models of Party Competition." *American Political Science Review* 57:368–77.

Stokes, Donald E. 1993. "Valence Politics." In Dennis Kavanagh, ed., *Electoral Politics*. Oxford: Clarendon Press.

Stout, Hillary. 1993. "Polls Shows Stunning Backing for an Overhaul, Giving President a Big Boost." *Wall Street Journal*, March 12, A1.

Sudman, Seymour. 1982. "Presidents and Polls." *Public Opinion Quarterly* 46:301–10.

Sundquist, James L. 1983. *Dynamics of the Party System*. Washington, D.C.: The Brookings Institution.

Tanur, Judith M, ed. 1992. *Questions About Questions: Inquiry Into the Cognitive Bases of Surveys*. New York: Russell Sage Foundation.

Tempe Tribune. 1993 May 23, A23.

Trefousse, Hans L. 1975. *Lincoln's Decision for Emancipation*. Philadelphia: Lippincott.

Truman, Harry S. 1955. *Memoirs*. Garden City: Doubleday.

Tsebelis, George. 1990. *Nested Games*. Berkeley: University of California Press.

Tucker, Robert C. 1981. *Politics as Leadership*. Columbia: University of Missouri Press.

Tufte, Edward. 1978. *Political Control of the Economy*. Princeton: Princeton University Press.

Tulis, Jeffrey K. 1987. *The Rhetorical Presidency*. Princeton: Princeton University Press.

Verba, Sidney and Norman H. Nie. 1972. *Participation in America*. Chicago: University of Chicago Press.

Walker, Scott. 1992. "Pennies for Thoughts." *Campaigns and Elections* 13:41–50.

Wall Street Journal. 1991. June 28, A14.

Walsh, Kenneth T. 1992. "All Dressed Up and No Place to Go." *U.S. News and World Report*:18 May, 11.

Warner, Lucien. 1939. "The Reliability of Public Opinion." *Public Opinion Quarterly* 3:376–90.

Warren, Harris. 1967. *Herbert Hoover and the Great Depression*. New York: Norton Publishing.

Washington Post. 1991. September 26. "Bush on Health Care; Case Study in Caution."

Wattenberg, Martin P. 1990. *The Decline of American Political Parties*. 3rd ed. Cambridge: Harvard University Press.

Weber, Max. [1918] 1946. *Essays in Sociology*. H. H. Gerth and C. Wright Mills, eds and comps. New York: Oxford University Press.

Weed, Clyde P. 1994. *The Nemesis of Reform: The Republican Party During the New Deal*. New York: University of Columbia Press.

Weinstein, Edwin A. 1981. *Woodrow Wilson, A Medical and Psychological Biography*. Princeton: Princeton University Press.

Wildavsky, Aaron. 1989. "Cultural Theory of Leadership." In Bryan Jones, ed., *Leadership and Politics*. Lawrence: University of Kansas.

Will, George. 1992a. "Perot Proves Public is Suffering from Cult of Leadership." *Arizona Republic*, June 1, A11.

Will, George. 1992b. *Restoration: Congress, Term Limits, and the Recovery of Deliberative Democracy*. New York: Free Press.

Wills, Gary. 1992. *Lincoln at Gettysburg*. New York: Simon and Schuster.

Wills, Gary. 1994. *Certain Trumpets: The Call of Leaders*. New York: Simon and Schuster.

Wilson, Woodrow. 1952. *Leaders of Men*. Princeton: Princeton University Press.

Winfield, Betty Houchin. 1990. *FDR and the News Media*. Urbana: University of Illinois Press.

Wittman, Donald A. 1983. "Candidate Motivation: A Synthesis of Alternative Theories." *American Political Science Review* 77:142–57.

Wlezien, Christopher. 1995. "Dynamics of Representation: The Case of U.S. Spending on Defense." *British Journal of Political Science* forthcoming.

Woodward, Bob. 1994. *The Agenda*. New York: Simon and Schuster.

Worcester, Robert, ed. 1983. *Political Opinion Polling*. London: The Camelot Press.

Young, John T. 1991. "Presidential Candidates and Public Opinion: Leadership or Followership in 1988." Paper presented at the Annual Meeting of the American Political Science Association, Washington, D.C.

Zaller, John. 1992. *The Nature and Origins of Mass Opinion*. New York: Cambridge University Press.

Designer: Linda Secondari
Text: Adobe Garamond
Compositor: Columbia University Press
Printer: Maple-Vail
Binder: Maple-Vail